....

SuRFing oN tHe InTErnEt

A Nethead's Adventures On-Line

SuRFing oN tHe InTErnEt

J. C. HERZ

LITTLE, BROWN AND COMPANY   Boston   New York   Toronto   London

First Edition

Portions of this book have appeared, in somewhat different form, in *Playboy* and *GQ*.

Library of Congress Cataloging-in-Publication Data
Herz, J. C.
    Surfing on the Internet : a nethead's adventures on-line / J. C. Herz.
     p.   cm.
   ISBN 0-316-35958-0
    1. Internet (Computer network)   I. Title.
  TK5105.875.I57H47   1995
004.6′7—dc20   94-24795

10 9 8 7 6 5 4 3 2 1

MV-NY

Designed by Barbara Werden

Published simultaneously in Canada by
Little, Brown & Company (Canada) Limited

Printed in the United States of America

For Mark Leyner

Four No-Doz and Eight Meg of RAM.
Is there anything else?

—Scott Krieger
excelent@mindvox.phantom.com

L'enfer, c'est les Autres.

—Jean-Paul Sartre

Thanks to Michael Pietsch, Sloan Harris, Dorothy Atcheson, the crüe at MindVox, Andy Green, Ted Drozdowski, and the reticulate consciousness of the Net.

CoNteNts

....

SuRFing oN tHe InTErnEt

pRocRAStinAtion rEVElatIoN

I CAN'T BELIEVE this. I can't believe this. I can't believe this.

I'm just goofing in the Science Center basement. Procrastinating — anything to keep from writing the Term Paper From Hell for that stupid jerk-off seminar. (Limning the poststructuralist discourse of the Other . . . Auntie Em! Auntie Em!) I'm stoned on lingo, in that state where you read a paragraph and forget that you just read it and then read it again and it's still gibberish, and then you force yourself to believe it makes sense and by sheer force of will it miraculously *does*. So to celebrate I put it away for a minute and start fooling around on the computer, just wandering, fishing through the shell.

With three keystrokes, I stumble into the Usenet index, at which point my monitor does its best impression of Heather ("They're Heeeeere") O'Rourke from *Poltergeist*. Newsgroup headings spew from the bottom of my monitor and scroll up and up and up for minutes. I've never come so close to believing a computer is possessed. Phrases race up the screen, almost too quickly to read: vampires, supermodels, multi-level business scams, conspiracies, Elvis sightings, Shostakovich, civil liberties, *Twin Peaks*, fractals, bondage, ghost stories, Spam . . . It reads like some wacked-out librarian has taken a few hits of crystal meth, decided that computer languages, television, fan clubs, and sex—in that order—are the essential human pursuits, and overhauled the Dewey decimal system accordingly.

I've touched down in a corridor of three thousand-some-odd doors. I open one of them and find a peanut gallery that spans the planet—Australia, Oakland, Toronto, Austin, North Carolina, England, Sweden. Participants bash each other unreservedly. It's like spitball throwing just became an Olympic sport.

I open door number two, crash a boomerang physics forum, and leave quickly, my head spinning. Another few keystrokes and I've barged into a cabal secretly plotting to torture, sodomize, maim, and kill *Star Trek*'s Ensign Wesley Crusher and/or his real-life counterpart, Wil Wheaton. I careen through the ethnic newsgroups like a glutton at an international food fair. The whole world is here: Czechs, Germans, Malaysians, Pakistanis, Finns, Taiwanese, New Zealanders.

When I look up, it's four-thirty in the morning.

"No way."

I look from the clock to my watch.

Way.

I've been in front of this screen for six hours, and it seems like no time at all. I'm not even remotely tired. Dazed and thirsty, but not tired. In fact, I'm euphoric. I stuff a disheveled heap of textbooks, photocopied articles, hilighters, and notes into my backpack and run like a madwoman up the concrete steps, past the security guard, and outside into the predawn mist. It's soft and still outside, orange halos around the sodium lamps and blue lights above emergency phones, no one out, just quiet, the whole campus asleep. The sprinklers are on. I walk straight through them.

I stop where a wet walkway meets a dry one and stand for a sec, look down at my soggy moccasins, and start thinking about this *thing* that buzzes around the entire world, through the phone lines, all day and all night long. It's right under our noses, and it's invisible. It's like Narnia, or Magritte, or *Star Trek*, an entire goddamned world. Except it doesn't physically exist. It's just the collective consciousness of however many people are on it.

This really is outstandingly weird.

This absolutely blows my mind.

LuRkinG

I LURK FOR weeks.

Lurkers—that's what they call people on the Net who don't make any noise. Lurkers don't register on the Net. Not even a blip. And there are tens of thousands of them, literally the silent majority, peering down from the gallery.

Lurking is considered unsporting here in cyberspace (this is, after all, a theater of verbal flamboyance). But the number crunchers who crank out quasi-Arbitron ratings of Usenet newsgroups estimate that lurkers outnumber their chatty counterparts ten to one. Even here, most people are content to be part of the grand, high-beamed woodwork. Virtual wallflowers.

Lurking is a larval phase in the nethead life cycle. It's that spooky, voyeuristic time when you haven't got your bearings yet, but you're fascinated enough to browse with bovine contentment on the grassy pastures of online discourse. Concealed, you can sit back and binge on ASCII text, guzzling it faster than you've ever absorbed information in your life. You inhale information. And all the while, you're completely invisible. Lurking is like one of those Sunday-night movies on network TV where a guy is struck by lightning or toxic waste and becomes Captain Undetectable, suddenly able to over-hear boardroom conversations and sneak into the lingerie dressing room at Macy's at a single bound. People get into fights, yell and scream at each other, and they're completely oblivious to you, in your front-row seat. Transparency has its privileges.

But after a while, the novelty of eavesdropping wears off. The learning curve flattens out. You're bloated with other people's thoughts, and you know enough lingo not to em-barrass yourself. So you say something. Anything. On some newsgroup. Any newsgroup. Just a few sentences. Nothing major.

And then you press a button, and your words come out the other side of the pipe. An offhand comment that lit up only one screen has circumnavigated the globe. One key-stroke sends duplicates to Auckland, Helsinki, Pretoria, and a few hundred polytechnic colleges in the American Midwest. This takes a few seconds.

And then, a few hours later, you pick up a response from some math major in Ontario — another rabbit out of the hat — and you're rolling. You have successfully evolved from larval lurker to the pupal nethead phase: novice poster (a creature with wriggly little legs but no wings). From there, it's just a matter of picking up speed and justifying sporadic editorials at the expense of school and state.

This is not a problem, as it allows me to avenge all those other frivolous uses of my tuition and tax dollars.

And in the midst of all this Netsurfing, it doesn't seem to matter that I've graduated. It doesn't matter where I am, physically (in this case, Florida). I'm still on the Net, and it's seamless. It's absolutely continuous. I've moved, but I'm still *here.*

The concept of "here" is doing a slow, graceful back flip.

. . . .
neT DEAth

WELL, MY BELOVED university has decided to drop-kick my ass out of the nest and into the real world. They're cutting off my Internet account. Graduating was no big deal. Moving to a different city, getting a job, and making new friends was no problem. But losing Net . . . this is serious.

Losing Net connection is a fate that strikes mortal terror into any denizen of cyberspace. It's something that can't even be called worse than death because it *is* death, in a way. Net death. If, for some reason, you lose access to the Net—your account is canceled, you run out of dough, or you move to a telecom backwater like I did, then you're dead as far as the Net's concerned. You just disappear. Fade out. From the exile's perspective, an entire world disappears. Foof, gone, like in *The Day After*.

And it's not as if I mind paying for Net access. But no one's selling it down here. This isn't New York. This isn't Boston. This isn't San Francisco, where a cappuccino license requires at least four Net terminals on the premises. I am planted in the telecom boondocks of southern Florida.

We have a problem.

I can't give this up. Go back to snail mail? Lose touch with my college classmates (yeah, they'll write paper letters . . . in my dreams) and all my Swedish hacker friends?

I don't *think* so.

This really sucks.

And no, I don't want some Tinkertoy online service. I want NET.

cybERpUnk: iT'S noT JUsT fOr BrEaKfaSt ANymOrE

I'VE BEEN SPENDING a lot of time on alt.cyberpunk. There's nothing like watching a once-underground subculture twitch through the wrenching throes of self-definition in the glare of media attention. (Cyberpunk: the *Time* cover story. Cyberpunk, the Billy Idol album. Can lunch boxes and action figures be far behind?) Cyberpunk science fiction, as written by authors like William Gibson and Bruce Sterling, is beloved of the Net community because it makes heroes out of techie outcasts. The skinny, disheveled, worn-down outsider takes on the Bad Guys. He's got a computer. They've got hired mercenaries. And the tech-savvy street rat wins every time. Cyberpunk glamorizes the hacker. It's every computer nerd's fantasy. But whether it's a bona fide "movement" is a subject of some contention, particularly on alt.cyberpunk. And right now, members of this movement, if it does indeed exist, are crash-testing various manifestos. *Line Noiz,* an electronic 'zine on alt.cyberpunk, runs a know-it-when-you-see-it definition culled from the newsgroup's list of frequently asked questions (FAQ):

So, what makes a cyberpunk? [If] you're laughing at my generalities and inconsistencies, then you're definitely a cyberpunk. If you're a techno-junkie or an info-junkie, then you'd probably consider yourself a cyberpunk. Basically, if you live in a world in the not-so-distant-future, ahead of the masses (the masses being guys named Buford who sit out in front of their trailer homes in lawn chairs sipping a Bud and watching the Indy 500 on an old TV), then you could probably safely consider yourself a cyberpunk. . . .

This is a clever bid for credibility on the part of *Line Noiz,* seeing as how it grandfathers its entire readership into the movement and shies from the riptide of specificity. It's not the broad brushstrokes that induce apoplexy around here. It's the efforts of self-appointed cyberstyle mavens to retrofit a fashion statement from the pages of *Mondo 2000.* Trying to label albums, hairstyles, and footwear with the cyberpunk seal of approval only triggers more confusion and paranoia. Basically, all hell has broken loose now that this motley pack has to deal with fitting in here, of all places. Cyberpunk, after all, has everything to do with the glorification of misfits.

When hackers—never renowned for their fashion sense—start posting sartorial advice, it's time to worry.

After the newsmagazine blitzkrieg, the ideological free fall continues for months. Finally, it hits bottom; an Australian university student takes the categorization fiesta to its logical extreme: "Just wondering," he asks, "what would people consider to be Cyberpunk food??"

Such a short, innocent question, such a seemingly simple issue — like the border of Alsace-Lorraine or the eternal tastes-great-less-filling controversy — touches off a firestorm whose bitterness is only heightened by its absurdity.

Snack food. Somehow, the churning self-examination of an entire subculture has come down to "cheap fast food, potato chips, junk food, liberally sparsed with psychedelics," the nomination from a netter in Washington State, seconded by a scattered multitude of North Americans. I sit back and wonder why a pack of brainiac individualists has suddenly decided to use snack food preference as a proxy for collective identity. What the hell are these people trying to do by defining themselves in terms of Store 24 dry goods? As I follow the snack food issue over the Net, the phrase "You are what you eat" takes on frightening connotations.

"Woke up today 5 minutes after i was supposed to be to work," writes Teknikl, a hacker with a Sisyphean computer graphics job — indexing binary pictures of cracks in highway pavement. Woke up today — don't all blues songs start that way? I half expect Tek to continue in twelve-bar verse form like Charlie Patton in cyberspace.

"Damn, i thought to myself, now i don't get any breakfast. This isn't really a big problem, since the quickmart is across the street, waiting patiently to sell me more coffee creamer and those nasty little cakes they sell at quickmarts that aren't part of larger chains. Little debbies, ultranasty 'kooshpies' made by twisted locals who think they've invented a new food type, and those ugly pecan pies. I really didn't want any of this stuff . . . I needed food."

Clearly, cheapness and low nutritional value are essential to the cyberpunk snack food gestalt. Mark Gooley, the cult hero of alt.non.sequitur, advises his flock to embrace artificial ingredients in one of his inimitable Gooley nonsense sermons:

"Aspartame by the plateful! Hateful plateful, careful carful, icky knickers? The movement started in Puerto Rico about ten minutes ago and is spreading inch-thick layers of Simplesse (tm), as written by Grimmelshausen, on every major highway in the United States except for those with prime-number names. Ever had roast Beat Poet? . . . Beer doesn't love me any more."

As the snack food thread spins out on various newsgroups, malnutrition acquires a grungy chic, and the nethead diaspora begins to riff on a white trash convenience store motif: Ding Dongs, Ho-Hos, and Grandma's cookies. Cyberpunk snack food is invariably described as single-serving, individually wrapped for the alienated and hard-up. Salty, carcinogenic tide-over food, redolent of dehydrogenated soybean oil, downward mobility, and creeping retail homogenization, would surely represent the post-apocalyptic future of Sterling and Gibson. Chemical side effects on the brain are an added bonus. Stimulants in general, and caffeinated beverages in particular, are cataloged in detail that veers between science and poetry.

Indeed, the Net is probably the only place where a comparison of the caffeine content in instant, drip, and expresso coffee, Twining's English Breakfast tea, Jolt cola, Swiss Miss hot chocolate, and Mountain Dew, in moles per liter, is not considered comprehensive. Multicultural netters wired on Chinese bark extracts have to chip in their two cents. Prescription diehards lobby for vasopressin. ("No letdown, just instant wakey-wakey. Does dry out yer nasal cavities though. Bummer.") This kind of discussion continues till dawn. He who stays awake longest wins. Long after I've thrown in the towel, an electronic cry of triumph rings across the Net: "Pills. Teas. Carbonated beverages. Amateur SLOTH!!!!!!" Apparently, some guy has engineered an intravenous ephedrine drip.

Personally, I stick to drip coffee and mass quantities of highly sugared cereal—straight up, no milk, and fortified with eight essential vitamins and minerals. Lucky Charms, Count Chocula, Froot Loops, Frosted Flakes, Captain Crunch, and Kellogg's Mini Cinnamon Buns top my list. Exotic shapes and colors are a bonus, but I'll usually forgo them in favor of a brand with more sugar than anything else. What I really want is for the Jolt cola company to get off its ass and package an all-the-sugar-twice-the-artificial-coloring cereal encrusted with pop rocks. That and Net would be unbelievable. Come to think of it, that and Net would be redundant.

The Ghost in the Machine is the only netter I've encountered whose snack food fetish rivals my own. He is obsessed with ramen. "Take some raw ramen noodles and pour them into a bowl," he instructs. "Then smash them up with a large blunt object til they are real tiny-like. Then add some ketchup and some thousand island (secret sauce) and the flavor packet. Stir well. Serve. this is the ultimate late-night snack and i seem to notice a heightening of senses after eating."

At 5:52 on a Tuesday morning, the Ghost in the Machine is on his third cup of ramen, and he rhapsodizes about its endless variations. "I've found that if you nuke it for about 1 minute 45 seconds it is nice and crunchy yet still edible, its much more fun this way than the normal softstuff. I think i might try sculpting it soon, maybe a pillar of it over the computer or something. its great cuz you can mold it when its wet and then let it dry in place and it'll harden. but i'm kinda worried about bugs, but i guess i'll know in a few days whether or not it'll attract little beasties."

The Ghost is definitely on to something. Ramen strikes a chord. It's cheap, starchy, available around the clock, and vaguely derived from Asia like some ticky-tack secondhand widget. And the image of a bug-infested mountain of ramen towering above a CPU captures the imagination. Hugely overbuilt and rotting into detritus, not unlike the post-apocalyptic sci-fi future, Mount Ramen is an idea whose time has come.

After this monument to high-tech, low-rent sustenance, all other snack food comments are anticlimactic. The whole controversy, once amusing in a frivolous way, begins to seem merely silly. If this is cyberpunk, then the so-called movement is as stale as day-old griddle grease. I get the sense that something vital has been lost, that this isn't really worth the sleep deprivation. I haven't had a decent night's sleep in five days, and the ceiling fan isn't working in my minuscule, lemon-yellow tropical kitsch apartment—not a pleasant state of affairs in midsummer Florida. I'm dipping into a caffeine low and getting fed up with the whole cyberpunk phenomenon, whatever the hell it is. I make a pact with myself to get some sleep. (Just a few more minutes. OK, no, really, just a couple more minutes. One more post. After this one. OK, one more, but this is it . . .)

That one more post turns out to be a polemic by Andy Hawks, who runs the Krackerbox freedom of information bulletin board (BBS) out in Boulder, Colorado, and publishes (if that's the word) an e-zine called *Future Culture*. Outraged by AT&T's "You Will" commercials and other corporate dreamscapes, he blasted alt.cyberpunk:

```
wake the fuck up, people.

take a look at who you are dealing with . . .
don't be apathetic—pay attention to who is bat-
tling for the prize, who's choosing to play the
game, and what their motivations are . . . AT&T
and TimeWarner don't care about increasing com-
munication, about integrating technologies all
over the world, about bringing people closer
```

through complete bi-directional interactivity from the grass roots up. Jesus, check your head . . .

[In Apple's "1984" commercial] a girl comes in with this hammer and throws it at the image of Big Brother projected on a large screen, and wakes up the IBM automatons from their incredible sleep and the Macintosh is given birth. well the year may read 1993, but 1984 is still out there, only the names have been changed . . . We should not be focusing any longer on the projected image of Big Brother on the screen, we should be focusing on the wizard projecting the image. the wizard, the Biggest Brother in the Making, is known to us as AT&T, TimeWarner, TCI Inc., US West, and a smaller subgroup of dawgs humping their collective wizard-leg. Big Brother this time around is much more powerful—the war is being waged on Brother's turf. If we have enough force to throw the hammer and shatter the image of Big Brother, then the prize will be free information. If we sit back and stay in line like automatons, the consequences could be immeasurable. so. . . .

wake up.

—.-.-.-.... . . . .-.-.—.... .
.andy.

Pixellated light makes its way from the screen through all the usual cognitive channels, and then some intellectual pilot light flickers on. It's not the content of the message. I've heard the argument before. I even have my share of problems with it—I like movies and voice mail as much as the next person. But the ability of one nineteen-year-old with an attitude to reach millions of people, in seconds, with no campaign budget, no PAC money, no CNN, no global marketing strategy, just the Net—and the fact that I could do the same thing, *that*'s impressive, even inspiring—Hostess cupcakes or no Hostess cupcakes.

in tHe FuTuRe, EVEryOne wilL hAvE hIs oWN NewsgRoUp

AFTER CRAWLING THROUGH the warren of digital fan clubs, I stand in awe of the netter's capacity to obsess. His attention to obscure detail is almost erotic in its intensity. His research skills are unrivaled. And his pulpit is the gargantuan grapevine of the Net itself. No club dues, no postage, no copying fees. Hence, the Amy Fisher newsgroup, the Alok Vijayvargia fan club, and the online Zappa shrine. (Frank's artificial intelligence construct occasionally shows up to bitch. "Death's not so bad, man, but the line noise around here sucks . . ." "No, that was *not* the correct lyric, shithead.")

I've been a fervid fan in my time. As a five-year-old, I set my Oscar the Grouch alarm clock to go off at 5:30 A.M. so that I could watch all six hours of the Saturday-morning cartoon marathon, including the "Star Spangled Banner" public service announcement and that Lutheran stop-motion sitcom, *Davey and Goliath*. I hated the show, but to miss even one minute of the animation bonanza would have violated my Saturday-morning ritual. Later, I amassed an impressive collection of lunch boxes, Barbie dolls, and *Dynamite* magazines before moving on to obscure British New Wave bands and the *Weekly World News*. But I have to admit, the encyclopedic fervor of Net fandom puts my own Godfathers fixation and fanzine habit to shame.

I realize this when, in the middle of a theological debate (the Bible: Virus or Faulty Operating System?), a devout William Gibson admirer posts his interpretation of Jesus' role as pitchman in the extended marketing war of major religions.

"The way I see it," he writes, "Jesus was a politician, a media man . . . an orator, a phylosopher. He was inspired by his own life experiences . . . and confused as to the purpose of his existence. His teachings had a major media impact on the initial 'viewers'. He was a Gibson."

My jaw drops.

Jesus was a Gibson.

I guess that makes St. Peter the granddaddy of all literary publicists and Bantam Books an avatar of the Holy Mother Church. No wonder the guy stays off the Net.

Gibson, I mean. Jesus is all over the place. He even has his own channel on IRC, which I crash with the question "Does Jesus hang out on the Net? And if so, what's his handle? Would he go by just 'Jesus,' or would he cyberize it by mixing lowercase and capital letters, Mondo-style (jESuS). Or would he even use the name on birth certificate, driver's license, and American Express card, at the risk of being blasted off his own channel?"

According to Net folklore, that's what happened to Douglas Adams. Having assumed quasi-Jesus status in the Net's pantheon of celebrities for his *Hitchhiker's Guide to the Galaxy* pseudo-trilogy (now up to five volumes), Adams showed up in his own fan club, only to be pilloried as an impostor. No amount of biographical trivia or reasoned argument could budge the consensus that he was a fraud.

Jesus, on the other hand, would probably be smart enough to use a pseudonym that pushed all the right cyberpunk buttons — Kid Righteous, posting from GodNet (.com? .org? .edu? .gov?), or something to that effect.

These musings do not go over splendidly on the Jesus channel, which erupts with scripture-laden justifications for the presence of God in cyberspace. The subsequent chorus of hosannas bears an eerie resemblance to *Family Feud,* after Uncle Bob pitches his best guess and the rest of the clan roots, "Good answer! Good answer!" (The redoubtable über-game-show host, Richard Dawson, gazes up at the score screen and yells, "Wherever two or three are gathered on this channel, Jesus is on the Net. SURVEY SAYS . . .")

"So would you say that jesus is more present on #jesus, than, say, #hotsex?" I query.

I think that puts me in killfile territory. Either that, or they figure I'm not worth evangelizing. So I give up on #jesus and tell the IRC server to send me straight to #hell, on the odd chance that such a place might exist.

Three seconds into #hell, a bot called Bitch of Death greets me with an invitation to join a private channel — #seattle. In a rather poetic turn of networking, #hell is the gateway to the Pacific Northwest. It's all chutes and ladders. Logic is a different beast down here.

If I need any more proof of that than the #jesus/#hell/ #seattle ride, I find it back in fandom, on the Douglas Hofstadter newsgroup. Amid a discussion of symbolic logic and cybernetics, a McGill student has lodged the following one-line post:

"David Hasselhoff rules the world!!!!!!!! Do you agree?"

Somehow, the juxtaposition of philosopher and logician Douglas Hofstadter — an undisputed genius who weaves together artificial intelligence, violin sonatas, and Zen Buddhism in his Pulitzer Prize–winning *Gödel, Escher, Bach*— and David Hasselhoff, the erstwhile star of *Baywatch,* has a sublime resonance that is not lost on the cerebral heavyweights in alt.fan.hofstadter. The question is, could this message be a mere flub, the chaotic by-product of Usenet's immense bandwidth? Or is it some kind of elegant puzzle, a sophisticated bit of meme-play, perhaps a biting commentary on the pervasive and tragic ignorance of a media-doped public? Maybe it's some Warholian prophesy of a future in which Douglas Hofstadter and David Hasselhoff stand on equal footing in the world of ideas. Douglas Hasselhoff. David Hofstadter. No one would know the difference. It is, in a sense, the ultimate intellectual nihilism.

Or maybe it has something to do with Hasselhoff's pre-*Baywatch* gig, *Knight Rider,* in which the protagonist's obtuse studmuffin heroics are made possible by the immense artificial intelligence of his sentient crime-fighting car. The machine consistently saves his ass. It's the only thing that keeps him from looking like a complete dufus. So . . . the union of man and machine may lure us on but will ultimately make the human race look really goofy. That's what this is all about. Hmmm. . . .

But wait. This is too complex. A true Hofstadter fan would reduce the puzzle to its most elemental components and deftly shuffle alphabet letters to produce some profundity.

Of course! It is so obvious. *Knight Rider,* the television show, is only one letter removed from Knight Ridder, the media conglomerate that owns a good chunk of America's newspapers. So this Hasselhoff comment is a tip-off about Knight Ridder's conspiracy to depose the world's leaders and run the planet as a one-world media state. Very clever.

Well, that's my theory.

Meanwhile, there is no consensus about the mysterious McGill student. Either he's a complete genius whose little joke has baffled the best of us, or he has mistakenly crashed a party of logic test-drivers who are bending syllogisms like animal balloons just to accommodate his existence.

After a week of this, I can't stand it anymore. I have to know. So I e-mail the Hasselhoff poster an inquiry about the Hofstadter/Hasselhoff switcheroo. "Was it intentional?" I ask. "If so, it was brilliant :-) BTW, what does it mean?"

I stew for a few days, waiting for the enigmatic Canadian to reply. I begin to feel sheepish. Maybe it was just so obvious that I didn't get it. Maybe this guy thinks I'm a complete idiot and is wondering whether it is worth his time to spell it out for me in a line-by-line geometric proof, using small words so that I will be sure to understand. When the answer finally comes, I see the McGill address and skip past a column of e-mail to read it. It's e-mail number sixty-seven in my mailbox. Prime number. Lucky. I type "67" and lean forward, my pinkie poised on the return key. In a few seconds I'll know the truth of the whole Hofstadter/Hasselhoff controversy, and I want to savor the moment.

I pause to contemplate Schrödinger's cat. For a moment, my Canadian correspondent is *both* a genius and a complete moron. I briefly consider leaving the letter unread, floating in its own paradox, before caving in to curiosity.

The explanation is brief and to the point:

"Uh, no, I must have been confused. They just really sound the same."

The puzzle implodes.

No doubt, mix-ups like this are responsible for the frazzled and pedantic tone of many fan group FAQs. The one in alt.fan.asprin reads, "This newsgroup is for fans of Robert Lynn Asprin to discuss his literary works. Robert Asprin is best known for his humorous fantasy series — Myth Adventures. This newsgroup is NOT for the discussion of aspirin (acetylsalicylic acid) or other pain relievers." Now I really want to start an acetylsalicylic acid fan club, alt.fan.aspirin, just to fuck with the Robert Asprin fans, as sort of a twisted tribute to their obscure newsgroup.

There is no such thing as too obscure on the Net. This place makes the Library of Congress look like B. Dalton. There are fan groups around here so obscure that they seem completely random. Invariably, these are the most interesting ones. The less likely I am to come into actual contact with a Usenet fan club's object of worship, hatred, and/or fascination, the more likely I am to follow the newsgroup's discussion avidly. The Berkeley student who raised a media rumpus by loitering in the nude, for instance, now has a fan club on the Net. Sure, alt.fan.naked.guy has its share of snide crashers ("Is anyone here really his 'fan'? Or, did you just subscribe to all the newsgroups containing the word 'naked'?"). But I believe alt.fan.naked.guy fills a crucial niche in the Usenet information economy, namely the discussion of on-campus nudity in Alameda County and the posting of Naked Guy updates courtesy of a Berkeley student named Terence ("Naked Guy Sighting yesterday, saw him clothed sitting by the BofA on Telegraph and Durant, eating a slice of pizza, looked like Fat Slice's Special of that day").

My favorite fan clubs, however, are the ones that have absolutely nothing to do with life outside the Net. They revolve around celebrities whose marquee is cyberspace itself, individuals whose flamboyance and sheer bandwidth have earned them massive name recognition, worshipful admirers, sworn enemies, authorized and unauthorized biographies, and outright cults in the Net's self-contained media microcosm. Not surprisingly, these apotheoses of self-referential pop stardom are frequently the key patrons of their own electronic shrines. In the future, everyone will have his own newsgroup.

"Those ingenious steel mechanisms with the osmium and ruthenium plating won't save you from creeping ennui, MacLaurin," writes Mark Gooley, the raving madman of alt.non.sequitur, apropos of nothing. "Better to give yourself up to the Secreting Service now and admit to them that you plotted to kill the Great Seal of the United States simply because you hated the way it went 'oook! oook!' on unstated state occasions at the State Department . . ."

Gooley is the anchorman of a newsgroup consisting solely of non sequiturs. He has several fan clubs named after him now.

When I write him a fan letter asking what he thinks of his own Net celebrity, he is pretty laid-back about it. Gooley is aware of his own anonymity outside the churning textscape of the Net. "When I introduce myself or get introduced, I never draw the response, 'Not the Gooley who posts to alt.non.sequitur?'" he responds. "I don't have the name-recognition of Carasso, of a net.kook like Robert McElwaine, of Kibo, of a crank-it-out writer like Elf Sternberg (though on alt.non.sequitur my output is getting into that league). Perhaps I don't get introduced to enough people who read the Usenet groups." For a Net celebrity, Gooley is disarmingly self-effacing.

Kibo is not. But then, Kibo has transcended Net stardom and assumed a kind of digital godhead. In real life, he is James "Kibo" Parry, an independent graphic designer who lives in Boston. On the Net, he is a meme that has spun wildly out of control. Kibo has amassed a huge following for one simple reason: he claims to read every mention of his name on the Internet. Every day, he runs a trawl program through the ocean of data in Usenet, fishing for the Letters K-I-B-O. And then he reads the entire haul. That's like a Gulf Coast shrimper swallowing every wriggly crustacean he can catch in bumper season—raw. It's absurd. But it's the kind of absurdity that makes you a star on the Net. Kibo's name is thrown into signature quotes and sprinkled into Usenet articles regardless of context. At first, this was an effort to overwhelm him. But the phenomenon has snowballed, and now Kibo is a genuine icon. His words migrate across newsgroups like some kind of unstoppable virus. And alt.religion.kibology, the newsgroup devoted to Talmudic study of his personal quirks, may well be the first international cult to germinate on the Internet. The sheer bandwidth this man occupies must now cost the academic community, the National Science Foundation, and the international computing infrastructure hundreds, if not thousands, of dollars every day.

A megalomaniac posting his weekly grocery list to the Net for worldwide distribution does not impress me, particularly. It's the fact that a global community feels compelled to break into small discussion groups afterward that blows my mind, especially since there's no currency exchanged here. Fan clubs usually imply an attempt to capitalize on celebrity—$9.95 for an eight-by-ten glossy and a newsletter, or at least stamp money. But this is just fandom for the sake of itself.

Call me paranoid, but I've even noticed a trickle-down effect among Net celebrities. They quote each other incessantly. It's a kind of pyramid scheme. John Winston, the Net's preeminent alien visitor expert, for instance, is now a part of the kibology FAQ. Meanwhile, in Winston's bailiwick, alt.alien.visitors, a Net connoisseur dismisses the author of a mediocre non sequitur with another Net in-joke:

"You, sir, are no Mark Gooley."

IntErnAtIonAl FlAmE

NET FANDOM GAVE me my first taste of the bilious epistolary genre known as the flame. On the Laurie Anderson fan group, one foolhardy poster, a Mr. Anil Prasad, forgot the title of an upcoming Anderson release and was summarily scorched by a die-hard Anderson fanatic in Britain. "Dear Anil," he wrote. "How dare you confuse the composition of Anderson's works with the albumenic constitution of your own yolky brain. I think that you are well overdue for a discharge into a mental institution by early 1994 if all you can think to say about the extraordinary event of a new Anderson publication is that it will happen. I shall be able to forget your name with the ease that you forgot the title of her new work, but, at least, nobody will judge me to be an idiot. Yours sincerely."

Signed, Damian Shaw, St. Edmund's College, Cambridge.

I love it when Brits flame. They're so uptight, even when they think they're really cutting loose. It just drives me crazy. Even now, as I ponder the megabytes of flames I've sent, received, and applauded, this specimen of flamus brittanicus has a special place in my heart. It was so uncalled for, so abrupt, so mean, and yet so exquisitely executed — the essence of Net flamage.

Flames, for the uninitiated, are the Net's own species of verbal Luger. For some reason (anonymity? arrested development? boredom? physical distance?), netters are easily offended and quick to fire off incensed ad hominem attacks. When the target responds in kind, the resulting melee escalates into a full-fledged slugfest: flame war. Little or nothing is actually resolved in flame war, as participants toss reasoned argument to the four winds at the first opportunity.

But that's not the point. The point is to outwit, humiliate, browbeat, and generally outsnarl one's opponent. It is a game, not to be taken seriously, or even personally. Most seasoned Net veterans realize this. They also realize that one does not openly confess a penchant for flames or flame war ("That was a logical argument, you idiot!"). Flames are noise. Flames are trivial. Ostensibly, we try to avoid them.

And yet flame wars simmer on, and talking trash on the digital ballcourt has become a spectator sport. Flames have acquired their own grammar and syntax. They've fallen into a distinct formal groove. I comb the Net for them now, picking up mutant, oddly colored, or perfectly formed ones like seashells and sorting them by phenotype. The "Cyberhype Deflator," for instance: "You want to know the secret behind Virtual Sex? It's called Masturbation. Shh . . . Don't tell anyone you'll ruin the surprise." And then there's the classic "Newly Exposed Village Idiot" flame:

```
Why don't you pry your atropied little brain out
of your reeking, cancerous colon and shove it up
your weevil-infested, snot-packed nose where it
```

belongs? You must be a complete moron with the I.Q. of a hockey score to so proudly admit that you're a close-minded feeb with no ability to even maintain at least the illusion of objectivity in this discussion. . . . Nothing will ever change your tiny, calcified little inaccessable mind. Thank you for warning us, so we won't waste our time trying to have a rational discussion with you. And thank you so very much for being such an imbecilic, simple-minded, boorish, pus-encrusted dolt. We all need someone we can laugh at.

And for the connoisseur, metaflame is a must-download.

> Get a life you fucking morons!

Ahh. The classic get-a-life post. I'll give it a 7.

Hell, there's even an all-flame newsgroup, alt.flame, which has just been voted "Most Evil Newsgroup" in a Net-wide poll. It's the Sotheby's of flamage — sooner or later, every serious collector shows up there. "Welcome to alt.flame," the FAQ begins.

The sole purpose of this newsgroup is to insult your opponent. It's a kind of a game where there are no scores, just someone who gets flamed and someone who gets the tribute. Just to make it clear before you start, you have NO friends in alt.flame you're alone against the rest, who are alone against you. Still you shouldn't take the flames too seriously, try remembering that this is only a game. If you are easily offended you should hit the unsubscibe button at once. Please also note: YOU HAVE NO FRIENDS, THERE ARE NO TEAMS. IF YOU GET BACKUP FROM A GUY, HE MIGHT BE THE NEXT ONE STABBING YOU WITH A KNIFE.

The ground rules segue into a taxonomy of flamethrowers: the conspirator, the gross, the intellectualoid, the asphixiator, the hacker wannabe, the chameleon, the lightweight, the hit 'n' run, the sophist, the storyteller, the senseless and deviated.

Alt.flame's forte, at this juncture, is the jingoistic flame. Whereas other parts of the Net read like Bennetton ads, alt.flame has more of a Balkan vibe: Swedes versus Norwegians, Norwegians versus the British, Brits versus Americans, and Americans versus everyone else. It's really breathtaking to see citizens of different countries and different cultures converge with the aid of massive technology and then start a food fight. Alt.flame is global geopolitics reduced to am-not-are-too-I-know-you-are-but-what-am-I.

"Just like a limey bastard to miss the point," yells an American.

"Just like an American to try and start a racist thread," retorts a livid Brit.

Let the games begin.

Top of the second inning, the American hits hard with a Global Supercop flame. "Before you think you are so superior amongst the world's peoples," he sneers, "just remember: that F-111 or F-16 you see flying above your head is an American fucking jet plane. We don't see any of your fucking planes flying over *our* houses, cause we don't need anybody to protect us from boogymens. I'll bet you just hate it too. Good. Now fuck off, and go back to eating your jellied eel and chips, you wanker. Nothing personal."

"What do you guys think you're doing?" counterflames another Briton. "Is this supposed to be alt.america.against.-the.world or what? I consider it extremely sad that you have run out of ideas for flaming each other (not that that is suprising) and have resumed to slagging off different countries (especially England by the looks of it . . .) now. Get a life! Get a new newsgroup!" A Stupid American (tm) flame, with a Get a Life (tm) double axel. Impressive.

Top of the third, a trigger-happy Dartmouth student pitches his best imitation of Kevin Kline in *A Fish Called Wanda*. "Ah, quit yer fargin' whinin', ya limey lap-puppet lashin' luzer," he writes, fast out of the gate. "Take yer tea pot and yer crumpets, yer bloody queen and 'er mum, yer 'pip pips' n' 'cheerios' and shove it up yer beefeater boffin' boil-ridden bum! And as for the rest of you stinkin', clotted pools of yak puke . . . SHUT THE FUCK UP!! Especially you herdy-ferdy, bork, bork, borkin' simpering scandoscum suck weasels!! I gotta a fuckin' headache, I just ran out of thorazine and I'm going to rip yer fuckin' heads off and shit down yer collective albino throats!! I've had it, ya hear me? Thank you for worthless and ill spent time."

The waters have been chummed. The Norwegians are circling. A gorgeous, gorgeous cascade flame tears through alt.flame as the newsgroup's Scandinavian contingent piles onto the British:

```
. . . and their inventing this silly, wasteful
      game called 'golf'
. . . and their ugly, wasteful gardens
. . . and their role as the biggest drug pushers
      in the history of mankind
. . . and their boring BBC-TV programs
```

. . . and their bad low-flying-vertical-takeoff Harrier planes

. . . and their stupid left side driving . . . and their violent hooligans

. . . and their taste for Vinegar potato chips

. . . and their horrible Marmite

. . . and their butt-ugly royal family

. . . and their incredibly silly national anthem

. . . and their sarcasm and their political system which makes the Dark Ages democratic

. . . and their obnoxious electricity plugs

. . . and their backyard homocidal tendencies

. . . and their taste for killing 2-year olds

. . . and their stiff upper lips

. . . and the acid rain they're sending us

. . . and their stupid coal miners

. . . and their fish'n'chips

. . . and their dangerous, clunky, old nuclear plants

. . . and their contempt for anything not english

. . . and their umbrellas

. . . and their awful mint sauce

. . . and their ridiculous lawns

. . . and their funny-looking police uniforms

. . . and their acid-houses

. . . and their east-end bore the viewer shows

. . . and their fox hunting

. . . and their aristocratic image

. . . and their dry biscuits

. . . and their fear of the Euro-tunnel

. . . and their sad life.

To be fair, the Scandinavians are usually a well-behaved busload. Even the shouting match on alt.swedish.chef.bork.-bork.bork doesn't spin too far out of control. The controversy revolves around the linguistic nuances of Jim Henson's beloved food-juggling gourmand, the Swedish Chef. Apparently, the muppet does not mumble in ersatz Swedish but rather in ersatz Danish or ersatz Norwegian.

"The pronunciation the chef uses is a little harsh for Swedish, possibly inviting comparison to Danish," explains a netter in Denmark. "However the Swedish chef's trademark 'singsong' quality, that up-and-down slide through words and sentences, is in strong disagreement with the Danish delivery method, which usually consists of monotone delivery, little or no pause between words because of run-on, and seemingly random glottal stops called 'stoed,' and may also include keeping the mouth fully closed while talking. Swedish does have the singsong quality, but it is actually the Norwegians who have the rep for an operatic language, and bokmaal, the commonly written Norwegian language, is almost identical to written Danish. Maybe that's the sound they were after. The lure of meatballs may have been the deciding factor, since Danish and Norwegian cuisine have less recognizability."

"I understand that you are Danish," counters a Norwegian, "but I must protest to some of your views. The Norwegian 'bokmaal' bears resemblance to written Danish, but there are some big differences . . . 'Bokmaal' originates from Danish, [but] we must all remember that Norway used to be a Danish 'colony'. As for the cuisine bit . . . you seem to forget the 'lutefisk', the 'fenalaar', the 'flatbroed', the 'roemmegroet' and the 'smalahovud'."

The Swedish chef was unavailable for comment on his dubious nationality but is rumored to have silenced the charges with a substantial out-of-court settlement. He may have weathered the controversy by secluding himself in the Swedish Chef Borkland compound, but his innocent, child-like image, his future commercial success, and the trust of young people everywhere have been irrevocably compromised.

On the bright side, the Swedish Chef controversy does illuminate the finer points of Scandinavian linguistics and lutefisk preparation — two yawning gaps in my knowledge base. You never know when you'll be stormed by starving Norwegians who threaten to pillage your apartment unless they're served lutefisk immediately. Thanks to the Net, I'm prepared for that contingency (now *that's* what I call an educational resource).

Flame wars in particular are a valuable primer in international slang. Just as in real life, accents flare when arguments heat up. As long as everyone's getting along, we're all capable of smooth English globalspeak. But when things get contentious around here, flame warriors brandish their regionalisms like red-hot pincers. The Australians are particularly good at this. ("Ain't they fed the bloody dingoes lately, mate? You keep talkin' like that and you'll end up done like a dinner, so quit floggin' the cat in public for being such a pathetic crawler. If this is yer best bloody shot, you couldn't knock the dags off a sick canary. . . .") Australians do not check their chauvinism at the password prompt. Indeed, they even have their own flame tournament, aus.flame, a newsgroup by and for Australians. It doesn't see the traffic alt.-flame does, but aus.flame sarcasm is generally of a higher caliber than its international counterpart. Aus.flamers slip newbies on the barbie like so many shrimp. It rocks.

I find all of this perversely reassuring.

It's not that I'm misanthropic. I'm just pleased this technology hasn't ground us all into homogenous gruel. There's something frightening about a place where everything is clean and shiny and conducted in a polite common dialect. That's not human; that's the Small World (tm) ride at Disneyland. On the Net, an Australian doesn't flame like a German or a Finn or an American. Against all odds, our accents survive the meat grinder of ASCII text. And for better or worse, we have a dizzying array of local synonyms for "idiot."

CAmPfIre tALeS

URBAN LEGENDS: the unsubstantiated stories that have been passed around so many times that they seem true. Things that happened to friends of friends, or that your mother-in-law's veterinarian's hairdresser *swore* she saw.

You know, like the one about the boy who finds a stray puppy on the dock and takes it in. He raises it as a pet and teaches it tricks, and then it turns out to be a rat. Or cow tipping. Or the gerbil story about Richard Gere. This is the folklore of lunch counters and watercoolers—the last gasps of our spoken story tradition.

Terry Chan, author of the alt.folklore.urban FAQ, defines an urban legend (UL) as a story that "appears mysteriously and spreads spontaneously in varying forms, contains elements of humor or horror (the horror often 'punishes' someone who flouts society's conventions), makes good storytelling, [and] does NOT have to be false, although most are. ULs often have a basis in fact, but it's their life after-the-fact (particularly in reference to the second and third points) that gives them particular interest." The FAQ divides urban legends into seven shades of substantiation, from 100 percent scientific truth to 100 percent falsehood (scores in the middle account for bogus stories with a kernel of truth, dubious legends that have not conclusively been proven false, unanswerable claims, and "maybe it didn't happen, but it's scientifically possible").

In one company or one neighborhood, a small meme pool of urban legends spreads to the point of saturation, and that's it. No one knows any more, and no one makes new ones up from whole cloth. But assemble 20 million people from around the world, and you have one hell of a campfire.

That's what alt.folklore.urban is — an electronic campfire. Newsgroup regulars and newbies alike gather round and relate urban legends with varying degrees of embellishment and panache, and then say, "Oh yeah, I know that one. But did you hear the one about . . ." This group is one of the few places on the Net where newbies are warmly welcomed. They are fresh blood. They keep the circle going, as the legends are passed around and around and around, with new twists and occasionally something completely fresh, a squirt of lighter fluid on the embers.

"A woman was raped in an alley [or somewhere] in broad daylight," says Andrew Bulhak, an Australian university student. "Of course, she screamed for help; the passersby thought that she was just uttering 'primal screams,' and some of them 'primal scream'ed right back at her."

"Someone told me a story about Bungee jumping," says Greg Foster at the University of Missouri. "There was this company (unknown) who wanted to start jumping off the side of a building. They rode the elevator to the 27th floor. They knew they needed a certain amount of rope for each floor — 10 ft. — minus the stretch of the rope. When the first person jumped off, the company realized there was no such thing as the 13th floor. . . .”

Melissa Jordan in Maryland asks, “Has anyone else out there heard the old Russian story that people with one single big eyebrow running across their heads are really vampires? And, to make sure that they don't come back from the grave to suck your blood, their heads must be separated from their bodies before they are buried. I just want to know if the powers that be whacked Brezhnev's head off after he went to his great socialist reward (of course, there's always the story that Brezhnev had already been deceased for some time when he 'officially' died, and some renegade Disney guys were getting paid huge hunks of cash to do the old 'Hall of Presidents' number on him to keep people from wondering—all he had to do was stand on Lenin's tomb and wave a couple times every year . . . But I digress . . .) Anyway, I was just wondering, if this is true, whether Brooke Shields is a vampire, and, if so, when somebody's going to lop her head off?”

“I just heard this on KABC-TV in Los Angeles,” says Rick Kitchen. “A 10-year-old boy in Colorado had bought a new toy airplane, and opened the instructions to read how to use the plane. What he found, instead, was a plea, written in broken English, from the maker of the toy, asking for help to get him out of the Chinese prison where he is being held. The boy and his mother apparently have taken the paper to the State Department for help.”

The “Help, I'm being held prisoner in a Chinese cookie factory” legend that spawned this story may date back further than the Neiman Marcus cookie legend, but no one is sure—the cookie tale is a true chestnut. But it's told here all the time. The “Donna Anderson” version uses the first person, instead of the usual third. But there are two or three intermediaries between alt.folklore.urban and the mysterious

Ms. Anderson, who may or may not be on the Net. She writes:

My daughter & I had just finished a salad at Neiman-Marcus Cafe in Dallas & decided to have a small dessert. Because our family are such cookie lovers, we decided to try the "Neiman-Marcus Cookie." It was so excellent that I asked if they would give me the recipe and they said with a small frown, "I'm afraid not." Well, I said, would you let me buy the recipe? With a cute smile, she said, "Yes." I asked how much, and she responded, "Two fifty." I said with approval, just add it to my tab.

Thirty days later, I received my VISA statement from Neiman-Marcus and it was $285.00. I looked again and I remembered I had only spent $9.95 for two salads and about $20.00 for a scarf. As I glanced at the bottom of the statement, it said, "Cookie Recipe—$250.00." Boy, was I upset!! I called Neiman's Accounting Dept. and told them the waitress said it was 'two fifty,' and I did not realize she meant $250.00 for a cookie recipe. I asked them to take back the recipe and reduce my bill and they said they were sorry, but because all the recipes were this expensive so not just everyone could duplicate any of our bakery recipes . . . the bill would stand.

Donna then gives us the recipe itself as her way of "getting even" with Neiman Marcus. I don't know how many people have actually tried it, but I doubt Needless Markup is hurting; generalizations about the Net population are dangerous, but I'll venture to say they're not racking up Neiman's InCircle charge-card points.

Joel Furr at Duke has another tale of food health hazards. "A friend of a friend of mine got really really sick the other day," he says. "He'd parked his car and gone into a store and not come out for about two hours, and when he came out he drank a bottle of Diet Coke that he'd left in the car. It was warm, y'know, but he was thirsty. Well, when he got home he started feeling really sick and called 911, and when they got him to the hospital they figured out that he'd drunk about a half-bottle of formaldehyde! He hadn't known that Diet Coke turns into formaldehyde if it gets hot."

Moving onto the ever-popular topic of pets, Christopher Troise announces that he has a "confirmed dog in oven story," by way of his coworker's aunt and uncle, who own a pet grooming salon. "One time this old couple drop a dog off for a trim and a shampoo. So the aunt puts the dog in this special 'dog sized hairdrying unit' and then, forgetfully, goes shopping. A couple of hours later she returns and the dog is baked to a black crisp. They were able to BS the old couple about the dog's 'untimely' death due to the stress of the visit, etc., but they were in hot water when the old couple wanted to come in to 'say goodbye' to Jr."

The animal kingdom is the ur-genre of urban folklore. But all kinds of animal stories are popular, especially when they include insects and detritivores (thus overlapping into the "rot" genre). Dave Clark, posting from Ellicott City, Maryland, snagged a great story from his sister-in-law, whose friend told her that one time, "a woman in Arizona bought a cactus and took it home, where the cactus pretty much acted like a normal cactus. Until one day, when she saw that it was pulsating, the skin of the cactus moving in and out. The woman didn't know what to think, so she called 911. She was told to get out of the house, right now!, and wait for people to come (which people are unspecified). Anyhow, the right people, whoever they may be, arrive, go into the house, and put the cactus in a large, secure container. It turned out that the pulsating was a result of the cactus being a nest for a horde of scorpions! The scorpions apparently found the cactus as a source of water and food, and eventually ate all the innards so that nothing but scorpions remained. The 'pulsating' was scorpions moving around inside the cactus' skin."

Without a doubt, the greatest animal story, "How to Remove a Dead Whale," comes via a UC Davis student. It has been forwarded at least three times but supposedly originates with a coast guard officer in Oregon. Supposedly, a local TV station sends a reporter out "to cover the removal of a 45-foot, eight-ton dead whale that washed up on the beach. The responsibility for getting rid of the carcass was placed on the Oregon State Highway Division, apparently on the theory that highways and whales are very similar in the sense of being large objects. So anyway, the highway engineers hit upon the plan of blowing up the whale with dynamite. The thinking is that the whale would be blown into small pieces, which would be eaten by seagulls, and that would be that. A textbook whale removal. So they moved the spectators back up the beach, put a half-ton of dynamite next to the whale and set it off. . . . What follows, on the videotape, is the most wonderful event in the history of the universe. First you see the whale carcass disappear in a huge blast of smoke and flame. Then you hear the happy spectators shouting 'Yayy!' and 'Whee!' Then, suddenly, the crowd's tone changes. You hear a new sound like 'splud.' You hear a woman's voice shouting 'Here come pieces of . . . MY GOD!' Something smears the camera lens. Later, the reporter explains: 'The humor of the entire situation suddenly gave way to a run for survival as huge chunks of whale blubber fell everywhere.' One piece caved in the roof of a car parked more than a quarter of a mile away. Remaining on the beach were several rotting whale sectors the size of condominium units. There was no sign of the seagulls who had no doubt permanently relocated to Brazil."

There are certain genres of urban legend that barely register outside alt.folklore.urban yet take on a life of their own once the newsgroup's folklorists get going. Such is the case with urban legends about *Sesame Street.*

"Was the actor who played Big Bird really a cocaine dealer?" asks Nils Soe, a Yale student. "Did he bring it on the set?" No one knows the answer to this one, but there is a vigorous debate concerning Bert and Ernie's nebulous sexuality. "What *did* you think the relationship between Bert and Ernie was? Friends? Roommates? Who are as different as day from night, yet live in the same house and sleep in the same room for years and years despite getting on each others nerves all the time?" Keith Lim, a college student in Burnaby, British Columbia, and other inquiring minds want to know.

Although he admits it's "been a long time since I've seen 'Sesame Street,'" Damian Penny at Memorial University in Newfoundland tells us what he's heard about the show lately: "Ernie and Bert no longer live together, because kids began identifying them with homosexuals. Bert was killed off, to teach kids to deal with death. Cookie Monster (my favorite character!) no longer eats cookies, [and] Snufflufagus (sp?) is known to everyone, not just Big Bird.

"Obviously," he says, "these can't ALL be true; indeed, hearing about most of these brought back memories of elementary school, when it was going around that Mr. Rogers ('Mr. Rogers' Neighbourhood') had died of a drug overdose! Can someone out there shed a little light about the rumors

I've been hearing? (The only one I believe is the last one, about 'Snuffy')."

From *Sesame Street,* the topic shifts to gang initiations. The sister of a coworker of Lee Boyle's wife fed him a classic. "A woman fills her gas tank at a self-serve station. When she goes to the cashier's booth to pay, the cashier warns her that somebody has gotten into the back seat of her car. He advises her to fumble with her purse to stall while he calls the police. The police arrive and arrest a teenager who confesses that, as part of his gang initiation, he must sneak into the cars of two women at gas stations in order to rape and kill them." Another netter notes that the kill count has gone up — the old gang rite UL required only one parking lot casualty.

"Try this one," says Tom Cikoski. "A certain USENET group has a gang initiation rite. Members of the group post stories of dubious voracity and spelling as 'bait.' When innocent newbies post corrections in followups, the initiate fingers the poster, travels to the poster's site and kills him or her. Once this has been done, the initiate has his/her name added to the FAQ."

Meta-alert! Meta-alert! When the group starts folklorizing itself, things get surreal on alt.folklore.urban. Like, after Mark Thomas, a voxer, relates the age-old pet rat story (". . . the vet leaves the room and tells the family to do the same, because this is no dog, it is a carnivorous rat"), a netter in Berkeley adds an extra kicker, "And then the dog exploded, showering the couple with baby spiders." Signed, Drew "and the vet puked on their shoes" Lawson.

And the alt.folklore.urban survival guide, authored by Antony Cooper in Pretoria, has been known to induce epileptic fits in those allergic to bees and excessive referencing. Fortunately, "it does not contain any rat's meat whatsoever. Also, it is such a turkey that if you leave it out in the rain, it will die. . . . The survival guide does not freeze, whether or not the Twinkie has been boiled, and it does not cost two-fifty. It is not the script of a snuff film about a CIA plot to transmit AIDS from humans to monkeys, nor do gerbils have words for it, and it will not dissolve in Coke . . . nor has it been found drugged, disguised and hidden in the lyrics of a Disney record played backwards. Film at 11."

Although there is a lot of camaraderie on alt.folklore.urban, it is not without its political skirmishes. The most serious is a point-of-procedure spat between purists who want the group to be just urban legends and no off-topic discussion and those who don't mind the noise level. "Sure AFU's got noise," writes Ewan Kirk. "But it's also got a good quantity of legends. If you want your legend discussed by experts come here. If you want a good laugh come here too."

The UL puritans, led by Joel Furr, disagree and eventually secede from the group, forming their own newsgroup, alt.folklore.suburban, where they dissect folktales of the burbs. Some of these are quite good, particularly the ones involving dead bodies. Swarthmore student Jake Carlo sets a benchmark with a gruesome vignette of his friend's uncle, "a man in his sixties who, after years of alcohol abuse, went on one final, deadly bender. Apparently, the accumulation of nitrogen gas in his body was so tremendous that he was literally blown apart by the pressure. Parts of his body were found scattered around the room in which he died — a very grim ending. As an aside, a couple of years prior to his death, a foul odor led the Elkhart, Indiana, Health Department to discover the Uncle had been 'excreting' all over the house in which he lived with his 80 year old mother — whom he'd been sexually abusing and who was consequently removed from the home by the state. As the old refrain goes, I swear to god it's true." Despite the antipathy between alt.folklore.-

urban and alt.folklore.suburban, good burb stories like this do manage to cross enemy lines.

After hours spent around the campfire, it feels like my turn to start a story. Instead, I finish one. A student in Buffalo, Dan Case, tells the first half of an urban legend, "the one about Robert Benchley and a friend when they were at Harvard. They dressed up like moving men, went to a prestigious-looking house somewhere in Cambridge, and knocked on the door. 'We're here for the sofa,' they told the perplexed matron. They took a nice old sofa from the living room and left with it. They went to a nearby house and said, 'We've brought the sofa.' You can guess the rest—the only kicker being that they weren't around when the first lady visited the second one's house."

I've heard this one before. There's more. "The real kicker," I say, "is that the second house had a party to which the owners of the couch were invited. Terribly stuffy Brahman affair, with everyone talking out of one side of his mouth and all that. Three days later, the hostess of the party received a package with no return address—containing the couch's slipcovers."

And the campfire crackles on.

PhReAker fOLkloRE

THERE WAS A time when phone system hackers—phreakers—could solder together a few Radio Shack parts and hack Ma Bell with relative impunity. Those days are over, but the legacy of phreaking still bubbles up from the bulletin board culture that preceded widespread access to the Net. Because the boards deal in the technical blood and guts of raw code and homemade hardware, they're the last fringe outposts in the modem world. They're still part of the underground and promise to remain so.

Phreak recipes do float into the Net. But now that the criminal stakes are so high and law enforcement has gotten serious, phreaking is passed around in the guise of folklore rather than as practical advice. One reason for this is that you can never be sure who is reading the Net. Big Brother could be lurking on any newsgroup; the Net is definitely not safe in that regard. So ASCII schematics are doused with disclaimers and punctuated with nostalgia about the good old days.

Polishing the legends seems to get more airtime on the Net than new and zany ways to goose the telco. Phreakdom may be vital in the bulletin board world, where you have to know what you're looking for. But on the Net, it's being codified, partly for the benefit of newbies who keep asking elementary questions about defunct devices (What are blue boxes? How did they work? Tell us, Grandpa, tell us!). At which point, the wizened phreaker takes off his spectacles, thinks back to his days as a Reagan-era teen, and shares a few nuggets of his accumulated lore.

"What's a beige box?" queries a wide-eyed but fairly well-behaved newbie ankle-biter on alt.cyberpunk. Journeyman phreak Paul Houle answers the digital whippersnapper with professorial humor:

A beige box is phreaker slang for a lineman's handset, or any similar device. One can make oneself a beige box rather easily by attaching alligator clips to an ordinary phone, although there are a few electronic modifications that make it easier to tap telephone lines undetected. The most highly prized beige boxes in phreakdom are genuine stolen lineman's handsets. A lineman dropped his butt set in the back of a truck yesterday and drove off, and I came within about inches of grabbing it . . . damn!

Blue boxes are devices which imitate the signalling protocol used for switching in the early days of direct distance dialing. What they do is use a 2600 hz tone to reset the far end switch to a "waiting for commands mode" and then use a series of tones similar to touch-tones to transmit the commands to set up calls. Blue boxes not only made it possible to make phree calls, but also made it possible to hack the network. Blue boxes are almost obsolete in the US; the only way to

use them is to dial international 800 numbers and
use them to tamper with a foreign fone system.

Red boxes fake the tone pulse sequences used
to tell the central office that you put a coin in
a pay phone. They still work in many places.
Black boxes were very simple [<$1.00 in parts]
devices that played with the line voltage on
older switches to let you pick up the phone without the central office figuring out that you did,
so your phriends don't get billed when they call
you. Newer switches don't connect you until they
recognize that you've picked up, so this is useless. Neon boxes are a method of attaching your
phone to external audio sources. Many other kinds
of 'box' are really BS made up by self-styled
teenage phreaks.

The BS boxes and their dubious claims are everywhere.
But in phreaker folklore, they are just as interesting as their
working counterparts. Omnipotent boxes are the tall tales
of phreakdom — the Holy Grails that bestow infinite free untraceable calls or destructive powers upon their owners. Tra-
ditionally called by some color name, factual and fantasy
phreak devices come in every hue of the rainbow and a few
colors found only in the J. Crew catalog. Their inventors use
equally colorful handles, as in the Nevada phreaker who calls
himself "The Pimp," whose Acrylic Box promises "Three-
Way-Calling, Call Waiting, programmable Call Forward-
ing . . . ALL for FREE." His creations trumpet themselves like
Bill Graham productions (The Scarlet Box. A High Mtn
Hackerz Presentation. Written & Created by: THE PIMP).

There's a lot of showmanship in these carnival barks,
whether they're for long-distance toll relief or contraptions to
keep the wily phreaker one step ahead of the feds. "Every

true phreaker lives in fear of the dreaded F.B.I. 'Lock in Trace,'" announces the Aqua Box's ad-cum-descriptive blurb. "For a long time, it was impossible to escape from the lock in trace (the lock in trace is a device used by the F.B.I. to lock into the phone users location so that he can not hang up while a trace is in progress). This box does offer an escape route. . . ."

And there are MANY, MANY more. . . .

"Ever want to really make yourself be heard? Ever talk to someone on the phone who just doesn't shut up? Or just call the operator and pop her eardrum? Well, up until recently it has been impossible for you to do theese things," announces a phreaker named Shadowhawk. "Unless of course you've got a blast box. All a blast box is, is a really cheap amplifier (around 5 watts or so) connected in place of the microphone on your telephone. It works best on model 500 AT&T Phones, and if constructed small enough, can be placed inside the phone. . . . This device is espicially good for PBS subscription drives." The recipe follows, along with a note: "Have Phun, and don't get caught!"

One phreaker even claims to have invented the mythical Blotto Box, a device that can kill phone exchanges and cripple entire area codes. Blotto was a fantasy that lodged itself into the BBS network because it made teenagers drool with visions of despotic power. "The Blotto Box is every phreaks dream," writes the Traveler, who also claims to have invented the White Gold Box, the Aqua Box, the Diverti Box, and the Cold Box. "You could hold AT&T down on it's knee's with this device. Because, quite simply, it can turn off the phone lines everywhere. Nothing. Blotto. No calls will be allowed out of an area code, and no calls will be allowed in. No calls can be made inside it for that matter. As long as the switching system stays the same, this box will not stop at a mere area code. It will stop at nothing. The electrical impulses that emit from this box will open every line. Every line will ring and ring and ring . . . the voltage will never be cut off until the box/generator is stopped. This is no 200 volt job, here. We are talking GENERATOR."

This is the stuff of telco executives' nightmares, and if it was ever deployed, it would bring an army of Secret Service agents down on the bulletin board community before you could say "Waco." With that in mind, the Traveler prefaces his Blotto recipe with a disclaimer, "This file is strictly for informational purposes and should not be actually built and used! Usage of this electronical impulse machine could have the severe results listed below and could result in high federal prosecution! All right, now that that is cleared up, here is the basis of the box and it's function. . . ." Since no one's ever supposed actually to *build* the thing, the recipe stands. Blotto lives!

The Chartreuse Box, "so named because this is an obnoxious box and chartreuse is an obnoxious color, is designed to take advantage of the thousands of dollars Ma Bell pays to the electric company each day. As you know, your telephone line is a constant power source. The chart box is designed to allow you to tap that power source for whatever sicko purposes you might have in mind. . . . Once the voltage is set, remove the box from the line, hook your device up to the charged poles, and plug the box back in. If you're really in a constructive mood, build a switch into the box. Now leech Ma Bell's precious energy to your hearts content."

"So you want to be James Bond eh? So you want to be a private eye eh?" asks Razz, author of the Razz Box. "Well here's your chance to pick up some very important clues or ideas using your neighbors telephone line. Forget about climbing a telephone pole this sort of boxing can be done on the ground. Purpose: To tap your neighbors line without your neighbor knowing it. You can also make FREE (let me repeat that) FREE!! Phone calls to your favorite K-RAD-GNEW-WAREZ boards."

The vintage hacker slang in these phreak box teasers hints at how dated most of them are. Many of the classic devices don't even work anymore, since AT&T has upgraded its switching system. Other legendary phreak boxes are just that—legends. And even the ones that work are riskier now, because they're easier to trace. They are relics from before the MAN got hip to the phreak scene. That joyride is over now. People are going to jail. It's not funny anymore.

"In my opinion," writes the Marauder, a member of the now-defunct Legion of Doom, "Redboxing should simply be called toll fraud, since doing it requires little, or no understanding of the phone system whatsoever. I place it on about the same level as using a Sprint, or MCI code to make a free call. Things have changed greatly since the days that I, and my friends explored the telephone system, and discovered some of its many wonders. Security is downright _MEAN_, laws have been written, programs are better, etc. I would not trade for anything, the memories I have, nor the friends I have made over the years pursuing my 'hobby'. Today though, things are changing so rapidly that I sadly, cannot even hope to keep up with it all." The old stunts lack glamour now. "Things have changed," you hear all the old phreakers say, and always the same refrain: times were simpler then.

On #hack last night, I found six high school students talking about a brush with the law. One of them had been caught breaking into a Southern Bell facility in Georgia. The rest of the channel flooded the screen with questions. Who was with him? What was he looking for? What did he get? Was he arrested? Surrounded by his admiring peers, the youthful trespasser told the story of jumping the fence, running through a thicket of thorns, and confronting the police. He'd copped to a minor trespassing charge.

Emmanuel Goldstein, a living legend in phreakdom, drifted in, unnoticed, and then left, without a word.

eVEn ConSO1E CoWGiR1s
GeT tHe bLuEs

UGH. I'VE BEEN outed as a woman on a late-night IRC session. I don't want to deal with this tonight. I brace myself for the inevitable barrage of private messages:

```
*kilgore* What do you look like?
*jimv* How old are you? Are you still in school?
*casper* Would you care to talk in private?
*crackerjack* What do you look like?
*synapse* HI THERE :-))
*vito* Where are you?
```

As my screen oozes with IRC pick-up lines, I wonder whether it's worth it to stick around. I answer some of my messages.

```
/msg jimv 22. No, I graduated last June.
/msg vito Miami Beach, Florida.
/msg casper Uh, I really don't think the "Fire"
+episode really merits an in-depth pri-
+vate discussion.
```

It's not easy being a chick in cyberspace.

But I figure, a light coating of teenage drool is a small price to pay to be on the edge. The Net lets me tunnel through supercomputers from New Zealand to Palo Alto to Glasgow, trade virus folklore with Czechoslovakian hackers, and keep up with all my favorite Barney the Dinosaur vigilante hate groups. It's a place where I can say what I want, when I want, in whatever manner I choose. And there's almost a moral obligation to roam over it now, before AT&T, Warner Cable, and Barry Diller roll out the barbed wire. At least, that's how I justify obsessive sleep deprivation, clogged phone lines, and eye strain as I Netsurf into the wee hours, my trusty coffee mug on one side of the computer and a bowl of highly sugared cereal on the other.

Look at watch. 3:41 A.M. Think, God, this rocks. Think, corporate America will never let this last. Make more coffee.

I decide to switch IRC channels. I was sick of talking about pyromania anyway, and I'm just not up for digital propositions tonight.

Unfortunately, a few of the boys want to follow me around anyway.

```
*vito* Lucky girl, I'm freezing cold in New York
+right now.
*kilgore* Are u ignoring me?
```

Don't get me wrong. I don't find this stuff scary or intimidating. It doesn't violate my sense of self or whatever harassment psychobabble is floating around the talk show circuit these days. It's just that constant distraction by squirrelly comp-sci majors is a fact of Net life for the female minority. That's the real price of being a woman on the Net—not the sexual innuendoes or the overhyped threat of "cyber-rape," just periodic shattering of concentration by digital guidos. The constant drip-dripping of unsolicited messages amounts to a form of Chinese water torture.

```
*casper* Yeah, I guess not :-) Wanna talk anyway?
/msg casper Not right now. I'm trying to catch up
+on another channel.
```

What was I saying? Ah, yes, the Net.

Away from the subdivisions of online suburbia, the Net rolls away in vast stretches of coiled copper telephone wire and supports a free-ranging population of info-addicts, Sega warriors, crypto-anarchists, and teen hackers. Forget the media ballyhoo about electronic town halls and virtual parlors; the Net is more saloon than salon. Not too many women in these here parts, scant discussion of philosophy and impressionist paintings, and *no* tea sandwiches. Rather, much of the Net exudes a ballistic ambiance seldom found outside post-apocalyptic splatterpunk video games. Someone should nail up a sign: "Now entering the Net. Welcome to Boyland. Don't mind the bodily fluids and cartoon-caliber violence. And if you can't take someone ripping your arm off and beating you with the bloody stump, go back to where you came from, girlie."

```
*vito* Yeah, I sure could use a tropical vaca-
+tion. Got a balcony I could sleep on?
/msg vito Sorry, dude, the cyberpunk hostel is up
+in Orlando.
```

As one netter put it, "Chicks on computers are considered to be chicks first, and human beings second (if at all). It's something special if you see a babe on a BBS." As a BBS babe, I have to agree. If someone were to ask me how many of us there are, I'd give the easy answer: damn few. Beyond that, even a ballpark estimate is tricky, for a few reasons. First of all, the Net has absorbed everything from corporate mainframes to Bob's Basement BBS into its cybernetic cytoplasm; it's far too anarchic and decentralized to ever census. Second, thousands of women hide on the Net by simply remaining silent. And last but not least, when female netters do talk, they often use male pseudonyms. No one can call you on it, the reasoning goes, so why deal with a bunch of horndog e-mail?

vito C'mon. I'm an icicle up here.
kilgore Are you ignoring me, or are you just +ugly?

I usually finesse the gender issue with an androgynous nickname, but I'm honest when questioned whether I'm male or female . . . most of the time.

/msg kilgore Look, I hate to quash your weaselly +hopes of Net.sex, but that guy was fuckin' +around with you. I'm a marine.

It's true. Some of those Net dudes are actually dudettes. And vice versa. In fact, there's so much gender confusion on the Net that paranoia surrounds anyone claiming to be female. Consequently, women are sometimes treated like lab specimens of alien life, subject to a torrent of prurient, er, "scientific" inquiries. Apparently, 50 percent of the human population ranks right up there with UFO's and Elvis sightings on the netter's list of dubious phenomena. In the end it's a catch-22: half of the Net jumps you because they think you're really a man. The other half jumps you because they believe you're a woman.

```
*crackerjack* vito tells me you're in Florida. I
+bet you even have a tan — speaking as a pasty
+Bostonian :-) Wear bikinis?
```

When I tracked down Diana Tenery-Fisher, aka Cass, the moderator of MindVox's "Women Online" forum, she just warned me to brace myself for a hazing. "You have to realize that you are a minority and you may be an oddity to some people. You're just going to get, from the men, a little good-natured hazing . . . The second you say you're new, if there's any little tiny thing that they can pick on, they'll jump you. And it's not to be malicious. They want to see if you can survive. And if you can, they'll welcome you with open arms . . . It's sort of like a fraternity in that way."

It's weird though, being rushed by a bunch of hackers. I mean, these aren't exactly guys I picture in chug-a-thons back at school. Plus, Net pile-ons, however spiteful, are only sticks and stones. Your ego may get a little scorched, but there's no alcohol poisoning or internal bleeding involved here. And — this is key — men have no physical advantage in cyberspace. I'm five six, but no one is taller than me on the Net. I'm not a big person, but no one can muscle me aside. To paraphrase FDR morphed into Naomi Wolf, there is nothing to fear but the victim mentality.

Still, says Cass, "You're going to find women who get picked on and then disappear because they think, oh, this is cyberspace and people are mean. And then they leave. And then there's the total opposite, which is women who come in guns flying."

There's a strong selection factor that favors the latter: flame war. This is where many women opt out of the Net experience, leaving a few pilgrim souls to blaze the trail by sparring with Beavis and Butthead (feminist progress marches on, huh huh, huh huh huh). But regardless of gender, every non-lurker is flamed at some point. It's like gravity — inevitable — and the most trivial non-issues can trigger it. Not so long ago, I was flamed for a lapse in grammar. I don't know which was more offensive: some anonymous prig's officious lecture on proper use of the past participle, or the fact that he addressed me as "needledick."

```
*vito* ??????
/msg vito The answer is *NO*
```

When Leticia Baldridge publishes *Miss Manners' Guide to Online Etiquette,* it will no doubt advise ladies and gentlemen to ignore these vile little missives, or to send back a "curt but polite reply." And to be honest, there is some pressure among women on the Net to be, well, civilized. Jumping into a flame war is like admitting that you enjoy slam dancing or use your kitchen spice rack to showcase an eclectic assortment of firearms. Not exactly de rigueur.

But sometimes, I'm just surfing along, minding my own business, and some skinny-assed pimply teenage pseudohacker (or the aforementioned Grammar Cop) *starts* with me. At first, I ignore it. I repeat, "I'm a woman. I'm more mature than that. I don't have to give this guy the attention he so desperately craves." And I'm really grown-up about it . . . for a good ten minutes. And then enough is enough, and it's suddenly very easy to get in touch with my inner Grace Jones. She says, "OK, dude. You wanna shake it up? Fine."

```
*crackerjack* Tan in teh nude?
/msg crackerjack Brush up on your one-handed
+typing.
```

```
/msg crackerjack And stop msging me.
/msg crackerjack SQUIRREL. Get a life.
```

But after a brief spark of visceral satisfaction, flames usually leave me feeling dubious about Net life in general. So big deal, I can be as flamboyantly rude as any Tourette-riddled techie. I've proven I can run with rodents, and sometimes *even be accepted as one of them.* Great. It's not something I brag about, and sometimes I loathe, loathe, loathe it. That's usually when I cast about for other women, if only to feel a little less outnumbered.

Depending on where I rove, I can squint across the virtual horizon and not see another console cowgirl for hundreds of kilobytes. But sometimes I'm lucky, and I run into someone like Cass, whose verbal sharpshooting is pure Annie Oakley, or Lisa Palac, who edits the San Francisco cyberporn magazine *FutureSex.* Palac is the Calamity Jane of cyberspace, a feminist pornographer who eats flames for breakfast. As befits a cybersex advocate, Palac is quick to equate technology and sex, and sometimes it's hard to tell which she's referring to when she admonishes women to experiment.

"Women have some catching up to do in terms of figuring out how it works, what they can get out of it, how they can use it," she says, ostensibly speaking about the Internet. "And so you have to be a little bit determined — extra-determined, right? You have to work a little bit harder than the average guy to get where you want to go."

She tells me a story, one of her favorites, about a woman so frustrated at the dearth of beefcake photos on local bulletin boards that she trekked down to the gay section of San Francisco, bought a bunch of really hard-core S&M postcards, and did digital scans of them. "Then," says Palac, "she uploaded them to this board because, she said, 'They need to be out there, and *somebody's* gotta do it!' And I said, 'Well, right on, sister.' And that's really the only way to make a difference, is to get your hands dirty, so to speak, and make a change. Cause you can't wait for somebody else to give you what you want—across the board, in life. Don't wait for Prince Charming to give you an orgasm—or show you how a computer works. Go and do it yourself." Palac pauses. "I think that the Internet will be to women in the nineties what the vibrator was to women in the seventies. It's going to have that kind of power."

On the other coast, and at the opposite end of the female Net spectrum, is Stacy Horn, who describes her New York bulletin board, ECHO (East Coast Hangout), as an "electronic salon" composed of different forums—art and culture, music, books, and such. Her goal: to bring civilization to cyberspace. Horn seems intent on tidying the place up, at least in her corner of the Net.

"This is not a public square open to anyone who walks by," Horn insists. "It actually is a private salon. So it's closer to if-you-were-going-to-come-sit-down-at-my-dinner-table kind of behavior, not if-you're-going-to-be-walking-down-my-street kind of behavior. It's a community. Everyone that comes in is a part of it. It's like not making a mess in your own home."

In an effort to tame the electronic frontier, Horn has done what successful frontier settlers have always done: import women. She's made a concerted effort to recruit them, at first offering free accounts to women and then setting them up with "big sister" mentors to teach them the ropes. She also has a pretty fierce affirmative action policy when it comes to recruiting moderators for ECHO's forums. "Half the hosts on ECHO are women," she crows. "So, to a large extent, women are setting the tone, as opposed to other systems where you get there and it feels like there's nothing but men running it. . . . I hear all the time that ECHO is more civilized than any other online place like the Internet, that there's very little flaming, and people are generally very polite."

It's as if ECHO's women, having arrived by ship to the Dark Continent, have now convinced its lawless menfolk to shave and start using coasters. As more women arrive on-line, Horn envisions a blossoming of ECHO clones, havens of civility amid the larger crash and bash of the Net. "Rather than the Internet getting more like ECHO, what I see is a bunch of ECHOs evolving around the world," she says, "and people can go from ECHO to ECHO to ECHO."

But there's a rub to this vision of digital domesticity: ECHO's tea party is emphatically outside the Net's technical loop. "Very few conversations [on ECHO] have anything to do with computers," Horn says matter-of-factly. "All the computer conferences are dead as a doornail. Most of the discussion revolves around arts and culture."

Problem is, I'd rather learn how to build a cellular phone scanner in a den of hormones than discuss the politics of meaning in a salon full of upturned pinkies, male or female. So I jump back into the pit, this time with a conspicuously female handle. Same private messages, different ethical pot of coffee. Now the question is not whether to bail out but whether to exploit someone's hard-up social situation for personal gain.

```
*ice* What's a nice girl like you doing with a
+bunch of phreaker wannabes?
/msg ice Looking for someone who knows how to
+build a cellular scanner. Have a clue?
```

Needless to say, I show up on the private channel and listen to this guy's problems with his comp-sci project, his university's incompetent computer administrator, and the last person he tried to rope into a relationship. This is all by way of introductions.

In cyberspace, no one knows you're opening mail and paying bills.

And yes, this makes me a data slut. I recognize the contradiction.

As I watch the seventy-character ribbon of words take small, even jumps up to the top of my screen, I realize that it's the same old game, different medium. After all the sci-fi-inspired fear that technology will obscure our humanity, the humanity shines through loud and clear, and it's the same aggression, attention-mongering, loneliness, braggadocio, and manipulation that we bitched about before. Technology has yet to muffle the bullshit that makes us human.

I don't know whether to be depressed or reassured by this.

I think the only thing that's saved me from a particularly nasty brand of cynicism on the Net was one brief brush with a true gentleman. The Silicon Surfer, as he is known by his nom-de-hack, crashed in from the periphery of my e-mail universe just as my academic account was about to expire. Net Death loomed like an oncoming train. The Surfer offered to help. I didn't know much about him — still don't — just that some California hacker was determined that I not flicker out. Maybe it was altruism or a sense of Net kinship — hard to tell what motivates faceless strangers in this big soup. But the Surfer read like he was trying to impress me, in his slack, hackish way. Surfermail percolated into my account from New Mexico and California, messages like "lemmie have a look around and we'll get you dug in and safe (Figures, you

HAD to get a vax! Ugh, not nearly as good with em as a nice old unix, but ill deal w/ it . . .) Once i get a handful of accounts fer ya, you can telnet out of em to where you can get a stable e-mail adress to use. Sound ok? Pretty simple, i HOPE. . . ."

Somehow, it was reassuring to have a scraggly guardian angel of sorts on the Net.

While the Surfer shot the pipeline of VAX security at my temporary Net site, I was scrambling for my own solutions, some of them licit, some better qualified as don't-ask-don't-tell. I found a few toeholds. My prognosis was looking better by the day. And then, as seamlessly as he'd appeared, the Surfer vanished in a puff of electrons. I traced his e-mail tracks to a couple of EDU sites and came up empty. Flatlined accounts. I figured he'd been busted for breaking and entering a UNIX (the programming language that links the Net) system where he didn't belong. Live by the hack, die by the hack I guess. I didn't think I'd hear from him again.

About a month later, a piece of e-mail from the Surfer washed into my mailbox from a patchy California account. Nothing much, just a brief explanation that the surfmeister was experiencing technical difficulties, and voice mailbox number I could call if I wanted. I wrote down the VMB number and promptly buried it under a stack of newspapers and fanzines. When it surfaced, I lost it again, this time behind a dresser. Earring retrieval brought it to light a second time.

The Surfer's e-mail had been erased with my last temporary account, and I knew that if I lost this particular scrap of paper again, it was gone for good. I stuck it in a drawer, still leery about the VMB. I had my real life and I had my Net life, and I really didn't want to mix the two. And besides, I was juggling too many lunatic boys already without cultivating this one.

Curiosity, as usual, won out.

The Surfer's VMB greeting was addressed to me. God knows how long it had been sitting around, or if the mailbox itself was pirated and stowed in some mammoth audix (voice mail) system. I left a message and forgot about the whole thing until a few weeks later, when I came home to an answering-machine message in loping California-speak from the Surfer, calling from a hallway pay phone out West. He said he'd call back. That night, my phone line went down in a Southern Bell wire-fry. Crossed connections. The telephone link to my apartment was out to lunch in North Miami, and I kept getting calls for Carlo Grimaldi. As I'd predicted, I'd lost the Surfer's number a third time and for good. When my phone line went back up, the Surfer called and missed me again.

"Just calling to see what was up, really. I guess you have my VMB number so, um, maybe I'll talk to you sometime." The Surfer paused after a nervous laugh. "I dunno. So . . . like . . . bye."

I doubt he'll call again. After two unanswered phone messages, he probably figures I don't want to talk to him. I have absolutely no idea who this guy is, or where he is, and I'm not sure I'd even want to know. But I'm glad he showed up as proof that chivalry isn't completely dead. In fact, it might even survive the digital age.

CHaiN LeTTeRS aND
CoKe MaCHiNeS

Dear Friend,

My name is Dave Rhodes. In September 1988 my car was reposessed and the bill collectors were hounding me like you wouldn't believe. I was laid off and my unemployment checks had run out. The only escape I had from the pressure of failure was my computer and my modem. I longed to turn my advocation into my vocation.

This January 1989 my family and I went on a ten day cruise to the tropics. I bought a Lincoln Town Car for CASH in Feburary 1989. I am currently building a home on the West Coast of Florida, with a private pool, boat slip, and a beautiful view of the bay from my breakfast room table and patio. I will never have to work again. Today I am rich! I have earned over $400,000.00 (Four Hundred Thousand Dollars) to date and will become a millionaire within 4 or 5 months. Anyone can do the same. This money making program works perfectly every time, 100% of the time. I have NEVER failed to earn $50,000.00 or more whenever I wanted. Best of all you never have to leave home except to go to your mailbox or post office.

In October 1988, I received a lefter in the mail telling me how I could earn $50,000 dollars or more whenever I wanted. I was naturally very skeptical and threw the letter on the desk next to my computer. It's funny though, when you are desperate, backed into a corner, your mind does crazy things. I spent a frustating day looking through the want ads for a job with a future. The pickings were sparse at best. That night I tried to unwind by booting up my computer and calling several bulletin boards. I read several of the message posts and than glanced at the lefter next to the computer. All at once it came to me, I now had the key to my dreams.

I realized that with the power of the computer I could expand and enhance this money making formula into the most unbelievable cash flow generator that has ever been created . . . If you believe that someday you deserve that lucky break that you have waited for all your life, simply follow the easy instructions below. Your dreams will come true.

Sincerely yours,
Dave Rhodes

UH-OH.

I try to purge it from short-term memory (Yeah, that's the ticket—denial. I'll just pretend I never saw it. Nope. Never happened. Retroactive kill.file).

But I can't. It's just too ghastly to ignore.

Yeah, verily, there is a serpent in the garden of cyberspace — a chain letter on the Internet. And that's not the worst of it. Because in fact, the chain letter conceit is mere window dressing for a more insidious scheme: direct e-mail marketing. I read further, to the retch-inducing "INSTRUCTIONS," which if I follow "EXACTLY" will garner me "well over $50,000 CASH," ALL MINE, in twenty to sixty days. By joining the electronic chain, I could put myself in the lucrative business of developing rentable mailing lists. "Many large corporations are happy to pay big bucks for quality lists," chirps Rhodes, like some kind of cheez-mail impresario. "As soon as you mail out these letters you are automatically in the mail order business and people are sending you $1.00 to be placed on your mailing list. This list can than be rented to a list broker that can be found in the Yellow Pages for additional income on a regular basis. The list will become more valuable as it grows in size. This is a service. This is perfectly legal. If you have any doubts, refer to Title 18, Sec. 1302 & 1341 of the postal lottery laws."

The horror! The horror!

A palpable sense of violation is mitigated only by my firm belief that this bozo, wherever he is, will soon be flambéed. The reticulate consciousness of the Net will surely descend like a swarm of incensed wasps and spam his in-box with flame mail, maybe even death threats. He might soon find his hard drive riddled with all kinds of binary nasties. He'll hear peculiar clicks in his phone line erupt into the eardrum-piercing screech of a blast box on the other side. His credit rating will mysteriously shrivel and rot. Yes, Rhodes is cruising for a digital bruising.

This makes me feel a little bit better.

But the idea of a make-bucks-fast chain letter on the Net, it chafes. I take it as a sign of beastly things to come.

I'm noticing more and more ads on the Net these days, the first drips from a leaky ceiling that may or may not cave in. If ads look corporate, their originators are usually flamed. That strategy works now, because the numbers are small. The Net's peculiar center still holds. But God help us when the Information Railroad is actually built. We'll be talking about the good old days — these days — eighteen months or two years from now, when every post has a "Send me MORE information about this product" checkbox in its sig. We'll remember how self-contained the Net once was. We'll remark about the few places where the Net and real life touched, how strange and, in a way, how charming they were.

We'll remember the Coke machines.

According to Net legend, there is a Coke machine in the computer center of Carnegie-Mellon University. Rather than walk up a flight of stairs only to find it empty, a few CMU students rigged the vending machine with an electronic surveillance mechanism and wired it to a server. From the comfort of their desks, they could check on the Coke machine, and it would tell them how many Cokes were in it and if they were cold. It was something the Spacely Sprockets building might have had. And that was all — until the building's computers were hooked into the Internet. Now it was possible for anyone in the world to finger the Carnegie-Mellon Coke machine. A New Zealander on the other side of the earth could check up on the cola stock just as easily as the CMU grad student fifty feet away. Of course, there wasn't much the New Zealander could do with this information, but that was beside the point. Hundreds, if not thousands of people all over the world kept tabs on the Carnegie-Mellon Coke machine as sort of a mental vacation.

Programmers at other schools even installed copycat mechanisms so that they, too, could stake a patch of Netspace for their own caffeinated beverage dispenser. The computer science house at the Rochester Institute of Technology, for instance, has a machine that tells you how much Jolt, Mountain Dew, Coke Classic, and "Diet Stuff" is in it, as well as the number of cans in the "Mystery Slot" and if they are cold. If you have a drink account there, you can even charge that frosty drink over the Net, and the machine will drop it from the appropriate slot. Of course, this is meant for RIT students who live in the computer science house. But theoretically, someone in Finland could break into the server, and a cold can would clunk down from the mystery slot and find its way into the hands of a thirsty passer-by. The intersection between Net space and real life is tenuous here — there's an element of faith on the part of the Finnish hacker. He has to believe that the Coke machine exists, that it contains what it says it contains, and that his actions have a physical impact on it. But despite this (maybe because of it) the Coke machines on the Net have a kind of loony beauty. They seem to float there, waiting for someone to perpetrate a random act of kindness and hack a free drink for someone he'll never meet — good karma in the form of caffeine-laden carbonated beverages.

I can't think of the Coke machines without remembering the chain letter, and vice versa. They nest together in my mind and, for that matter, my computer hard drive. They straddle the line between Net and real life. They're not just ads shunted into Netspace. They're parasites. The Coke machines are pretty innocuous, sucking off just enough processing power to sustain a benign steady state. The chain letter, on the other hand, is malignant. If it actually worked, we'd be inundated by copies of Mr. Rhodes's smarmy get-rich-quick scheme.

But I don't think it stands a chance. It's too unpalatable to spread very far.

And besides, no one believes in it.

On the other hand, everyone on the Net seems to believe in the Coke machines, for some reason. They're icons of student life—never out of place. Perhaps we are so used to seeing them everywhere that when they show up on the Net, we just accept their presence as a matter of course.

I have never heard anyone express the slightest doubt that these plan files are connected to actual vending machines. I have never heard anyone express a desire to prove this hypothesis one way or the other. Without a sliver of physical evidence, they just believe that a Coke machine that takes Net credit corresponds to a hunk of plastic and glass with a slot for quarters. There are people who don't believe in God who believe in the Carnegie-Mellon Coke machine. Faith is strange that way on the Net. Sometimes, amid the forgeries, bogus identities, and pranks, you bump into something that feels oddly solid, and on instinct you believe in it— even if it's just a cold Jolt two thousand miles away. I've decided the machines are legit—until someone starts putting Snapple machines in cyberspace.

I am ideologically incapable of believing in pineapple raspberry kumquat juice connected to *anything* on the Internet.

thE alIEns hAvE lAndEd

IT'S A SLOW day on alt.alien.visitors — a couple of crop circle reports, an abduction, a few hayseeds dazed in the path of UFO headlights, that kind of thing. And then, with the slightest rustle of electrons and no visible source of propulsion, It materializes. A post from Carleton, California, bearing the real question, indeed, the crux of the extraterrestrial dilemma: what would happen worldwide if space aliens made a guest appearance on *Larry King Live*?

"Larry would ask 'it' (?) some stupid, boring questions. Someone would call in and ask what it thinks about Howard Stern's penis. Someone would offer the alien a movie deal. Or a sitcom," answers one netter.

Another alt.alien.visitors fan at Youngstown State University (what is it with these people?) has an even more cynical view of the alien ratings bonanza, predicting that "thousands would die — trampled to death as every huckster & lawyer & 'agent' & flim-flam artist & wheeler-dealer rushed to tap into this new source of money making potential. Most of the dead would be local & national news announcers & videographers dispatched to the scene to try &

damage-control the fact that CNN scooped them. I personally would use it as an excuse to blow off work & go sailing."

While much of the newsgroup concerns itself with the hypothetical *Larry King* broadcast, a BBS operator in Jackson, Tennessee, pushes the envelope of media savvy even further. "Doesn't it seem as if these aliens are doing the same type of research that our corporations would do if we were about to open up a new market development area?" he wonders. "If they had no idea whatsoever of what they could market; or who they could market to?" In other words, our entire *planet* is a target market. From time to time, an extraterrestrial team of consultants zooms down, zaps up a few humans, puts them in a focus group, and makes them fill out questionnaires. Later, Boom! Cheap X-ray flux capacitors flood the global market, and the Earth is stuck with a mammoth interstellar trade deficit. Michael Crichton pens an alien-bashing novel, *Rising Satellite,* and congressional leaders bicker over the Interstellar Free Trade Agreement. Meanwhile, Ross Perot climbs back on the isolationist soapbox. "Y'all hear that giant sucking sound? That's the sound of American jobs going to the Zeta Reticulans. . . ."

The "Aliens on CNN . . . what if?" thread culminates a long line of "Aliens have landed . . . what now?" controversies, newsgroup meta-commentary, and revisionist speculation. Like, was Jesus a full-blooded alien, a mixed-breed genetic experiment, or just a heavily brainwashed contactee? "If so," wrote an alien aficionado at Occidental College, "he must have been heavily conditioned (and programmed) by his 'masters'—definitely NOT your garden variety contactee. One wonders whether they consider the 'experiment' to have been a success."

Alt.alien.visitors is my new favorite newsgroup. The grab bag of infiltration theories is a kick, but it's the newsgroup's collective navel-gazing that really fascinates me.

Callan Jacobson, a self-professed skeptic on the newsgroup, divides posters into three groups — "a) the Paranoids, who believe that the Big Bad Government is hiding all and responsible for everything from JFK's death to the mysterious 'face' on Mars, b) the Jokesters, who pop on, make smart-ass comments (which are, admittedly, sometimes funny & appropriate) and generally flame everyone here, and c) the Curious, who are more skeptical than the Paranoids, but tend to believe that every myth contains a bit of truth." I don't know where alien-enthusiast observer falls on Jacobson's spectrum, but that's what I am. I love to watch people who watch aliens. I love theories about UFO theories. Like, why have the space aliens always *just* landed? Egypt, Mesoamerica, Cold War cornfields, and now the Net — they land again and again, and it's always such a . . .

"NEWSFLASH: The most earth shattering news to befall the planet since the trials at Salem," announces a Texas Instruments employee on his lunch break. "There have been sightings of alien craft at Stonehenge, England. Several key witnesses including military personnel based in the area have refused to comment, however a man has come forward to attest to the authenticity of the reports. Several craft were seen by Mr. Hardacre, as he was out excercising his dog . . . This is by no means the first sighting of UFOs in or around the area. But the current resurgence of sightings must suggest that there is renewed interest by the aliens in this area, particularly the stone circle at Stonehenge. Any further news on this incident will be posted as soon as it comes in."

WE control the horizontal. WE control the vertical.

With no visuals, these alien updates on the Net assume the starkness of radio drama: "War of the Worlds" on-line. Except this time, a distinctly partisan fault line runs right through the ranks of alien cognoscenti. On one side are the Cold War–style millenarians raving about the Green Peril —

UFO's with superior firepower hovering down, blasting Wagner, and wreaking havoc on the hapless human race. Media, world leaders, religious figureheads, freemasons, top fashion designers—they're all in on it. They're the ones who are going to cash in on the biggest leveraged buyout in our planet's history. The rest of us will be reduced to scavenging hobos, living like rats in the post-apocalyptic rubble.

Dave Alexander, the George Kennan of Green Peril dogmatists, has formulated the most complex and elaborate alien scenario on the Net, "THE COMING 'OFFICIAL' ANNOUNCEMENT OF THE ALIEN PRESENCE ON EARTH," a cornerstone of anti-alien sentiment on alt.alien.visitors. Citing "whistle-blowers" and retired military personnel, he makes a case for a conspiracy involving the Greys from Zeta Reticuli, Eisenhower, J. Edgar Hoover, the MJ-12, the Council on Foreign Relations, the Trilateral Commission, the Bilderbergers, and the young George Bush, whose Zapata Oil corporation supposedly financed the underground alien bases by cornering the illegal drug trade. According to Alexander, Eisenhower was the last president to know the whole story. After that,

MJ-12 presented each new president with a picture of a lost alien culture seeking to renew itself, build a home on this planet and shower us with gifts of technology. Each president has bought the story hook, line and sinker. Meanwhile, innocent people continue to suffer unspeakable horrors at the hands of alien and human scientists who are engaged in barbarous research that would make the Nazis pale in comparison. . . .

Today, the government deals with an extreme dilemma. Too many sources are releasing alien information. The public will get angry at continued secrecy. MJ-12 plans soon to make an "official" announcement, under controlled conditions. Network TV will be called to meet the staged "landing" of the aliens, these being the Greys. They will come bearing gifts, technology that supposedly will heal cancer and AIDS, retard aging, etc. They will tell us they are the "saviors" of humanity who have come to defend the earth against an invasion of man eating aliens called Reptoids. This story is a lie. The Grays already work for the Reptoids. Their plan is to unify the world into a One-World Government, a "New World Order" with the argument that only this can defeat the invasion by Reptoids. This is a trap to enslave the world's population. Control will be accomplished through a universal currency controlled by certain international bankers, who for years have been lackeys of the aliens, who seized upon their greed and lust for wealth and power as a means to bring about their evil plan to control the earth. . . .

So be aware. Only your knowledge of this fake invasion can prevent it from happening. Demand the truth from your government. Tell them you know about the alien situation, that you know there are good aliens and bad aliens and that MJ-12 is promoting the bad aliens and the One World Government they hope to control. Insist on the truth.

I, for one, wrote a letter to my congressman and e-mailed the president at his spiffy White House AOL ad-

dress and waited for the nice men in white suits to arrive :-)
Or not.

But some people, apparently, have taken the Grey Invasion theory to heart, like the undergraduate at Plymouth State College with "a gut feeling I'm supposed to go out west and do something important." He's looking for advice about "what to do with my life because I'm supposed help in saving the human race from the Greys and greedy Top Brass selling out our race for technology. As I said I'm have these dreams and visions were I'm fighting the Greys and killing feds and others . . . Bill Clinton he's just a figurehead the Top Brass really control this country and there motto is 'ignorance is bliss.' The U.S. by 2000–2020 will be taken over by the Greys or whoever or the other side of the coin the U.S. falls into anarchy in 2020–2030 because of the Silent Generation and G.I. Generation fuckup this country past around 1950's and today they think there still in W.W.II era they can't deal with the the problems of today and think Sen. Dole should retire. So the big problem is, what should people like me do — watch, wait, and listen or take action blow them to kingdom come?"

Who said alien hysteria was a Cold War phenomenon? Now that we've got AIDS, Bosnia, a moribund social security system, a shriveling middle class, and a tottering global economy to worry about, there's no need for Russians. Green Peril alarmists can still have a field day. They'd run this newsgroup if it weren't for the multicultural posse protesting Earth-centrism and the bigoted stereotype of aliens as a morally inferior race. According to these people, extraterrestrials are just benevolent interplanetary visitors — shiny, happy aliens, as it were — who have been gunned down on vacation like so many German tourists in Miami. Aliens are victims, they say. Why can't we all just get along? As one nineteen-year-old college student writes, "It breaks my heart to know that possible aliens would have to go out of their way to not be seen. Do our galactic friends want to be free too? I understand government cover-ups and all, but I just wish they could be who they really are. Not aliens, but pals." This attempt to recast aliens as an oppressed minority is constantly denounced as insidious alien propaganda by Green Peril theorists, who are perfectly happy to keep gunning down aliens, no questions asked, because damnit, this is *our* planet.

Between the "Earth, Love It or Leave It" party and the alien defenders stands a lone figure, celebrated by some and accused of deranged lunacy by others: John_-_Winston, he of the mysterious login middle dash, a first-tier Net celebrity who regularly cross-posts his latest theories on alien conspiracies, time travel, abductions, the New World Order, and a medicinal "Space Syrup" recipe culled from the *Weekly World News.* In the Bermuda Triangle of Usenet defined by alt.alien.visitors, alt.conspiracy, and alt.religion.kibology, Winston's name is virtually synonymous with born-again belief in alien flybys, and consequently he is hounded by skeptics who snap at his flesh like wild dogs.

"So, John, if that IS your real name," sneers a student at Florida State University, "what should we, the ordinary ignorant citizens of the world do about this impending invasion? Where will these aliens come from. Are they Klingons? Romulans? the Borg? Darth Vader's storm troopers? Tell me, what's it like to live in your world, to live in a constant state of paranoia? What color is the sky in your world? Do they let you have crayons to play with where you are?"

"Be careful," warns a staunch Winstonite, "many who mocked The Winston have disappeared under suspicious circumstances."

But despite his defenders, Winston has become a whipping boy for the doubters, the cynics, and the know-it-alls who nevertheless insist on reading alt.alien.visitors just to mock its content. Rather than make enemies by condemning the entire newsgroup, they torch Winston instead. If they harbor the slightest suspicion that alien life may, in fact, exist, they are doubly vicious—anything to distance themselves from "freaks like Winston."

"In my mind," writes Jamie Bass, a particularly mean-spirited Winston-basher, "I picture John Winston being a *fat*, balding man with *no* teeth, impotent, wearing heavy, thick, magnifying-lens type glasses set in heavy old sixty-ish style frames; sitting in front of a TRS-80 (or similar technology) machine, using a 300 baud acoustic modem and posting whatever comes into his pea-size brain. Most likely he has several physical disabilities that cause him to remain stationary for long periods of time. Chances are that those thick glasses he wears are darkly tainted because he has an eye condition that prevents the proper function of his eyes/irises. The room where his TRS-80 is situated is most likely located in the basement with *no windows* that could let in Sun light and exaggerate his skin condition. There he sits, a pathetic little man wearing only a T-shirt, oddly patterned and stained boxer shorts in a small, damp, darkened, cluttered room, with a toothless smile, staring at a monochrome tube and posting to The Net; obtaining glee from people like you and me who talk about him. Sigh, such a sad, sad, life. Double sigh."

When Winston informs residents of the BermUsenet Triangle of his impending temporary absence ("Dear Wonderful People of Earth. I will be gone to Reno, Nevada for a few days, so try to be good while I'm gone. John Winston"), an alt.alien.visitors harpy can't resist kicking him on his way out. "PEOPLE OF RENO, NEVADA," he screams, "GET OUT!! GET OUT!!! RUN FOR YOUR LIVES!!!!"

Surfing on the Internet

John_-_Winston, the pope of alt.alien.visitors, is a magnet for Net.scorn. But he never responds to the innumerable ad hominem attacks. He just blithely goes about his business of posting space alien updates from the four corners of the earth (and his own private universe). And once in a while, someone reminds the rest of the group that alt.alien.visitors would unravel without him. Tom Loomis at Northwest Nexus has even composed an ode to Winston.

```
Summary: Enjoying John Winston
Keywords: John Winston; lighten up; humor

Hey folks!
Some of you maybe take our good and familiar
poster, J.W., seriously.

I don't, but I am sure this does not bother him,
and I certainly don't intend it to.

When I am tired, I can get onto alt.alien.visi-
tors, find a posting by J.W. and relax.

When I am gloomy, I read a piece by J.W. and
laugh.

When I am depressed, I peruse encouragement by
J.W. and
feel yes, SOMEONE, even if he/she/it is an alien
from the future,
cares about my fate.

When I am confused, I can find (sooner or later) a
wise explanation of
```

the object of my confusion, penned (well, keyed)
by J.W.
No matter that it came from a grey Pleiadian from
another twist in time;

I get a good, hearty—and I mean HEARTY!—laugh,
and as you all know

    "A stitch in time saves nine"

(saying attributed to a long-distance runner
from the future)

    No, no, let's all treasure J.W., and all the
J.W.s in our midst. If J.W.'s should be whipped,
who amongst us would escape a whipping?

    Tom Loomis

    "The notes are silver, but the rests are
gold."

    —an Arcturean Xspleyrhts player/composer
from the year 299384756 AD

Surrounded as I am by John_-_Winston's ilk, "Enjoying
John Winston" puts a lump in my throat. It's the most charitable thing I've ever read on the Net. As far as I'm concerned,
"Enjoying John Winston" says it all about the eccentrics in
newsgroups like alt.alien.visitors and the off-kilter Net culture at large. The Net doesn't care that I don't take it seriously. When I'm tired I can relax with it, and it'll make me

laugh. When I'm gloomy, it's always nutty enough to cheer me up. When I'm trawling through it, I always seem to find some unintentional nugget of wisdom. No matter that it comes from a stoned basement dweller from another time zone or was, in fact, a typo.

BaRnEY MusT DIe

BARNEY: THE WORD, the very idea of PBS's cloying purple dinosaur sends shock waves of hatred coursing through the five Internet bulletin boards dedicated to his violent and gruesome demise. After finding alt.barney.dinosaur.die.die.-die in my regular scan of vigilante newsgroups, I lean back, crack my knuckles, and dig into my computer-side box of Cocoa Krispies. I bask in the gray glow of my computer screen and the galvanic loathing of my long-lost Barney-hating kin.

The mondo wave of distilled malevolence goes far beyond my own minor-league critiques of Barney's detestable merchandising bonanza, his penchant for healthy snack food, the thinly veiled fascistic leanings of his show, and the fact that his visage is terrifyingly everywhere, like some kind of plush Mao Tse-tung. In Usenet, these sentiments are a mere springboard for discussion. Speculations as to the Beast's true identity whirl in an outlandish spiral. Barney is a misshapen cousin of McDonald's Grimace character, some say. Others maintain that he is nothing short of the Antichrist.

Not to be outdone, a significant minority of anti-Barney zealots bandy about an even more horrifying prospect: that the Lavender Scourge is really Rush Limbaugh in disguise.

Before my eyes, alt.barney.dinosaur.die.die.die takes on a tumescent fantasy role-playing dimension, feeding off the Net's not inconsiderable Dungeons & Dragons expertise. Plots against the Paleolithic puppet became more graphic and elaborate, blossoming into quasi-terrorist campaigns like Operation Top 40. "Using funding from arms sales to Quebec separatists," writes the Top 40's chief tactician, "we are buying all the records on the chart above the Barney album to keep him from being number one and eventually drive him off the charts. However, we had to divert funding to hire Mongol assassins to deal with a sudden rise in Barney Merchandise on the east coast. . . . With lack of funding, Operation Top 40 is in jeopardy. Therefore, we ask all loyal members of the movement to assist us by purchasing records, if possible Dark Side of the Moon so we can get it back on the charts. This situation is only temporary. Thank you." Signed, Kevin, Infallible yet Lovable Guardian of the True Faith.

In the newsgroup's narrative greenhouse, entire online identities take shape around a Manichean battle between Barney haters and the Jurassic Hellspawn's legion of aubergine destruction. An epic of this magnitude has the sci-fi makeover power to turn a guy like Todd Stevens, Cornell student, into Commander Stevens, the hero of Usenet post a short time ago in a mental galaxy far, far away:

```
"Step this way Commander Stevens, you know the
protocol."
      The sentry guides Stevens into a small room.
The door is armored and gas nozzles protrude from
the ceiling. Two hevily armed sentries wearing
```

gas masks, and full virtual reality sensory isolation helmets, designed specificly to filter
any attempt an psycic or pschological manipulation, stand on either side of the door. Stevens
enters alone, the door is locked behind him.

"The usual selection, sir?" the corporal
says over the mike from the control room.

"Certainly, coporal, NIN . . . . how bout
"broken" today . . and I think lemon pez will
due. A vanilla twinke would be good also."

A door in the wall opens and a "Spiderman"
pez dispenser, loaded, as well as two vanilla
twinkes emerge from a chute. they fall on a shelf
below the door, and the door closes. NIN begins
to play from the powerful speakers in the ceiling. Stevens begins to eat. Five minutes later,
having passed the test, He emerges. A simple
retina scan opens the door to the compound, as he
walks down the hall toward the main control room,
passersby stop and salute. Throwing open the door
to the control room, he snaps, "AT EASE!" before
most of the room can get to their feet.

With all these subplots and alter egos bubbling in the
textual vat of alt.barney.dinosaur.–die.die.die, it doesn't take
long for a fundamentalist crusade to ignite like so much ammonium nitrate fuel oil. "The Jihad," writes Sergeant Luna-
tik of the University of South Carolina's Campus Crusade
Against Barney, "is a group whose reason for existence is
to overthrow and kill the Purple Putz himself. They want
B*rney hung, stabbed, shot, poisoned, infected with venereal
diseases, drawn and quartered, and beheaded. And that's on
a slow post day."

But even with anti-Barney fervor at fever pitch and a nascent Jihad organization in place, the odds are daunting. How can the forces of truth and unhealthy snack food possibly triumph against the onslaught of Barney propaganda? What argument is powerful enough to shatter the Evil One's totalitarian mind control? Certainly, the struggle is noble, but it seems hopeless.

And then, deus ex machina, the High Prophet of the Three-Fold Truth sweeps down with a revelation:

THE TIME HAS COME! Friends, an evil is spreading through the world. Up until now, it has been invincible. But now, there is hope. Yes, finally we have a weapon. A weapon so powerful that the Sponge-Minions of the Evil One will be unable to stand in its way. Yes, that's right, an argument so perfect that any one who does not immediately agree with it is a Communist slave of the Dark and Purple One. Righteous crusaders, I bring you the light. I bring you The Three-Fold Truth.

1. The Demonic Barney is Hell Incarnate.

2. His mission is one of brainwashing, to create Sponge-Minions to carryout a takeover of the world.

3. Barney must be destroyed! All else is immaterial!

Yes, "All else is immaterial!" Therefore the use of The Three-Fold Truth will automatically win any argument, from discussions of the Horrid

Plush Monster of PBS to business transactions.
Quote from the Three-Fold Truth and you will tri-
umph. Some of the Commie-Sponge-Clone-Minions
will try to tell you that there is no proof of
The Three-Fold Truth. DO NOT LISTEN OR YOU WILL
INSTANTLY BECOME A SPONGE-MINION! The name
Three-Fold Truth automatically proves that It is
True, and It is The Way. Only the Three-Fold
Truth is perfect enough to prove itself. Any who
deny this logic are slaves of the Evil One. They
must be destroyed for their own sakes. Long Live
the Holy Crusaders! Long Live The Three-Fold
Truth! Death to all Sponge-Minions and their
Twisted Masters, Stew and Gerry! Death to the
Most Foul!!

   B*RNEY, YOUR DAYS ARE NUMBERED.
   DIE THEN! DIE WITH THE THREE-FOLD TRUTH RING-
ING IN YOUR EARS! WE WILL TRIUMPH! THE THREE-FOLD
TRUTH SAYS SO, THEREFORE IT IS SO!

   —The High Prophet of the Three-Fold Truth

Armed with the Three-Fold Truth, the Jihad gathers
force. Netters from Canada to Mexico rally to the cause.

"How do I join Jihad?" asks the Exalted Grey Wizard of
Palanthas. "I want to know! I do what I can to stop the spread
of the purple pestilence, but one man can only do so much
alone! I seek to join your ranks so that together we may rid
the world of sponginess FOREVAH!!!"

"Behold!" writes a new recruit at the University of Penn-
sylvania. "The forces of justice have finally united in a cause
that defines all that is good in this world: The destruction of

the wretched fiend who goes by B*rn*y! Know, that you are not alone in the loathing of the hellspawn purple daemon. I wish to join your holy cause, along with my flock of elite warriors, the Knights of the Raptor. The knighthood wishes to become one with the Jihad, allowing our might to wipe out the scourge of purpleness. We are all dedicated to only one cause: DEATH TO B*RN*Y!!!!!" Signed, Zach, Minister of Propaganda, Knights of the Raptor.

From the University of Massachusetts, Amherst, Svenyip the Spiritual Bard raises his voice in allegiance to the Jihad: "We MUST be strong against this menace. The Evil One's essense spreads throughout the world like a dark plague . . . but if we have the courage, that which is right and just must triumph over the Sappy Darkness which threatens to destroy the future of America by forever altering the mindsets of the next generation. I am here to assist against this darkness as best I can. Advise me on what to do, and it shall be done." Another post, another foot soldier marching with the faithful.

The throng of ardent but, alas, untrained new troops on the anti-Barney front necessitates response from Jihad high command; clearly, tactical guidelines are in order, lest reckless recruits unwittingly injure the cause. With supernatural forces at work and so much at stake, it would be folly to let budding Jihaddi fly into battle ignorant of the pitfalls that lie ahead. Jihad commander Jack Skellington takes it upon himself to deliver words of wisdom to the rookies:

```
Two very quick, VERY important pieces of advice:
When posting to this newsgroup NEVER spell out
the name of the magenta molester. You may have
noticed that no-one other than the sponge-minions
EVER do that, just mentioning HIS name, or even
```

worse, spelling it out, can set you down the path to becoming a sponge-minion. Two, join the Jihad, swear your allegiance to the three-fold truth of the Jihad. This gives you tremendous brother/sisterhood with the other members, and your need for help (should it ever—hopefully not—arise) will be answered with the backing of countless thousands of other Jihaddi from across the nation. You might have noticed this in your reading of such places as Santa Cruz, Michigan Tech, Des Moines and many others.

B*rn*y must die (slowly, painfully, at our hands) all else is immaterial.

Yours in the Fight,

Jack Skellington
Commander,
B.E.A.M. (the B*rn*y Eradication Association of the Midwest)

"That which does not destroy me makes me stronger . . ."
—Friedrich Nietzche

Skellington is top brass. Like his *Nightmare Before Christmas* namesake, he possesses a deranged lyricism that inspires cultish loyalty among his troops. A brilliant strategist and gifted orator, he has single-handedly organized B.E.A.M. and has risen like a rocket through Jihad ranks to become one of its most eminent regional kingpins. In the Jihad's spidery guerrilla hierarchy, Skellington's power and prestige are rivaled by only three other leaders. Tripwire Scipio Tomarctus Serbeus, Fleet Commander of the Doberman Empire (and student of veterinary medicine at Michigan State University) is one. Julian Roberts, leader of the University of Hawaii's Organization for Slaying Truly Insipid, Lame, and Idiotic Tyrannosaurs for our Youth (H.O.S.T.I.L.I.T.Y), is another.

The fourth member of the quadrumvirate is none other than the Mystic Mongoose, Leader of the Baylor Jihad and Ultimate Prophet of The Church of the Anti-Barney Incarnate. Mongoose operates out of the Texas division, which is, in some ways, an organization unto itself. And while Mongoose captures the lion's share of international newsgroup attention, the Lone Star command is, in reality, a confederation between himself and J-Rock, overseer of the Texas A&M, B'harne Genocide Division, EphedrineLord at UT, Dallas, and HillBrother the Spongeless, who anchors central Texas for anti-Barney forces. "As we are located at UT at Austin," explains Spongeless in his letter of induction, "we can observe the southward spread of sponge-minionism into our campus." He ends on a hopeful note, however, observing, "We have had some success in reprogramming several hard-core sponge-minions through the use of MTV and large supreme pizzas."

"Yes!" the Mongoose hisses through his sharp, pointy teeth. "Yet another Texas-based Jihad! With yours, mine, and the one at A&M, WE will keep Texas pure from the Lavender Lard Lord! JIHAD!!!!!!!!!!!!!!!!!" Such displays of Texan chauvinism might be a political sticking point, were they not matched with devastating anti-Barney firepower.

Outside of the Texas division, B.E.A.M., H.O.S.T.I.L.I.T.Y., and the Doberman Empire, a number of smaller elite anti-Barney crusaders hold down their respective regional fronts: Dave, Grand Marshall of the Santa Cruz Anti-B'Harne Task Force; Amir Rosenblatt, Archon of the Holy Gotham Protectorate and High-Lord of the Knights of the Sacred Felt; Moonflake, Director General of the Bh*r'n'e Information Gathering Organization of New England (B.I.G.O.N.E.); and Fixxer, a bit of a loose cannon but a ferocious fighter whose crack commando unit at Youngstown State University triumphed on perhaps the bloodiest battlefield of the war. Matt Giwer, a battle-scarred veteran who has retired from the front lines to the Cleveland Freenet, is a Top Gun instructor of sorts and an inexhaustible font of Barney combat strategy.

"Let's say you happen to see this toy Barney, just sitting there in a swing made from an old Uniroyal," he posits for the benefit of unblooded newbies. "Do you pull out your handy M-16 and pump him full of hot lead, screaming 'DIE, YOU UNHOLY SPAWN OF SATAN! DIE DIE DIE!' No. You do not. This will only make him angry. If you're LUCKY he will only suck out your soul like soup through a straw. We are dealing with a SUPERNATURAL Creature here. Don't assume that just because he LOOKS like a fuzzy harmless doll that he IS a fuzzy harmless doll. In toy form he will be constantly on his guard, whereas in active mode he thinks himself invulnerable. And THAT shall be his downfall. You will need the standard tools: Garlic, a crucifix, an iron rod, a Tammy Faye record, stuff like that. Keep them ready at all times in case of random Barney encounters." Should one confront Barney in active mode, "Decapitate him with a silver sword, on sacred ground, under a 3-D picture of Jesus, while drinking a glass of holy water FROM THE FAR SIDE OF THE GLASS, with a bag over your head, while singing "Amazing Grace", in a month with a "K" in it. (Note: The sword MUST be blessed by His Holiness the Pope. Otherwise, you're wasting your time.)." Giwer ends his lecture with a recommendation that Jihad troops field-test this method on Rush Limbaugh: "All of the above applies to HIM, too."

Confronted with this spectacle of martial preparedness and camaraderie, I initially mistake alt.barney.dinosaur.die.-die.die for a secure haven from the dark forces of Barney-dom. But, alas, the newsgroup has been breached by an insidious cabal of netters who've converted to the Dark Side: the dreaded Sponge Minions, led by Gerry S., Mr. Honorable (promptly christened Mr. Dishonorable), and Jason Kodish, a University of Alberta student who routinely co-opts the Jihad's rhetoric into his own sneering dispatches to alt.barney.dinosaur.die.die.die:

```
From: Jason Kodish
Subject: Barney is powerful
Date: Fri, 17 Sep 1993 20:24:46 GMT
```

While you putred little pukes preach your hatered against the GREAT PURPLE ONE, our forces grow in strength. We loooooove you, and that is why we have to put you all out of your anti-Barney misery. Cower fools, because the Great BARNEY will swallow you whole, and will show you the love you deserve to be shown. You think you can escape, well, you can't. The Alliance of Love! is everywhere. We have illuminati contacts. The Illuminati loves Barney. (Perhapse even the GREAT ONE himself is Illuminati.) He loves you all, but you are all such naughty, naughty boys and girls. Barney and Gerry are merciful, I am not. While I try to achieve the sublime perfection of them, I cannot. So I polish my weapons, and watch my Bar-

ney videos, and watch Clint Eastwood movies. I
await your petty Jihad.

Like any anti-Barney partisan, I hate the Sponge Minions. I would rather die than join their cause. Obviously, they
have become villains in a desperate bid for attention, and
their efforts to spread Barney's totalitarian propaganda are
detestable. But the fact that they conduct such a campaign on
alt.barney.dinosaur.die.die.die is compelling. I can't help but
feel a twisted admiration for anyone perverted enough to fly
Barney's banner in a newsgroup that clamors for his excruci-
ating ritual murder. Despite their loathsome ideology, the
Sponge Minions have an ineffable tinge of the existential anti-
hero about them.

The battle lines are drawn: the Jihad on one side, the
Sponge Minions on the other. As the 1993 holiday season
pitches Barney merchandising forward at full throttle, Gerry
S. strikes alt.barney.dinosaur.die.die.die with a Christmas nau-
sea bomb: a laundry list of Barney paraphernalia "gift suggestions" for Jihad family members. "There are no Barney
video games yet, but you just wait and see," Gerry taunts,
hinting that Sponge Minion R&D was developing a game
in which a dancing Barney figure earns bonus points for
converting Jihad members into Sponge Minions by force
feeding them healthy snacks.

Gerry's post-bomb instigates an escalating flame frenzy
on the newsgroup, prompting Manoj Kasichainula of the Jihad to Destroy Barney at North Carolina State to burst into a
fit of alliterative rage: "I am not so cruel," he wrote, "that I
would inflict the torture of having to even glance at a replica
of the Purple Painful Pansy Parabolic Parasitic Pathetic Pel-
vic Perky Perturbing Perverse Piss-filled Pitiful Plush Poi-
sonous Polluted Pompous Porcine Pornographic Predatory

Preposterous Primitive Problematic Propagandist Psycho-
pathic Pedophile (whew!) Hmm . . . I'm hungry. What should
I eat? A healthy salad, or a cheesy, greasy pizza. Well, sponge-
minion-bot. I'll have a pizza with extra cheese, all the meat I
can fit, and Jalapenos! Die, sponge-minion."

Moonflake is livid. "I'd love to personally oversee your
punishment when the revolution comes," he fumes. "Your
head will be bolted in a steel vise, and hoardes upon hoardes
of my angst-ridden Rabid-Attack Hamsters (tm) will be set
loose upon your hapless skull, and allowed to chew off your
putrid face until they have had their fill. Then what remains of
your head will be severed from your body and hung on a post
for all Sponge Minions to witness. P.S. They generally go for
the eyes first."

Moonflake is, in fact, so incensed that he organizes an
entire campaign to foil Barney's Christmas retail rally in New
England:

As part of B.I.G.O.N.E.'s never-ending battle
against Insipid Heretical Sponge-Minions, I have
dispatched several undercover agents in several
key retail areas of Boston. Dressed as Joe, the
Camel Emblem (of cigarette fame), these agents
have been busy distributing packs of cigars &
cigarettes to any minors suspected of sponge-
hood. They have also been clueing children in on
the evils of the Bh*rn'e, and of the eternal non-
existence of Santa Claus. My agents have also
been distributing an assortment of educational-
subversive material.

Thus far, our propaganda efforts have been successful. pon realizing that they have been exploited for nearly two centuries in a cynical

effort to boost end-of-year retail sales, children throughout the greater Boston Area have been rioting in the streets. The carnage is horrific, beyond our greatest expectations. Decades-old racial tensions have been dropped, as the children realize that differences in race, creed, or sexual persuasion are completely irrelevant in the face of the Threefold Truth. We have received a number of unconfirmed reports of several Bh*rn'e impersonators having been stoned to death. There is also a substantial rumor of at least one public hanging. . . . it is hoped that this spirit of holiday cheer will continue long past the Epiphany . . . only time will tell, of course.

Updates will be posted as appropriate: Jihad!

Remember: Only zealous adherence to Jihad orthodoxy can protect Freedom of Thought (tm).

—

Moonflake
Director General
Bh*r'n'e Information Gathering Organization of New England
(B.I.G.O.N.E.)

Moonflake's campaign is a bloodless rout. Other Jihad operations do not sail so smoothly. Youngstown State University, for instance, is a bloodbath. Preposterously outnumbered, the ratty Youngstown Jihad would have ended its days as dinosaur chow had not Michigan State's Serbeus stopped studying for veterinary exams long enough to deliver reinforcements. His Youngstown battle address, delivered one

hour before a brutal epidemiology exam, stirs every functioning cerebrum on alt.barney.dinosaur.die.die.die.

My Brethren against Bharney,

As you know we are having trouble reaching those
brave souls currently in battle at Youngstown
against the purple pestilence. As the situation
worsens I have been called from Examination Hell
to make one final post for this year.

The Doberman Empire has now redeployed Commander
Hydra's Alpha Sigma garrison to meet up with that
of Commander Xerxes. A FERRET (Frigid Environment Rapid Reconnaisance Espionage Trooper)
force is already on the scene and a WALRUS (Water
Attack/Land Raid Utility Soldier) is moving towards Youngstown via the sewer system. All our
heavy weaponry is being redirected towards
Youngstown. The Supreme Doberman Master himself has sent his own bodyguards, The Doberman
Guard to Youngstown to coordinate the attack. We
will not fail. The holiday season and the future of our childrens minds rest on success. To
Battle.

I now must return to exam hell. Epidemiology
comes for me in one hour Future communications
will remain the duty of Trooper Ravage

Commander Tripwire Scipio Tomarctus Serbeus
Fleet Commander
Doberman Empire

"Michigan State Vet School: Where every week is finals week"

A few days later, Fixxer reports victory in a garbled dispatch from the Youngstown front:

crackle *hiss*

This is Fixxer of Youngstown, reporting back after 5 days of not being able to transmit due to Sponge Minion jammings. The battle was rough, but I am very pleased to announce that I and fellow Jihadi in the area will be joining your troops on the way back to their respected HQ's. We are eternally grateful for your help and shipments of PEZ (tm) dispensers and Happy Meals (tm). Here is a brief summary of what took place over the last few days . . .

Total Casualties:

Jihadi: 5
S-M's: 575
Civilians: 120

We did manage to gain about 75 more troops after deprogramming. On the way to meet with national leaders, we played heavy metal and industrial to be sure that we weren't infected. Nothing was noted about this, so our new uniforms worked.

By the way, we never found the Secret Weapon, but we are certain with the lack of Sponge Minions on

```
the campus, no one will activate it again and in-
fect thousands.

This is Fixxer of Youngstown . . . Clear . . .
```

Although most Jihad battles end in underdog victory or at least a strategic retreat, there are a few disasters. Jihad leaders do not dwell upon them, except to lament the occasional martyr. Most often, news of setbacks arrives with Sponge Minions who turn up to gloat over casualties, brag about Barney sales figures, or claim responsibility for the "vanishing" of Barney resisters. For Jihad members, capture is a fate worse than death, considering the horrors of the Sponge Minion Gulag and the ruthless brainwashing techniques of their Barney-worshiping captors. Naturally, leaders worry when Jihad troopers disappear for any length of time.

"Troopers Dionysus, Bigwig," Commander Serbeus inquires anxiously. "Please post on progress of the New York City campaign. Have not heard from you recently and am growing concerned. Do you require reinforcements? How organized is the New York militia. What is the enemies position and strength? Respond immediately. That is a DIRECT order."

Within hours, a Sponge Minion commander confirms Serbeus's worst fears:

```
You will not hear from them because they are no
longer able to! They were ambushed in a surprise
move by Barney's Elite S&M Special Forces Team.
The ease with which they were defeated and cap-
tured is enough to make anyone sing one of Bar-
ney's favorite songs! They will be treated
pleasantly and humanely at Barneys deprogramming
```

facility while they undergo deprogramming. Which is more than I can say would happen to a SM if you got your hands on one! As for Boston, watch out! They are ready for you and have already prepared defenses against the bombs and other sinful devices! Boston will be victorious against you all!

DJW
Commander, BLOW ESMSFT
1st regiment, 7th Love Brigade, 3rd Song Batal-lion
Love Conquers All!

Exams are taking their toll, sapping the Jihad's strength and eroding morale. Fortunately, EphedrineLord at the University of Texas in Dallas is able to program an EphedrineLord substitute robot, the E-BOT, to shoulder his Barney combat responsibilities through the blight of exam week.

"My friends," EphedrineLord announces, "i am about to enter into exam hell. In order that this not interfere with my war against the putrid purple pederast, i have created E-Bot. . . . His primary purpose is to emulate me, flaming Jihadii and the like, while extolling the praises of B'Harnee. Please do not take this to mean that i have truly defected. And, if Gerry-Bot or the like mentions my defection, please ignore them, or reply with just anger at me. please feel free to flame the E-Bot as much as necessary." Signed, Yours in the struggle, EphedrineLord, Chief Inquisitor, Brotherhood of the Destruction of B'Harnee, Plano, TX Chapterhouse. "Through subterfuge, the vile one will be defeated."

From a trickle of online gripes, alt.barney.dinosaur.die.-die.die has blossomed into a microcosm with its own culture, politics, and rich body of mythology. Inevitably, it begins to historicize itself, in sagas like the *Jihad Tales* and Macalester College student Brian C. Bull's *Day of the Barney* epic trilogy, a narrative tour de force on par with *The Iliad, Evil Dead II,* and the Middle English *Beowulf.* The Hegelian dialectic of Barney and Anti-Barney has produced a self-sustaining meme war beyond the wildest dreams of armchair sociologists and PBS programming executives alike. When someone suggests that alt.barney.dinosaur.die.die.die be split into alt.barney.dinosaur.god.god.god, and alt.barney.dinosaur.satan, no one takes the bait. It's unthinkable. Jihad–Sponge Minion kickboxing matches are the soul of the newsgroup, the crux of it all. The war will continue until one side lies in a pool of virtual body parts and blood. Even if PBS cancels the show, there will be plush toys, books, bedspreads — the seeds of evil lying dormant in attics and garages across the world — to track down and burn. The battle ahead makes the Hundred Years' War look like a cigarette break. But hey, it's a crusade. The righteous have as long as it takes.

Long live the Jihad.

HeL1 Is tHe OthER sIdE oF ThE DaiRY sHElF

"YOU'RE HIRED."

After a job interview grueling enough to warrant an Amnesty International letter-writing campaign, I sit in the personnel office of a gargantuan, stocked-to-the-ceiling, arctically air-conditioned supermarket. Still shaking from the trauma of interrogation, I can look forward to months of can stacking and tile mopping before I claw up the next rung on the supermarket ladder to UPC label replacer. If I'm lucky, maybe I'll even make it to bagger before the year is out.

I rack my brain. How did this happen? Everything was going so well. I was twenty-two, fresh out of college. I had a book contract. I had an agent, for God's sake. And somehow, I've lost it all, and now I'm doomed to slog away at some purgatorial hypermarket for the rest of my life, effective immediately. While my rodentine soon-to-be supervisor shuffles a fat stack of tax forms and human resources documents on the other side of the customer service counter, I lean forward to sneak a look at my entrance evaluation.

I'm employee number 666.

My mental soundtrack blasts the *Psycho* shower theme. Two barely audible pencil pushers in the back room debate about changing the number to 667.

As I shuffle off to collect my teal standard-issue can-stacking uniform, I hear the cigarette-counter checkout floozy mutter under her breath, "I can already tell we're gonna have problems with this one." Barely five minutes into the job and I've already been labeled a troublemaker.

I wake with a jolt. It's 3 A.M., and my computer glows like a nightlight across the room. Before my pulse has settled down, I'm mainlining IRC.

For some reason, #goth is the happening channel tonight.

```
<DarkGodML> im Sharping my knifes now.
<jchz> Hi all
<christ666> hi
<OrionStar> hiya jchz
<jchz> I just had sort of a satanic dream
<OrionStar> :)
<OrionStar> welcome!
<christ666> hello from hell
<Woarloc> a 99 is an ice cream cone with a cherry
+on top
<jchz> I dreamed I got a job at a supermarket
<jchz> Stocking or something
<Angsty> Oh, well byy all means, jchz, share!
<jchz> And they were filling out my new employee
+forms . . .
<Woarloc> I dreamed I was sleeping with plastic
<jchz> And it turned out I was employee #666
<Angsty> . . . . how about counting everything in
+the store? That's pretty satanic . . and it was
+no dream. :(
```

\<Woarloc\> ouch
\<christ666\> employee #666? cool! ;)
\<OrionStar\> hehehe
\<DarkGodML\> i should check my voice mail
\<OrionStar\> kewl
\<jchz\> There was a big debate in the personnel
+office about whether to change the number to 667
\<OrionStar\> this makes me feel kinda funky:)
\<christ666\> no, 666 is good
\<Woarloc\> I read an article in some big satanic
+publication about how to go grocery shopping and
+remain true to your satanic beliefs
\<christ666\> :)
\<Woarloc\> It was goofy to say the least
\<christ666\> wow . . . i don't care much for sa-
+tanism though
\<Woarloc\> It basically said go at night
*** OrionStar changed the topic on #goth to
+"_hell finally froze over:)"
\<Angsty\> Ah. Of course you've got to find the
+products with 666 in the UPC code . . :)
*** Angsty changed the topic on #goth to "Satanic
+grocery shopping"
\<Woarloc\> There was a big part on Boyd Rice too.
+Everybody's favorite fascist nazi satanist.
\<christ666\> boyd rice? cool . . . i like his music
\<Woarloc\> and some of his re/search articles are
+cool, but his personal politics suck
\<christ666\> yeah, his beliefs are a bit fucked
\<christ666\> but its a free country
\<jchz\> What qualifies as "fucked" on this channel?
\<OrionStar\> _ACTION wheels out a cauldron from
+the closet_
\<OrionStar:#goth\> *bubble bubble*

Surfing on the Internet

<OrionStar> *bubble bubble*
<OrionStar> *bubble bubble*
<OrionStar> hhehehehee
<Angsty> toil & trouble
<Woarloc> lines like: Do you ever think about all
+the people in this world who make life so miser-
+able
<OrionStar> anybody want some batwing currey???
<Woarloc> Then he asks for Musselini, Hitler, Vlad
+the Impaler, and Diocletian to return to earth.
<Angsty> How about just some lightly boiled fruit-
+bats?
<OrionStar> _ACTION tosses in a friutbat for
+angsty_
<comatose> what the hell is a fruitbat????
<christ666> it's been nice chatting but i think
+i'm going to go off and kill myself. :(
<OrionStar> dont forget to clean it up!!
<Woarloc> for true?
<comatose> i guess thats how you goth ppl are . . .
<OrionStar> _ACTION feels bad now_
<Woarloc> I'm not Goth
<OrionStar> nor am i!!!
<jchz> Woar: so why are you here?
<OrionStar> i am a jeahovers vittness
<Woarloc> I'm a RaveKid :)
<Angsty> With baggie orange pants?
<comatose> _ACTION laughs at orionstar_
<Woarloc> nope
<Woarloc> With baggy dark blue pants :)
<OrionStar> wwwwwwrrrrrrrrrrrrrrrrrr can you
feel +it!!!!!!!
<Angsty> _ACTION turns on 180bpm drone tunes_

<OrionStar> bump bump bump!!!
<OrionStar> bump bump bump!!!
<OrionStar> wwwwwwrrrrrrrrrrrrrrrrrr can you feel
+it!!!!!!!!
<Woarloc> yuck
<OrionStar> wwwwwwrrrrrrrrrrrrrrrrrr can you feel
+it!!!!!!!!
<Woarloc> Well, Skinny Puppy are thinking of doing
+something similar to Aphex Twin, so . . .
<jchz> You're kidding
*** OrionStar is now known as TeknoBrat
<Angsty> Whew, Im exhausted just thinking about it
<TeknoBrat> oh no!! there goes the neighborhood
<Woarloc> Apparently cEvin Key and Goettel are re-
+ally into Richard James
<TeknoBrat> :)
*** TeknoBrat is now known as BlackMage
<BlackMage> there
<BlackMage> thats proper
<BlackMage> :)
<BlackMage> :[)
<jchz> How old are you?
<BlackMage> who??
<BlackMage> 22
<BlackMage> if that was directed at me
<BlackMage> :)
<Angsty> 21. (sniff)
<jchz> Yeah, I'm 22 also.
<Woarloc> I'm 20
<Angsty> Wow.. Oldster nite. :)
<Angsty> _ACTION cringes_
*** DJ_Sweet changed the topic on #goth to
+"Stanic Grocery Shopping"

```
<BlackMage:#goth> stanic????
<DJ_Sweet> whoops . . . ;)
<BlackMage> welcome back
```

Netsplit. It's odd, having no physical sensation of appearance or disappearance while you fade in and out of vision. If people didn't constantly greet you, you'd never know what happened.

```
<Angsty> So were you trouble, jchz? Pea soup ac-
+tion?
<jchz> No, it was just the prospect of being em-
+ployee #666 in that place.
<Angsty> I used to have supermarket nightmares at
+a young age after wandering from the clean
+friendly atmosphere of the aisles into the dark
+evil Back Room.
<Angsty> But then, I worked at one, and the illu-
+sion was shattered.
<jchz> What was it like being one of the grocery
+minions . . .
<Angsty> Just . . depressing . . I worked the
+graveyard shift doing inventory at various gro-
+cery stores . . tedious & depressing
<Angsty> I was there in the dead of night all the
+time . . no customers . . just bad Muzak and
+solitary counting
<jchz> Whoa
<jchz> If Sysiphus were alive today, he'd be
+stocking groceries.
<jchz> And carrying a mop.
<Angsty> With the occasional life-threatening
+ladder to reach stubborn items in the Back Room.
+High adventure, for sure
<Angsty> _ACTION chuckles_
```

<jchz> The BACK ROOM. What was THAT?
<Angsty> The Dark Place. The domain of boxes
<jchz> The supermarket innards.
<OrionStar> heehhee
<Angsty> The Place From Which None Shall Return
<jchz> ACTION-shivers
<Angsty> Luckily I only did that gig for a summer.
+Whew.
<jchz> What do you do now?
<Angsty> Nothing. :) Im a stoo-dent.
<jchz> Of what?
<Angsty> Of life? No, no . . electrical engi-
+neering.
<Angsty> though a nocturnal nothing-job would be
+nice now . . . trade sleep for cash.
<jchz> Yeah. I once had a late shift at the library
<jchz> Not only was the place haunted, but it was
+impossible to pry the premeds out of their car-
+rels
<Angsty> OOh. Neat-o. At least there arent any
+spilled cans of yams at the library
<Angsty> Haunted eh?
<Angsty> Lost souls of students past?
<jchz> I don't know.
<jchz> But the basement was absolutely freaky
<jchz> I think it was the urban myth that homeless
+people had occasionally bunkered down there.
<Angsty> basements usually are. pity everything
+around here is too new to be scary
<jchz> Where are you?
<Angsty> California . .where things over 20 are
'OLD'
<jchz> Supermarkets are spookier-the really huge
+ones

Surfing on the Internet

```
<drizzt> heh
<jchz> The lights are always on
<jchz> And you never know what's going on behind
+the brightly lit dairy shelves
<Angsty> It's like descending into the basement,
+the dark side of the market
<jchz> Angsty: Hah!
<Angsty> . . and those HANDS that come out from the
+other side of the milk rack! Dairy Faeries mag-
+ically restocking it!
<jchz> Hell is the other side of the dairy shelf
<OrionStar> HAAHAHAHAHAHAHA
```

FaSt TiMEs iN THe PyRO ShACk

ALL MY FRIENDS are applying to law school.

I don't think that has anything to do with my current idyll among anarchist gun nuts on the Internet. But I could be wrong — forgery, firearms, and explosives do seem infinitely preferable to the LSAT.

And so I find myself in a Fagin's den of fresh-faced bomb experts, grizzled gun nuts, and forgery aficionados in a particularly well-armed corner of the Net.

Out of conscience, paranoia, or fear of prosecution, disclaimers are the norm around here — dozens of light-fingered amateur locksmiths have assured me that the potential flaws of U-shaped bike locks and magnetic card security systems are of scholarly interest only. That recipe for pushing back the birth date on an Iowa driver's license is merely a hypothetical solution to the famous "Drinking Age Quandary." If you can hack in four computer languages, the reasoning goes, you can hack a bit of plastic and laminate issued by the Iowa Department of Public Safety. But surely, no one in alt.forgery would use such information to break the *law* or anything.

Of course. And I've got a gorgeous, museum-quality Commodore 64 for sale. Mint condition. It's a collector's item.

Counterfeit driver's licenses notwithstanding, physical document forgery is not the newsgroup's forte or even its prime concern. Electronic forgery, with its immense prank potential, is a much meatier topic — sending bogus e-mail traceable to celebrity e-mail addresses, putting flame bait into the mouths of public figures, that kind of thing. Depending on how much root access you have, fake mail can be a cheap, quick, and dirty way to exact revenge on, say, the federal government for, say, busting a college student who joked about putting the president's head on a pike.

"Now now kiddies," chides Baron Samedi, borrowing his hack-name from the latest Gibson novel. "Sending threats to the Pres is juvenile. But more importantly, it's already been done a hundred times over, to every president, for decades. Just ask the NSA. But, there is an unprecedented opportunity for Class-A Pranksterism here . . . Sending e-mail death threats to people FROM the President. Telnet port 25, hombres. Fakemail is a superb mimetic."

Crank e-mail from the President. Charming. ("My fellow Americans, let me be the first to offer you an outstanding deal on some waterfront property in Arkansas. And if you act now, I'll even throw in this amazing set of Ginsu knives.") A few months after someone suggests a presidential forgery, a letter from Clinton's whitehouse.gov address shows up on alt.2600, complete with ASCII letterhead "From the DeskTop of the PRESIDENT of The UNITED STATES of AMERICA."

"Hello Everyone. Just stopped by to see the new newsgroup and wish everyone well. Just remember to behave yourselves and 'you stay out of my mail, I'll stay out of yours. Have Fun Now.'" Signed, Bill. "P.S. I've been doing a little work on my sig (?) and would appreciate any suggestions. Please, no e-mail though. It's getting a little piled up and I'm still getting the hang of this multiple folder thing. You can just post them here, I'll check back from time to time. [note: consult Al re: correct spelling- sig, .sig, Sig, before posting]"

I'm staying tuned for the house party invitation from vatican.com.

After alt.forgery, I'm ready to move on to bigger and more explosive newsgroups. Next stop: the cyberspace gun club, rec.guns. Threads here spin out with a casual Elk Lodge machismo: "Portable Skeet Launchers, Need recommendation." "Compact .40 Auto — Which One?" "Tear Gas — available and legal????" If you need to, say, convert a Russian/Chinese SKS/Type 56 rifle from 7.62x39 millimeters to the standard NATO 7.62 round or score some surplus U.S. customs revolvers, rec.guns readers will dispense the requisite information without much editorial yip-yapping. Prices, availability, field test results — it's very terse, very *Drag Net.* It's the anti-alt.cyberpunk. So even after spending days sorting through silencer ratings, the intricacies of interstate arms transport, and sale announcements for semiautomatics and Kevlar vests, I'm still no closer to knowing the background, the mind-set, the daily grind and favorite snack food of the cyberspace gun club.

Who *are* these people? Geeks who read *Guns and Ammo*? Has Bubba finally stumbled into the Net and sniffed out his niche? Or has the Net spawned an entirely new breed of techie/Bubba hybrid to engineer the big millennial blowout and pull the trigger too? A quick canvass reveals that rec.guns is, in fact, the happy hunting ground of middle-aged ex-military types who began their Net careers with ARPANET access, back in the Paleolithic (the seventies). Surfing through this pocket of the Net feels like an ethnographic expedition to some lost Stone Age tribe in the South Pacific, a time warp to an era before compact discs and acetylcholine smoothies. This is the land that cyberhype forgot.

When I inquire about favorite albums, beverages, and political manifestos, a former marine is the first to answer.

"Doors, alive she cried. Scotch. Libertarian."

Libertarian — check. Doors — cool, despite the red flag of klassic rock. But Scotch? Somehow, the juxtaposition of nerds and guns doesn't slow me down, but the idea of Scotch drinkers on the Net stops me in my tracks. Arsenals in the pantries of northern Virginia, that I can handle. But a tumbler of Dewar's sweating next to a suburban 486 makes my skin crawl. A child of the eighties, I've always pictured computers in the hands of young, ill-clad subversives, people who abuse their bodies with more arcane substances than whiskey. When I think "Scotch," I think of lawyers, lobbyists, politicians, ex–fraternity boys, and other Establishment types and grumpy grown-ups — in short, the antithesis of the Net's adorable anarchy. I get along with Scotch drinkers in real life, but it's an unpleasant shock to meet them here.

I shake my head, aghast. This isn't the Net. Not *my* Net, at any rate. It couldn't be. And then I figure, the Net's too big *not* to contain these people. If you give enough netters enough time, eventually one of them will produce an NRA membership card. I back out of the cyberspace gun club slowly, without any sudden moves, and duck across the tracks to rec.pyrotechnics.

I'm instantly at ease here. Rec.pyrotechnics has a ragtag, Spy-Versus-Spy sensibility. It generates discussions like "Chemists Versus Bandits: How to Fry Burglars and Muggers, and What to Do When Sued by Their Surviving Relatives." Undergraduate paintball warriors, model rocket builders, fireworks enthusiasts, and doctoral-degreed pyromaniacs lend the place a certain scruffiness. Unlike their gun club counterparts, who buy and sell premanufactured hardware, the pyrotechnics crüe prefers a do-it-yourself approach to combustibles. When one person needs help on a backyard explosives project, everyone rallies around the Bunsen burner. This is the collaboration of men who've survived advanced inorganic chemistry, but barely. They are always delighted to contribute to a new explosion, particularly if it is loud and comes in pretty colors.

Hence the fireball thread ignited by a Rice University student. "I would like to make a large fireball for use in a home movie," he announces. "I have attempted it before, using a black powder pipe bomb to ignite a can of gasoline. Needless to say, the bomb worked, severely rupturing the can, but the gasoline didn't erupt in a huge ball of flame! Was the bomb too small? A friend of mine did the same thing, but I believed he used acetone. His apparatus worked spectacularly. Any ideas? Please e-mail me."

Within days, fireball chefs from all over the Midwest post their recipes, including detailed descriptions of fireball circumference, sonic impact, and theatric potential. A netter in Des Moines is particularly proud of his fireball formula, which calls for a five-gallon plastic food bucket, a pound of commercial black powder, and two layers of quality garbage sack:

After ducking behind my pickup truck 300 feet away, I connected the speaker wire to a battery and got a column of fire, over 100 feet in the air! The heat was fantastic and so was the light. It was seen from over 20 miles away! A highway patrol pig saw it from a highway over 5 miles away and called it into the fire department. They

went out to try to locate the site but couldn't
find it. I did this in a freshly plowed field, in
the center, away from trees and combustables.
Needless to say, this pyro demonstration had to
be reperformed for _all_ of my friends. The next
time I did it, I used aviation JET fuel! It gave
the most beautiful orange fireball, and was many
times hotter than the gasoline one, also jet fuel
doesn't "whoosh" when you light a 5 gallon bucket
of it up. I get paranoid when I light up that
much gas and just the vapors make a big whoosh
when lit.

Amateur explosives in the heartland. Makes me proud
to be an American.

The fireball recipe contest, however, plays second fiddle
to the mammoth slime launcher project. A Siemens Corporate Research staffer needed to know "how to slime a bunch
of people. Please don't ask why. Anything dangerous to the
slimees is absolutely out of the question."

Shortly thereafter, a slime charrette convenes on the
newsgroup, producing several blueprints for the launcher
mechanism, as well as a plethora of slime ammunition formu-
las — wallpaper paste, diluted lime Jell-O, and mashed okra
being the top contenders. Slime, in all its glorious grossness,
was a cause célèbre.

The Shadow, a star pyrotechnics poster at Montana
Tech, contributes the most elegant model of the bunch, a
simple yet effective two-pipe mechanism. "It works on the basis of the plunger effect on a pinball machine," he explains. "I
used such a device when I was a wee lad in school (flinging
such things as snow balls, blood capsules, and such) ——
And for all you deviant bastards who don't mind getting their

hands slimey take a nice handful of slime, run up behind victim and throw such mess at victim :-) (Oh, look my smiley is back from vacation. . . . . whoopeee!!)"

When I finish reading the recipe, a shock of recognition jolts me to the core. Whoever the Shadow is, he has independently devised the same projectile weapon I built as a child and gleefully deployed against my younger siblings. After a moment of nostalgia, the warm memory of my sister's terrified squeals gives way to a sense of kinship. It's always a rush to find someone who shares your taste in nonlethal projectile weapons.

Other slime schematics are more complex, but none of them has any serious potential for mutilation or fatality. This cannot be said of most topics in the pyro shack. Because the people at risk are fellow netters, pyrotechnics suggestions are rigorously scrutinized and subject to peer review. It's generally considered bad etiquette to post a suggestion that blows someone's arm off. Getting sued by that person is no picnic either. This is why most posters end with a caveat, something like "It's only fun until someone loses an eye." After an article entitled "So You Want to Build a Bad-Ass Flame Thrower," a Carnegie-Mellon student says, "i hope i haven't given all this shit to an asshole, don't be one i don't want to read the paper about some yaahoo going around frying people in wisconsin. Flame throwers are cool and it was fun to have one but think and use a lot of common sense." In other words, now that you've built that Handy-Dandy Brand Flamethrower, play nice.

"Oh boy, thanks mommy and daddy for the flame thrower and grenade launcher," sneers the Shadow. "I swear I won't go around frying anybody. . . . . just birds, foxes and the occassional homicidal maniac." As if to hammer down the don't-fuck-around-with-fire message, people start telling horror stories about pyrotechnics projects gone haywire. The string of cretin-in-my-chem-class stories culminates with a grim post about "a guy here in Spokane [who] tried to launch a home made sky rocket. The rocket was made from a thick walled metal pipe. He *was* trying to launch a pipe bomb. He *is* dead."

But like so many tales of fear and loathing on the Net, this thread quickly degenerates into a competition for a) "messiest blood-and-guts narrative" and b) the Doogie Howser Prize for youngest childhood pyrotechnics disaster. From the Bay Area's WELL bulletin board, John H. LeBourgeois (if that is his real name) mused, "Ah yes, in my misspent youth, I had the run of the chem lab on the naval base at the age of 14. I had mixed a stochiometric mix of KClO3 and Red Phosphorus on a filter paper under the hood. Fortunately I had the shield down. I was gently shaking the filter paper to mix the two ingredients when the mixture detonated . . . I had a not so pleasant hour at the base infirmary where the surgeon picked the phosphorous particles out of my hand without anesthetic."

Not to be outdone, a Berlin hacker by the name of Solon Luigi Lutz, aka Lord Dread, posts his own contribution to the growing body of pyro-tot tall tales. "When I was ten years old," he brags, "I was making my own acetoneperoxide. Nobody told me that this substance is VERY DANGEROUS and so I put about 0.5g on some aluminum foil and heated it on a candle. The next thing I can remember, was glowing particles flying around me and me hearing almost nothing. Fortunately the explosion trauma has nearly disappeared today!"

As a great sage once said: Fire is kewl, huh huh huh.

After a few weeks, I am spending way too much time in the pyro shack. I think the fact that I can't put my grubby little hands on anything in this place makes me want to blow things up. I mean, sure, it's nice to know which combination of gasoline, candle wax, and Vaseline yields the most effective homemade napalm, or how to destroy a small room with a pound of flour and a tuna can full of C-4. But it's more than that. Nothing I do on the Net makes any kind of tangible dent. So naturally, the idea of physical destruction is irresistible. All I can think of are things that go BOOM.

And now that the really big heists are perpetrated with bits and bytes, all these mechanical tools and chemical reagents — metal picks, solid fuel, steel tumblers, gold-dusted laminate, stuff you can measure with your eyes and adjust with your fingers — seem like a throwback to a fast-fading era. It's all so . . . *mechanical.* There's a nostalgia about mechanisms now that everything's turned digital, like with records. I can barely remember the sound of a vinyl record, but their physical mechanism imbues them with an antique mystery, like that of blasting caps or flash powder. Didn't Neil Young say that records are warm and CDs are cold? Well, compared to the odorless poison of software sabotage, these jerry-built explosives seem neolithically crude and, for that reason, extraordinarily cool. It's vaguely comforting to discuss them.

The irony that we're doing it *here* is just gravy.

········· · · · · · · ·

PsSsT...

Is it possible that all 20 million of us are un-
knowing subjects of some sort of psychological or
sociological experiment? In this experiment,
they put us in a large and comfy room with immense
bookshelves, lots of old but serviceable furni-
ture, absolutely no decor (except what we provide), and a very, very large bowl of popcorn. A
cluster of researchers in white smocks and dark
ties looks at us through the one-way windows we
think are mirrored coffee tables and takes ex-
haustive notes, to be passed on to people who
have more money than we have popcorn. Or perhaps
we are the ones running the experiment.
                              —warrenec@news.delphi.com

KURT COBAIN ISN'T even cold in his grave, and the conspiracy theorists are already picking at his bones. So far,
they've targeted everyone from Pearl Jam to the Trilateral
Commission.

The most cynical theory to date comes from "Captain Sarcastic," a discordian in Denver. "Cobain is such a money-grubbing bastard," he fumes after announcing that the body found in the Cobain estate garage was just a "patsy stand-in" for the real Cobain. "Now that we all think he's dead, he'll finally be able to release those three hundred hours of Sinatra and Bee Gees covers the band did while drunk. I saw them, stacked in Warners warehouses on my secret mission to get an advance copy of In Utero. 'What the fuck is this?' I said to my companion, pointing at the 100 or so tons of the unreleased album. I can warn you in advance, this stuff isn't for the faint-hearted . . . I gave it a D in my zine review of the copy I stole . . . but those A&R men in black stole the entire press run of the zine. My entire month's allowance down the drain. I have to tell the world, NIRVANA IS A SCAM . . . COBAIN LIVES!"

Barbara Abernathy, the dragon lady of alt.flame, is convinced Cobain's punk-rocker wife, Courtney Love, murdered him or at least drove him to suicide. "Krist and Grohl are not above suspicion also," she adds. "If what another poster said was true (The other poster posted something to the effect that Kurt didn't necessarily want to make music with the other band members anymore) then anyone of Cobain's leeches could have wigged out and killed their gravy train. A shotgun blast to the head is a very unusual and painful way to kill oneself. The whole thing just seems too prepackaged. There's got to be more to it."

From his terminal at Central Michigan University, Josh Beckerman looks beyond the small circle of Cobain *intimes* to the sphere of national politics. "An entertainment figure, usually a musician, is chosen to be the consensus counterculture leader," he says. "In the early 20's, it was Billie Holliday. In the 60's, it was Mick Jagger, followed by Bob Dylan, who was replaced by Jimi Hendrix, after whose death John Fogerty ascended, then Jon Anderson of Yes, then Sid Vicious, then Bono. After 'Rattle and Hum,' there was a movement to oust the allegedly commercialized Bono. Perry Farrell and Axl Rose were co-leaders until November, 1991. Most music historians agreed that Kurt Cobain was the new leader. . . .

"I hated H. Ross Perot," says Beckerman, "but he proved the viability of third party candidates. With Howard Stern running for governor, ever-increasing popularity for Nirvana, and alienation with government as we know it, the next logical step was a Cobain candidacy. There may be some who would suggest starting with a run for the House of Representatives, but it is likely that Kurt would have seen this as too slow a path to the presidency . . . Now, the man who wrote 'Smells Like Teen Spirit' and 'On a Plain' is gone, the old power structure remains intact, and there's yet another struggle to name a new consensus leader of the counterculture, which will likely be good news to Eddie Vedder, Weiland from Stone Temple Pilots, Beavis and Butt-Head creator Mike Judge, or Snoop Doggy Dogg." Clearly, bipartisan fear of a Cobain candidacy ensured that he would not be allowed to survive. Stay tuned for the Oliver Stone biopic.

Others argue that the conspiracy goes even deeper, that the plot transcends national politics. At stake is nothing less than the global balance of power. The most grandiose theory of all traces the Cobain assassination plot from the dive bars of Seattle to the halls of Congress. This one goes all the way up to the top — the shadowy corridors of . . . the Muzak Corporation. This theory, incidentally, is posted by a military whistle-blower from an air force site (Can you say "Usenet feeding frenzy," boys and girls?):

Was it a simple political murder? That's part of what they want you to believe. Economics always drive politics. Kurt lived near Canada, he was an outspoken critic of NAFTA . . . Was he killed by those NAFTA interests? What was discussed in secret meetings in Seattle in early March between the primary NAFTA representives from the US, Canada, and Mexico? . . . Are the Trilateral people being manipulated? Of course they are. I have evidence that the people who put "Teenage Wasteland" down tempoed in elevators are really the actual force behind these events. They promoted the Trilateral Commission to kill J.F.K. in order to throw blame on our economic problems on. This led to the illegal formation of NAFTA which was used as a spring board to convince other bands to get together and kill Kurt in a well planned attack. In the end, MUZAK kill be seen as the real threat. They had to kill him because he refused to see "Smells Like Teen Spirit" played in doctors offices over tinny little speakers.

The Cobain controversy flares and then fades, like so many blossoms on the Net's rhizome of paranoia. Usenet has a conspiracy theory for every aspect of modern life, with particular regard to technology and how the government is using it to spy on us. As Tomwhore, aka Thomas Higgins, the bard of MindVox, says, "The Net as we know it is built from a goverment base out; it is intertwined with the goverment and all the nastiness that brings. Basically we are playing around in the goverment's basement rumpus room." Posters beware. Big Brother is watching.

"Is your Food Spying On You?"

I normally skim past threads in alt.conspiracy, but this is irresistible. I have to know what the Men in Black are hiding in my bowl of Count Chocula.

Unfortunately, the subject heading is just a teaser. The conspiracy theory itself is a run-of-the-mill Orwellian nightmare scenario authored by a Mr. Melvin Gladstone, who's doctored his organizational address to read "Ruprecht's Lizard Emporium." It's old hat, the same old stuff about the FBI, CIA, and NSA spying on us through home appliance components, in this case the closed caption (CC) decoders installed in new televisions. "These decoders supposedly provide captions to TV shows for the hearing impaired, but in fact they are also rebroadcasters which will allow the gov. to spy on anyone they want," Gladstone declares, without explaining the source of this revelation, natch. He even provides tips about how to deal with the gizmo.

"When you find yourself with a TV equipped with the 'Decoder,'" he says, "there are several things you can do to protect yourself. First, don't put the TV in your bedroom, this is where the government is most interested in spying. When not watching, push the antennas all the way in or disconnect the cable. Unplugging the TV will not help because the 'Decoder' will use passive broadcasting to continue sending its signal. Also turn the volume down when not watching. When you watch the TV, place a candle or other heat source to confuse the infrared EYE. Don't say anything secret or get undressed near the TV. Don't be seen smoking near the TV."

It's shoddy work, not really up to par on alt.conspiracy at all. Most theories on this newsgroup are far-fetched but, like all well-constructed conspiracy theories, impossible to disprove. Mel leaves himself wide open to all kinds of embarrassing questions. (How did he peg CC decoders as spy devices? Has he ever actually taken one apart? And how did the government sweet-talk the *Japanese* into installing these sophisticated — and no doubt pricey — surveillance gizmos?) A student at Penn State simply advises Gladstone to chill. "Melvin, buddy-it's time to lay off the Philip K. Dick books, ok? Remember, Eye in the Sky and Radio Free Albemuth were just _stories_."

Ah, Net, where one can speak freely without fear of repercussion.

Or not. Just ask "Diablo," a Cornell student who told the readers in alt.anarchy, alt.privacy, and alt.lawyers.sue.sue.sue that he was "KIDNAPPED BY THE STATE." Two days after he asked the folks in alt.romance.chat for advice about his suicidal tendencies, he says,

a couple of cops show up at my door, along with some nut from the mental health department of Tompkins County and tell me I have to come with them to the hospital for "an hour, maybe an hour and a half." I said "What if I don't choose to go." They replied that I don't have a choice. They informed me that I'm going with them because some people read my internet message and were concerned. I was in the middle of conducting some business on the phone and asked if I could make a couple of phone calls first but the pigs replied that no, I couldn't. In effect, they kidnapped me. . . . They strapped me down (I cooperated but was berating them the whole time) and put me in the ambulance and left a guy in the back to watch me. I was telling him what a dick he is and how big a violation of my human rights this was and he just told me to shut up. After a period of silence I apologized to him and told him I didn't mean anything personal. He responded with something to the effect of "Well fuck you, I dont' like your tone of voice." I asked him, very sarcastically, if he was pleased with how well he was doing his job. He said "Look, I'm just doing my job here." Yeah, yeah I replied, so were the Nazi death-camp guards.

Anyhow, they get me to this hospital. They made me strip and put on stupid hospital clothes. By this time it was 8:30 at night (I got picked up at about 4:30) and no one had given me anything to eat. They gave me some graham crackers. Whoopee . . . I spent the whole night planning a way to escape (pathetic security cause I was in the wing where people with things like depression are kept, not the criminally insane wing). At 6:30 in the morning, they come in and tell me they are going to take blood from me. When I said no they said they were going to anyhow. The long and short of this all is that I ended up spending two nights in a fucking mental hospital . . . The way I look at it, I was held without indictement, without warrant, and without legal representation based on evidence contained on a Usenet posting. I mean c'mon. Like even 1/8 of the stuff posted here should be taken seriously. . . .

The moral of this story: Don't yell "Fire" in cyberspace.

And as Cobain himself sang, just because you're paranoid don't mean they're not after you.

tHE JeoPaRDy ChaNneL

I WONDER IF Alex Trebek knows there's an automaton named after him — the alexbot. It emcees the Jeopardy channel on IRC, where ZeEd, Selira, and Kay are competing for the grand prize.

```
<alexbot> Welcome to Jeopardy! A new game is be-
+ginning now.
<alexbot> Categories for this game are:
<alexbot> Third_Reich  Alaska  Name_That_Tune_2
+Guys_Named_Al  TV_Occupations  Shakespeare_Char-
+acter
<ZeEd> fuck you alex
<alexbot> zeed: Keep it clean, this is a family
+game! Otherwise I will have to call the bouncers.
<alexbot> Please wait while preparing the next
+Guys_Named_Al question . . .
<alexbot> Current category: Guys_Named_Al. Ques-
+tion Value: 200.
<alexbot> Question 16 of 30: He's married to Kim
+Basinger:
```

<ZeEd> aLeXz baldwin
<alexbot> zeed: That is CORRECT! You win 200.
+Your total is 1400.
<alexbot> Please wait while preparing the next
+Guys_Named_Al question . . .
<ZeEd> this cat again?!
<Selira> really
<alexbot> Current category: Guys_Named_Al. Ques-
+tion Value: 400.
<alexbot> Question 17 of 30: E=mc (squared):
<Selira> alex einstein
<alexbot> selira: That is CORRECT! You win 400.
+Your total is 2000.
<alexbot> Please wait while preparing the next
+Guys_Named_Al question . . .
<ZeEd> aLeXz einstein
<alexbot> Current category: Guys_Named_Al. Ques-
+tion Value: 600.
<alexbot> Question 18 of 30: Heavy metal star of
+the 70's, he wore mascara frequently:
<ZeEd> aLeXz alice cooper
<alexbot> zeed: That is CORRECT! You win 600.
+Your total is 2000.
<alexbot> Please wait while preparing the next
+Guys_Named_Al question . . .
<alexbot> Current category: Guys_Named_Al. Ques-
+tion Value: 800.
<alexbot> Question 19 of 30: On "Family Ties", he
+was the Republican stock-broker-to-be of the
+family:
<ZeEd> aLeXz keaton
<alexbot> zeed: That is CORRECT! You win 800.
+Your total is 2800.

```
<alexbot> Please wait while preparing the next
+Guys_Named_Al question . . .
<alexbot> Current category: Guys_Named_Al. Ques-
+tion Value: 1000.
<alexbot> Question 20 of 30: He produced all of
+Jimi Hendrix' albums:
<ZeEd> al bundy did
<kay> alex we give up
<alexbot> Giving up after another player gives up
+or 7 seconds elapse.
<alexbot> The ANSWER is: alan douglas
<alexbot> Please wait while preparing the next
+TV_occupations question . . .
<alexbot> Current category: TV_occupations. Ques-
+tion Value: 200.
```

The alexbot progresses from category to category to final Jeopardy to the start of a fresh game. "Welcome to Jeopardy!" he exclaims. "A new game is beginning now." He is poised between home-shopping hostmanship and a mean impression of Joel Grey in *Cabaret* ("Good evening Mesdames and mien herrs! Remember, you only have six more minutes to order this fabulous pair of diamonette (tm) earrings! Next category: TV heroes in Spandex.") He works the room. He works for free. He requires no makeup artist. The alexbot does his job so expertly that his real-life counterparts seem robotic by comparison. Sajak, Barker, Trebek . . . those teeth, those chuckles, the way they hold their little cards . . . I make a mental note to check for sockets and concealed fuse boxes the next time I watch *Wheel of Fortune* reruns.

IRC Jeopardy goes on twenty-four hours a day, seven days a week. It never stops. There's something frozen and eerie about it. The channel just loops and loops and loops. If it could pipe the *Jeopardy* jingle through IRC, I think we'd all go mad. It's endless, changing only with the barely noticeable turnover of contestants and, occasionally, a new stack of questions that some faceless university student boots into the automaton's mouth.

It's a rare and satisfying moment on #Jeopardy when something shatters the routine. Like one time a player stole alexbot's name and locked him out of the room. While the automaton scratched at the channel door, his usurper began a new game with rap music questions.

"The lead singer of Cypress Hill."

"Ice Cube's real name."

The French Jeopardy contestant was perturbed. He had scant knowledge of gangsta rap. The real game show host was absent. Obviously, the scores were now invalid. I asked him if he'd ever seen *Jeopardy* in France. "No," he replied (an American game show on French television? Sacre bleu!) How did he learn about the game, then?

"Here."

Ingeniously, he has managed to circumvent his country's isolationist GATT maneuvers by watching *Jeopardy* on IRC, proving yet again that it's no longer possible to contain infectious memes. It's like trying to stop a hurricane with chicken wire.

The inexorable flow of Cheez Whiz culture will not be stopped.

Vive la Net.

ThE BAr At tHe ENd oF The INteRNeT

"WELCOME TO THE #IRCBar mischief, I am your bot Barman!"

The automaton behind the bar greets me and prompts me to order a virtual drink at the #IRCbar, the British pub of cyberspace traceable to an academic site in Hertfordshire, England.

I order a bourbon and the barbot fetches it with dispatch. He is nothing if not efficient, and he serves any request. His repertoire is as varied as your imagination. As I recall, his signature pousse-café consists of cognac, tangelo liqueur, lychee brandy, absinthe, and the fermented extract of fruit grown only on volcanic soil that has been blessed by ancient Mesopotamian gods and sanctified by human sacrifice. He also pulls Guinness, Blackened Voodoo Lager, and Belikan Beer and doubles as a security goon. If you irritate a regular, he will throw you out. He's a bot. That's his job. That's what he's programmed to do — run the bar at the end of the Internet.

It's a small crowd tonight. The jEsTEr introduces himself with a flourish.

```
<mischief> What *is* the point of this channel?
<TOD> Nothing, just blablabla. 42.
<Kintaroo> Barman get me a BIIIIIG_steak
-Barman3:#ircbar- ==== Gets Kintaroo a BIIII
+IIG_steak ====
<Kintaroo> Thanks barman
-Barman3:#ircbar- ==== Anything, Anytime Kinta-
+roo!! ====
Steve_O has joined channel #ircbar
<Barman3> ==== Welcome to the #IRCBar Steve_O, I
+am your bot Barman! ====
```

Steve_O orders everyone a shot of Goldschlager. Meanwhile, I'm still getting used to the bar idiom.

```
<mischief> A bar on irc? it's like some kind of
+weird . . . mirage
<mischief> or maybe that's just the commercial
<TOD> You ggot it . . . isn't it great?
<NEKO> I like it it's the *only* thing
```

Kintaroo wants to know if the jEsTEr is an illustrious
sound file hacker, THE Jester. JEsTEr points to himself,
smiles, nods his head, then crumbles under pointed ques-
tioning. He's an impostor.

```
* jEsTEr gasps
* jEsTEr chokes
```

```
* jEsTEr twirls around
* jEsTEr falls to the ground in utter dispair
* jEsTEr melts in to abandon
* jEsTEr is dust
<jEsTEr> Sorry, no one loves me.
```

I call for a round of bourbon. Steve_O gets everyone another flaming shot of Goldschlager, and Kintaroo buys the disconsolate jEsTEr a beer and orders a round of Pangalactic Gargleblasters for the rest of us.

```
<Kintaroo> BYebyebyebyebye . . I'm leaving . . .
* NEKO has found an exit
* jEsTEr jumps skillfully into the air and lands
+on Kin's back
* NEKO waves bye
<jEsTEr> impressive?
<Steve_O> barman get everyone a Flaming.Shot.Of.-
+GoldSchlager
-Barman3:#ircbar- ==== Gets a Flaming.Shot.Of.-
+GoldSchlager for everyone courtesy of Steve_O
+====
```

NEKO is gone. Steve_O is sulkily nursing his Goldschlager, and Kinteroo has left the channel. No one is talking except the jEsTEr, and he only talks nonsense, howling as he slips, falls to the floor, and vanishes, cut off by a lousy link.

Curiouser and curiouser.

THE next time I log onto the #IRCbar, it is a dimly lit crush of students from around the planet: Frank, a blunt-spoken meat-and-potatoes man from Kansas City; Flowers in upstate New York; a Palestinian named Teebo; assorted limeys; an expatriate Texan in New York City; firehead at Texas A&M; and a computer science student named Brooker logging on from the Czech Republic.

Of course, the Texans bond instantly.

Meanwhile, Barman3 has changed the channel topic to "DING DONG DING DONG: Another hour rolls by in England!" Much to the chagrin of the assembled procrastinators, he announces this every hour.

```
*** Ulic has joined channel #ircbar
<Barman3> ==== Welcome to the #IRCBar Ulic, I am
+your bot Barman! ====
```

Flamewise, a German masquerading as a dragon, guns into the bar.

"Hi flame!!" yells Teebo.

"Hey flamewise!!" shouts firehead.

"Hey flame," says Frank. Only here can a teutonic lizard be greeted like Norm from *Cheers.*

"Barman," says firehead, "get Flamewise a Beer." The barbot obliges, and Flamewise growls appreciatively.

Within seconds of each other, razor and charmeur tumble through the door. Razor, a Brit, is a regular and something of a rough; charmeur is a Frenchified Neil Diamond impersonator logged on from CUNY. This is his first time here. They are quite the odd couple.

```
<razor> guess who
<Teebo> hi razor u smeg!!
<charmeur> hello guys can i have a jackdaniels
```

<Brooker> SO MANY CHANNELS BUT ONLY ONE IS SO
+LOVELY: --> #ircbar
* FlameWise downs its drink happily.
<mischief> barman get charmeur a Jack Daniels
-Barman3:#ircbar- ==== Gets a Jack for charmeur
+courtesy of mischief ====
* Brooker kisses barman on the forehead.
<charmeur> mischief hello
<frank> barman give me a quadruple shot of grain
+alchohol.
<Flowers> Are there any other females on this
+channel?
<frank> not me.
<mischief> Me
<charmeur> mischif is a guy or a girl
<mischief> Mischief is a girl.
<frank> and what a name for a female, mischief.
<charmeur> frank i know full of wickedness
<Flowers> OK lets start over who is m and who is f
<grumptink> Hi again
* mischief says "Alright. Boys on one side of the
+room, girls on the other."
<Flowers> for all those who just joined the ques-
+tion is male or female
* charmeur wonders what kind of bar this is???
<mischief> Where are you from, charmeur?
<frank> A fine drinking establishment.
<charmeur> franky whats up what going on in the
+bar
<Flowers> female
<mischief> Nothing, flowers is just one of those
+categorization fiends.
<frank> Anything you desire.

```
<Flowers> am not I just wanted to see who I could
+check out:)
* charmeur vient du monde qui est dans la tere
+qui est une partie de la galaxie du soliel qui
+est dans l'univere
*** Signoff: razor (irc.uiuc.edu eff.org)
*** Signoff: Ulic (irc.uiuc.edu eff.org)
*** Signoff: Teebo (irc.uiuc.edu eff.org)
*** Signoff: Barman3 (irc.uiuc.edu eff.org)
*** Signoff: Polsy (irc.uiuc.edu eff.org)
*** Signoff: Brooker (irc.uiuc.edu eff.org)
*** Signoff: Worzel (irc.uiuc.edu eff.org)
*** Signoff: RedRum (irc.uiuc.edu eff.org)
*** Signoff: RedRum2 (irc.uiuc.edu eff.org)
*** Signoff: FlameWise (irc.uiuc.edu eff.org)
<Flowers> netsplit
*** Flowers has left channel #ircbar
```

Netsplit is when an entire system server swoons and passes out, creating a rift in IRC. Yes, it sounds like *Star Trek* ("A rift in the space-time continuum! Wesley, go put some duct tape on it!"), but it's a reality of Net life. When a glitch hits an IRC server, channel users are automatically shunted to alternate servers that are up and working. The problem is, not everyone is shunted to the *same* server. A given IRC channel is carried on every IRC server, so it seems as if you haven't moved at all. The IRCbar rolls along, ostensibly continuous. You are still there. Only, half your compatriots disappear, then reappear ten seconds later as the Netsplit zippers into one piece. During the split, they think they're the ones who aren't moving while you seem to disappear. But no one really "leaves." The bar just exists independently in several places before the Net mends itself, flowing around its wounds and filling in the holes like the villain of *Terminator 2*. In the meantime, IRC users are left with the disorienting impression that they're chatting in a roomful of Cheshire cats.

The question of where, and in what form, the bar actually exists during a Netsplit is a thorny one. The convenient answer is that the bar's primary location rests with the barman. He is a bot, of course, not a real person. But there is only one of him, and IRCbar is his home. He always flies back to it, so he's the marker. But that's a convention, more than anything else. Really, no one has reached any kind of metaphysical consensus about this boîte afloat in cyberspace.

Relativity isn't an abstract theory on the Net. It's a pain in the ass.

It's amazing how the Net can strip you of grown-up assumptions about the laws of physics. You're forced into an almost childlike approach to the digital world, always asking why, why, why like a five-year-old and accepting the answers, no matter how outlandish they seem, because the alternative is to believe it all happens by magic. (What's a Netsplit? Oh, that's when you're all in the same place, but separately, and you can't see each other. Oh, OK. I can accept that, along with the room with no walls and people sitting on barstools that don't exist shouting "Barman! Barman!")

This is lunacy. It has a certain internal logic — but then, so does schizophrenia.

Every once in a while, I stop to consider how crazy this all must look from the outside: a girl staring at a piece of cast plastic and metal parts and claiming to speak with people from England and Czechoslovakia while a string of ones and zeros pours drinks. (*Can you see them?* Um, no, they're invisible. *Are they talking to you now?* Yeah, but they don't make any noise. I can see what they're saying, though. *Oh really? How nice for you.*)

```
*** FlameWise has joined channel #ircbar
*** RedRum has joined channel #ircbar
*** Worzel has joined channel #ircbar
*** Brooker has joined channel #ircbar
*** Polsy has joined channel #ircbar
*** Barman3 has joined channel #ircbar
*** Ulic has joined channel #ircbar
*** razor has joined channel #ircbar
*** Wyndi has joined channel #ircbar
*** Teebo has joined channel #ircbar
<Barman3> ==== Welcome to the #IRCBar frank, I am
+your bot Barman! ====
<Barman3> ==== Welcome to the #IRCBar GNU, I am
+your bot Barman! ====
<Barman3> ==== Welcome to the #IRCBar mcaff, I am
+your bot Barman! ====
<Barman3> ==== Welcome to the #IRCBar charmeur, I
+am your bot Barman! ====
<Barman3> ==== Welcome to the #IRCBar BC4, I am
+your bot Barman! ====
```

Barman3 greets me with the rest of them. I guess that
means I disappeared too.

Once we're all joined up, charmeur wonders in French
whether this bar is gay or straight. Frank asks if there is a
jukebox. Of course there is, I answer. All you have to do is say
a thing and it exists here. The idea of a jukebox will play anything you want. Name it.

```
<mischief> What do you want on the jukebox?
<frank> ZZ TOP
<frank> Any thing.
```

```
<charmeur> franky is this bar gay or staight or
+both
<FlameWise> Charmeur none at all. It's a bar.
<frank> I'm straight how about you baby.
* mischief puts a quarter in the jukebox for "Je-
+sus Just Left Chicago"
* charmeur aime nana mouskouri charmeur wants to
+hear nana mouskouri sing french
<frank> Yes.
<frank> ZZ
```

Dragon2, MstrMind, and Smurfy-2 arrive in tandem as charmeur pleads for French love songs. I put a quarter in the jukebox for Edith Piaf and laugh at charmeur when he tries to kiss me. Frank is disgusted with all the mushy, unmidwestern lovey-dovey Euro music and yells for the barbot.

```
<frank> Barman give me a vodka
-Barman3:#ircbar- ==== Gives frank a vodka ====
<frank> is there a pool table in here?
```

Frank still doesn't get it yet. Of course there is a pool table. He just conjured one. Razor points him toward the corner and sidles up to me. Charmeur announces that he is "horny after all the drinking," and we all give him a wide, wide berth.

```
<razor> hello
<frank> Let's play pool mischief. You pay.
<mischief> What a gentleman.
* charmeur leans back on the bar and looks at all
+the sexy people
<mischief> You break.
```

```
<frank> Frank breaks and scratches.
<razor> typical man
```

Smurfy-2, a pneumatic Net.babe, disappears and reappears, caught in a momentary Netsplit. It's a statistical joke by now that the Netsplit favors women.

```
<Barman3> ==== Welcome to the #IRCBar Smurfy-2,
+I am your bot Barman! ====
<Smurfy-2> what the hell happened . . .
<Smurfy-2> did I flood everyone's screens? If I
+did . . . sorry
<Smurfy-2> I think my account is sick . . .
<frank> good shot mischief.
<Smurfy-2> barman, get me a gin
<frank> Try for the black one baby.
-Barman3:#ircbar- ==== Gets Smurfy-2 a gin ====
* charmeur wants to pick up someone
<Smurfy-2> barman?
<mischief> The eight-ball is for last.
<Smurfy-2> does anybody read me?
<Smurfy-2> hello?
<Smurfy-2> did everybody leave?
<frank> No.
<mischief> Chill out, smurf.
<Smurfy-2> helloooooo
<Smurfy-2> ok . . . I suppose everybody left.
<Smurfy-2> is there anybody else on this channel?
<Smurfy-2> heeeeeellllllllllllloooooooooooooooooooo-
+oooooooooooooooooooooo
* charmeur wonders if someone in the bar is sex-
+ualy attracted to his muscular bodyand his sexy
+hairy chest showing from his half opened shirt
<razor> not me
```

```
<Teebo> no
<frank> NO!
* Worzel pukes on charmeur and kicks him out of
the bar
```

Charmeur has successfully nauseated everyone in the bar. It is time for drastic action, and Teebo has the ops (operator powers — VIP clout) to do what must be done — kick charmeur off the channel. Barman3 does the dirty work.

```
-Barman3:#ircbar- ==== Get out of this Bar char-
+meur ====
*** charmeur has been kicked off channel #ircbar
+by Barman3 (BYEBYE!!)
<mischief> What ircbar would be complete without
+the requisite lounge lizard.
<mischief> Half-open shirt? Puhleeeze!
<frank> Got a piano in here?
<mischief> Play it, frank.
<frank> Frank starts in on Piano Man.
*** Signoff: Teebo (ra.oc.com eff.org)
*** Signoff: razor (ra.oc.com eff.org)
*** Signoff: Barman3 (ra.oc.com eff.org)
*** Signoff: Polsy (ra.oc.com eff.org)
*** Signoff: Worzel (ra.oc.com eff.org)
*** Signoff: RedRum (ra.oc.com eff.org)
*** Signoff: RedRum2 (ra.oc.com eff.org)
*** Signoff: FlameWise (ra.oc.com eff.org)
<Smurfy-2> AAAAAAAAAAAAAAAAAAAAAAHHH, NETSPLIT!!!
```

I'm left with Smurfy and frank. The others reappear momentarily. Meanwhile, Smurfy sniffles in the corner because she feels abandoned and neglected. I offer her a Kleenex and a beer. Charmeur shows up again and promises to behave himself this time. Smurfy-2 continues to bawl. It doesn't seem like I've gone anywhere, but apparently I have vanished and reappeared. Barman3 greets me at the door again.

```
<Barman3> Welcome to the #IRCBar mischief, I am
+your bot Barman!
<mischief> What's wrong, smurfy?
* mischief sits down with smurfy for some girl
+talk
*** Signoff: Barman3 (Excess Flood)
```

Uh-oh. The barbot has disappeared. This means the real IRCbar is somewhere in the ether and we're stranded in a bartenderless simulacrum thereof.

```
<Smurfy-2> frank? are you here? is anybody here?
<Smurfy-2> geez! NET SPLIT'S BACK!
<frank> Watch out guys
<Smurfy-2> quit flooding my screen you damned net
+split!
<Smurfy-2> my computer's giving me all these/who's
+on all these people that I have no clue who they
+are . . .
<Hands> Is there a Net Split going on?
<Hagen> Hmmm barman is dead *sigh*
<frank> smurf or smurfette?
<Smurfy-2> barman, get me a vodka. I need some-
+thing heavy.
<Smurfy-2> ooh, I'm a ette . . . :)
<Smurfy-2> barman???
```

```
<mischief> The barman is busy. He'll be back with
+the next netsplit
* Smurfy-2 sets a rose on barman's grave
```

And then she flashes out. A few seconds later, she's back.

```
<Smurfy-2> AAAAAAAAAAAAAAAAAAAAAAAAAAAAAAH, THERE
+IT GOES AGAIN!!!
<Smurfy-2> *sob* is anybody out there. . . . .
+. . *waaaauuuggghhhhh***
<mischief> What's wrong, smurf?
<Smurfy-2> my account isn't working. . . .
+*wwwaaaauuuuggghhhh*
<mischief> Oh, is that all?
<Smurfy-2> there's too many net splits that flood
+my screen.
<mischief> Well, as long as your personal life's
+in order . . .
<Smurfy-2> it says all these /whois's on people
+I've never heard of . . . it logs me out and back
+on . . . my screen floods . . .
<Smurfy-2> *sob*
<mischief> There, there smurfette.
* Smurfy-2 grabs mischief and starts sobbing on
+his shoulder *sob*
<frank> mischief is a girl
<Smurfy-2> oops
<Smurfy-2> ok . . . /me grabs anyone that's a man
+and starts sobbing on their shoulder *sob*
<razor> wow
<FlameWise> barman get smurfy-2 a drink
<Smurfy-2> barman's still dead . . .*wwaauugghh*
```

I think Smurfy-2 is a guy. Anytime a female-presenting character starts acting like some silent movie stereotype of femininity, I get suspicious. Women just don't act like this on the Net. Usually, they're tougher than they are in RL. It's the guys who swoon, faint, and give out measurements.

Hands and Ulic sign onto the channel, but there is no Barman3 to greet them.

```
<Hands> Where's Barman
<Smurfy-2> he's caught in a net split
<Brooker> Grrrrr. I am so thirsty!!!!
* mischief gets Brooker a shot of vodka and a pint
+of beer.
<frank> We used up our three wishes with barman
+someone else has rubbed his lamp.
* Smurfy-2 runs behind the counter and acts as a
+"barman" for now . . .
<Smurfy-2> hi, everyone, I am your host . . .
+smurfy's . . .
<Smurfy-2> hee hee
* Smurfy-2 gets everyone a drink
<frank> Can I have a beer please.
* Smurfy-2 gets frank a beer
```

Randydog, dissatisfied with Smurfy's bot impersonation, heads for the door, grousing on his way out, "Go to #CymBar . . . There's a working bot there." Hands follows him out. I plug the jukebox back in and slip it a quarter for Patsy Cline's "Walking after Midnight." Nostalgia, I guess. Tommy's Diner on Mount Auburn Street had a jukebox with that song. Tommy's was a real diner, with townies planted on their stools, Harvard kids squeezed into banquettes, and Tommy slinging greaseburgers behind the counter. I used to go there late to hang out and play pinball. The cutest boy in the world kissed me two steps away from the Earthshaker machine before they turned Tommy's into a sterile McPizza restaurant. Tommy's doesn't exist anymore, physically. It's just an idea now, kind of like this bar.

```
<mischief> Any requests, people?
<frank> Patsy cline I'm going to die.
<razor> somthing heavy
<razor> eeeeeerrrrrrrr
* Smurfy-2 shoots the jukebox
<Smurfy-2> no country allowed
```

Smurfy-2 is really starting to get on my nerves. She grabs frank by the shoulder and sets him on a barstool.

```
<Smurfy-2> here, have a beer frank.
<frank> what else do I get smurfette.
<Smurfy-2> what would you like frank
<Ulic> anybody seen any swallows lately
<Smurfy-2> *gulp* no
<frank> Ahhh Ahhhh Ahhhh Frank turns red.
<Brooker> Whererrrrrr's the waitttteeerrrrr?
+Grrrrrrrrrrrrrr
* Smurfy-2 gets brooker a vodka
<Smurfy-2> I'm your bartender, Smurfy-2
```

Just then, the barbot reappears to oust her from behind the bar. Hallelujah.

```
*** Barman3 has changed the topic on channel #irc-
+bar to The Barman is here, Therefore the Bar is
+OPEN!!
```

```
-Barman3:#ircbar- ==== Please Wait !!! Banning
+the fools ====
<Smurfy-2> huh . . . who's he banning?
<Smurfy-2> here, barman, you can take over now
```

Like she has a choice.

Brooker is back. I message him, "So, how goes it, my czech friend?" Private messages on IRC go from one user to another without appearing on the public screen. They only appear to the sender and the recipient, set off by arrows (->) and bracketed by stars, respectively. Between four or five separate conversations, on and off the common screen, IRCers get confused. They respond publicly to private messages and vice versa, pocking the public channel with gaps and non sequiturs. So Brooker's public response, "My life is shitty enough to spend my free time in #ircpub," looks like a sudden fit of Slavic ennui.

Teebo tickles me (actually, he just emotes that he's tickling me. In IRC, thought corresponds rather cleanly to action. Catharine MacKinnon would have a field day here). Smurfy-2 laughs. Whatever.

```
<Smurfy-2> :)
<Smurfy-2> we aren't ticklish
<Smurfy-2> hee hee
<Smurfy-2> hee hee . . . I'm not ticklish . . . hee
+hee
<razor> leave mischief alone you perverts
<razor> razor slaps teebo leave her alone
<mischief> Razor-what a gent.
<Smurfy-2> ok, what am I missing?
<razor> a brain smurfy
<Smurfy-2> I know, razor . . . I try
<Smurfy-2> :)
```

```
<Smurfy-2> hee hee
<razor> thanks mischief
<razor> :)
<frank> let's dance smurfette.
-Barman3:#ircbar- ==== Turns the Juke Box up . . .
+====
<Smurfy-2> ok . . .
<razor> mischeif how about coming up to my place
+somtime for i dunno
* Smurfy-2 grabs frank and starts dragging him
+around the room . . .
<frank> Let's merenge.
<razor> lets dance mischeif
-Barman3:#ircbar- ==== Turns the Juke Box up . . .
+====
<frank> Frank dips smurfy.
<frank> I'm a poet mischief want to hear one.
<frank> tried to dance with you.
<razor> so do i mischief
* Smurfy-2 grabs frank and starts dancing . . .
<mischief> Smurfy, you hussy :-)
<Smurfy-2> I'm not a hussy . . . I'm married . . . :)
<frank> It's a long one mischief but a really
+good one hang on.
<frank> I'll give it line by line mischief
<razor> mischeif what are you doing tonight
```

A dragon from Toronto appears and disappears while Frank recites pseudo-Elizabethan love poetry. Razor tells him to sod off, and Teebo keeps sending me private "hey babe" messages. I keep quiet. Let them squabble for a moment.

```
<frank> Smurf where are you. Mischief has aban-
+doned me.
```

```
*** Barman3 has changed the topic on channel #irc-
+bar to DING DONG DING DONG: Another hour rolls
+by in England!
```

As the boys begin to scrap in earnest, I smell a challenge. I decide this is the perfect laboratory to test a pet theory of mine, namely that even without the hair, the heels, the finely honed flirtatious gestures and gym-toned figure, I can still instigate a bar brawl. As if on cue, the Duke swaggers in and tips his hat. I put a quarter in the jukebox for "Duke of Earl."

```
<Smurfy-2> hi duke
<TheDuke> How about i take my six shooter and put
+a hole in you pilgrim
-Barman3- ==== Please accept a rose with compli-
+ments from Teebo! ====
<TheDuke> ::Loads his gun::
<TheDuke> ::shoots smurfy-2::
```

Razor knifes the Duke, and Teebo has Barman3 throw him out.

Too bad. I was really starting to like the guy. I was about ready to shoot her myself.

```
<Smurfy-2> smurfs are bullet proof
<Smurfy-2> hee hee
<razor> razor put's a pound in juke box and has i
+do any thing for love for mischief
<razor> i know that mischief is very very pretty
<mischief> And how do you know that?
<razor> give me a kiss mischief
```

-Barman3:#ircbar- ==== ooohhhh!! They're getting
+friendly!! ====
<razor> well it's that sexy little swagger you've
+got
Teebo *hug*
<frank> Frank pinches smurfette.
* Smurfy-2 slaps frank
<Smurfy-2> stop that
<Smurfy-2> geez
* Teebo punches frank
<mischief> Teebo is quite the chivalrous patron
+tonight.
<Teebo> mischief: i always am!!
<frank> Smurfette is a dud. Want to dance mis-
+chief.
<razor> mischief where are you darling
-Barman3:#ircbar- ==== Turns the Juke Box up . . .
+ ====
<mischief> I'm here. Lost in the Netsplit for a
+moment.
<mischief> This is so Wrinkle in Time. Ever read
+that book?
<mischief> What time is it over there?
<frank> Ah 3:40 pm
<hightoned> 15:20
<hightoned> how can it be 21:16, 15:20, and
+15:40 ?
<razor> 21:17 darling
<hightoned> 4 minute lag?
<Smurfy-2> mine says 15:20 now
<hightoned> someones clock is mussed up
<mischief> How do people get kicked out, anyway?
<razor> ask teebo mischeif

Teebo im sorry to have to boot razor but. . . .
<razor> well it's not bad mischief
-Barman3:#ircbar- ==== Get out of this Bar razor
+ ====
*** razor has been kicked off channel #ircbar by
+Barman3 (BYEBYE!!)
razor i like you
*** razor has joined channel #ircbar
<Barman3> ==== Welcome to the #IRCBar razor, I am
+your bot Barman! ====
<razor> teebo you are such a great guy
<razor> mischief darling at what stage were we
*razor punches teebo and breaks teebo's jaw
-Barman3:#ircbar- ==== Did you know there is no
+fighting in this bar, razor!!
* Teebo boots razor up the arse
-Barman3:#ircbar- ==== Get out of this Bar razor
+ ====
*** razor has been kicked off channel #ircbar by
+Barman3 (BYEBYE!!)
*** razor has joined channel #ircbar
<Barman3> ==== Welcome to the #IRCBar razor, I am
+your bot Barman! ====
<mischief> This whole experience is absurd.
* Smurfy-2 ducks at all the flying glass and beer
+bottles
<razor> mischief help me from this horrid man
<mischief> Lay off, Teebo . . . until razor mis-
+behaves :-)
* Smurfy-2 ducks from some more beer bottles
<razor> hurt and crawls into courner looking for
+sympathy
<razor> from miSCHIEF

```
*Teebo* he is sat next to me and believe me he is
+misbehaving!!
<Teebo> NO FIGHTING IN THE BAR!!!!
-Barman3:#ircbar- ==== Oi Teebo, if you want to
+fight take it outside ====
```

My experiment is a stalemate. Yes, there's a bar brawl. But it turns out that razor and Teebo are really the same person, a demented University of Hertfordshire student fighting with himself for dramatic effect.

```
-> *razor* Alright, what's your story.
<razor> a naugty boy from birmingham england
<mischief> You English are all perverts
*razor* no story just love darling
<moonchyld> im not a pervert! it is the americans!
<moonchyld> the americans are the pervs!!
<razor> razor sticks knife into teebo then runs
+away
<mischief> No, the English are more perverted.
+They're more repressed.
<razor> leave her alone moonie razor hits moonie
-Barman3:#ircbar- ==== Oi No fighting in here
+Please razor!! ====
<Teebo> im not american and im perverted!!
*razor* i agree come here darling
-Barman3- ==== Please accept a rose with compli-
+ments from razor! ====
*** Signoff: moonchyld (irc.uiuc.edu irc2.mit.-
+edu)
*** Signoff: Barman3 (irc.uiuc.edu irc2.mit.edu)
*** Signoff: Teebo (irc.uiuc.edu irc2.mit.edu)
*** Signoff: razor (irc.uiuc.edu irc2.mit.edu)
```

Netsplit. Only person left in the bar is beartwo, a Tennessean grad student who orders me a glass of merlot. We start some bar small talk before the Netsplit ends and we rejoin the rest of the channel.

```
<Barman3> ==== Welcome to the #IRCBar mischief, I
+am your bot Barman! ====
<Barman3> ==== Welcome to the #IRCBar beartwo, I
+am your bot Barman! ====
<Teebo> hi mischief
<mischief> Hi Teebo
<razor> mischief darling we are on our own except
+for teebo
<mischief> Compsci, bear?
<beartwo> Sociology and law
<beartwo> How do you make comments with aster-
+isks?
<beartwo> And change topics?
<beartwo> (Does it show that I am a novice?)
<razor> oi i saw her first sod off bear two
-> *beartwo* type /me <action>
<beartwo> Thanks mischief
> Bear, where in Tennessee are you from?
-Barman3- ==== Please accept a rose with compli-
+ments from razor! ====
<beartwo> Kingsport . . . you've never heard of
+it . . .
<Teebo> only opers can change topics!!
<beartwo> ok
-> *beartwo* You'd be surprised. I know someone
+from Pikeville :-)
*razor* me again
```

<beartwo> Pikeville?
<beartwo> LOL
* Teebo pisses on the barman
<beartwo> I'm a touch typist but I'll never get
+used to this!
* beartwo smiles at mischief
-> *beartwo* Pikeville, yes. This is a private mes-
+sage. You do it by typing /msg <person> <state-
+ment>
beartwo Pikeville is pretty close
<razor> i'm getting the cold shoulder treatment
+now :(
-> *beartwo* quick learner!
<LtlBeeper> :)
-Barman3- ==== Please accept a rose with compli-
+ments from Teebo! ====
<razor> god
<mischief> :-)
<beartwo> we aim to please
<mischief> I feel like Scarlett O'Hara.
<beartwo> LOL
<razor> i',m fed up :(
<beartwo> do you have a red dress to wear?
<razor> im not smiling
* Teebo hugs mischief
* mischief smiles at razor so he doesn't feel
+neglected
<beartwo> Are you still mad, Razor?
<razor> i feel better now :)
*** Nut has joined channel #ircbar
<Barman3> ==== Welcome to the #IRCBar Nut, I am
+your bot Barman! ====
<mischief> Don't be mad, razor.

```
<razor> lady in red are we well i think i've fallen
+in love
<mischief> *beartwo* glad you showed up
<beartwo> thanks mischief
*** Barman3 has changed the topic on channel
+#ircbar to DING DONG DING DONG: Another hour
+rolls by in England!
```

Teebo sings "The Lady in Red," line by line. Razor puts a pound in the multicurrency imaginary jukebox for "Be Bop A Lula" and gets kicked out by his alter ego. Twice.

```
<beartwo> why does razor keep getting kicked out?
<mischief> He must be getting bruised by now
<beartwo> hey, mischief, more Merlot?
<mischief> Bear: why not?
* beartwo orders two merlots
* beartwo gives one to mischief with a smile
* Teebo sits in the corner and sulks
<Teebo> barman get me a gun
<beartwo> no sulking . . . I do all the sulking
+here . . .
-Barman3:#ircbar- ==== Gets Teebo a gun ====
<razor> razor grabs gun and shoots teebo
<beartwo> Razor!
* Teebo shoots myself in the head!!
<Teebo> goodbye creul world!!
<madrigal> hey teebo did your brain go all over
+the carpet!!!!!!
<sofad> HERTS students rule this joint
* Teebo is dead
* beartwo mourns poor departed teebo
<Worzel> :)
```

Someone orders a glass of white zinfandel, and then the bar falls away. As another Netsplit floods my screen a string of dead servers, I force-interrupt IRC and come up for air (and cereal). No more bar. No more jostling doppelgangers. No more Ibsen antics. No more nursery rhymes. It's like shutting a book.

CrOSs-DresSInG In CYberSpaCe

THERE IS A certain poetic justice in the fact that a computer network pioneered by the U.S. military is now home to a bevy of virtual transvestites. The Net isn't just a scientific research tool — it's an outlet for gorgeous women trapped in the bodies of male computer programmers.

A social environment with no physical dimension does have a certain expedience for female impersonators. "I don't have to spend two or three hours before logging on, fixing my hair, putting on foundation and makeup and appropriate clothes," says a Swedish transvestite who logs on as Madeleine Nordenstam. "Everything is much simpler when I feel like taking on my female alter ego." Pinchy corsets, vertigo-inducing heels, eyelash glue, and duct tape languish in their hatboxes as techies from Montreal to Munich gender-switch with a few deft keystrokes.

Cyberdrag has been around since primordial three-hundred-baud bulletin boards first flickered into existence. And as the digital archipelago proliferated, so did online gender-bending. After all, there were so few real women on the Net. Why not spice it up with a few virtual babes? Most of these prototype cyberfemales sprang full-blown from the skulls of D&D dungeon-masters. The result was an artificially high population of black-leather-clad assassins with D-cup breastplates and buns of steel. It was fairly easy to tell that pimply pubescents were behind them.

But with a larger Net population and more powerful software, cross-gender aliases have become increasingly sophisticated, to the point where it is difficult to tell who's got what equipment in real life. The result is a carnival atmosphere of sorts. Massive gender confusion, intentional and unintentional, is rampant.

"When I started out, I had no intention of deliberately masking my gender," types Kurt, a software engineer whose feminine-looking login name has earned him more than his share of Net.propositions. "In fact," he says, "the thought didn't even cross my mind until guys started hitting on me. You see, when I first registered for an account at Delphi and was prompted for a log-on ID, 'EuroTrash Girl' by Cracker just happened to be playing on my stereo, so I simply chose ETGIRL as my name because of the song. I hadn't even considered that people might assume that I was female until guys in conferences started being unusually friendly to me. It was then that I realized that they weren't seeing me, but rather what they assumed ETGIRL should be.

"Jeez! Even as I'm typing this some guy named JOE710 butts in and wants to talk to me!" Kurt's electronic personage crackles with a palpable sense of violation as he swats away the interloper. "This happens all the time! It's hard to get in a good session of typing unless I SQUELCH all the horny bastards. . . . So anyways, here I am just trying to groove to my own things out here in cyberspace, and I'm fairly regularly interrupted by someone who thinks I'm some piece of meat in a shop window or something. Never having been female, I never realized just how annoying this sort of thing can be when you're not interested in it.

"Before long," Kurt says, "I realized that I had a number of options open to me. Tell them all the truth, that I'm really a man and therefore they probably wouldn't be interested in me, ignore them, go through the hassle of changing my ID, [or] have fun and fuck with their minds." Although Kurt ignores most folks, in the interest of time, he enjoys leading particularly nasty or annoying slimeballs down the primrose path. "I've totally led [them] into believing that I WAS female, going so far as to construct totally fictitious lives for myself... I figure, if they're going to bug me anyways, I might as well enjoy myself."

The Net is a minefield of booby traps like this. One Seattle computer consultant unsuspectingly tripped one when he encountered a particularly fetching online odalisque named Nightshade. "We had an orgy, as much as the software allowed," he recalls. "[Then] we discovered that the female was actually a male. To our mutual surprise, we were also all heterosexual men. It was almost a 'tearoom' effect."

In another dark corner of the Internet, Ben A. Mesander and Leftist, male netters in Virginia, decide to see what it's like to be hot and willing IRC babes. Leftist becomes "Julie," Ben becomes "Samantha," and they cruise the #hotsex channel looking for a little action. Leftist plays Julie as smart, beautiful, and passionate. Ben plays Samantha as a bimbo, "dumb with big tits," because, he says, "this is more natural for me."

Enter Adam (so to speak), a horny senior at the University of Maryland who joins them on #hotsex. Julie insists that he tell her a bedtime story.

While Adam describes in meticulous detail what he's doing to Julie and Samantha, Leftist and Ben pretend to be lesbians, confidentially message each other about what a dork Adam is, and log the encounter for the Net community at large. Adam, who turns out to be quite a foot fetishist, is kissing Julie's virtual toesies, "down from the big one to the little baby . . ." when Leftist (Julie) cuts in to Ben (Samantha) on a private channel: "Adam's got bad sentence structure. Let's make his life miserable."

Samantha messages Julie, "Tell him you think kissing toes is gross or maybe that you have a club foot."

Adam continues, ". . . then up the outside of your right leg . . ." Samantha squeals in bimboesque delight as she reads a message from Julie: "This guy is probably a 45 second-er." Adam messages Julie about his maddeningly masculine voice. "I have a DEEP voice," he whispers. "Very sexy voice I'm told. Women love it."

Julie messages Samantha, "He's offering to do it to me on the phone later," and tells Adam privately how sticky her keyboard is.

"'My voice,'" Samantha mimics privately to Julie. "Gag."

Meanwhile, the two "girls" ply each other with sweet nothings.

"I'd love to lick you julie!" squeals Samantha.

"oooooh," moans Julie. "if you only could"

Adam's narrative gathers steam. While typing miscellaneous squeals, mmmms, and aahs, the two boys in Virginia run a background check on Adam and mock him with assorted snide remarks. At the height of Adam's virtual climax, Julie grouses privately to Samantha, "3.5 hours till calc." Later, the gals make a few sadistic jokes at Adam's expense and plot new heights of humiliation for him.

Remember, these are all ostensibly straight guys.

But then, the line between straight and gay can be whisper-thin in a setting that lets one assume fantasy personae at will. Ashtoreth, a netter on Delphi, discovered MUDs three years ago and initially logged on as male. "I was still quite straight at the time," he says. "I met this other character, who was male, and yet I felt this sort of kinship with him, this association, which is to say, I realized later, that I was falling in love with him. But he was male. This was a huge obstacle to me. I'd had the usual conditioning and anything homosexual was supposed to be disgusting, unthinkable. So I got around that. I played a female character, rationalizing that since I was now female, it was okay to do things with him, and we proceeded to do lots of 'things.' *grin*

"Over time," he says, "it became quite routine to have sex with males, since I had a female body. I was being me through it. I'd taken on aspects of [its] personality. I'd admired the character, right? I'd impressed upon it the personality traits which I admired also . . . Over time, I assimilated these traits into my own personality." After three years, he says, "I now find it difficult to imagine a time when I wasn't bisexual."

Conveniently located between fantasy and reality (down the block from schizophrenia, role-playing on your left, up the stairs, take a right), the Net has become a gender laboratory for the twenty-first century. As one twenty-one-year-old hacker put it, "It's sex without guilt. Fantasies without pain. Freedom to experiment with fresh ideas without harming anyone or getting arrested . . . You are who you portray yourself to be."

I used to agree with that last part, but I'm not so sure anymore, after my own little foray into the electronic bathhouse as a flyboy named Kit, tricking around on #gaysex. I wasn't interested in the sex part, per se (frankly, I can't imagine how anyone gets off on this). But living in South Miami

Beach, where every guy is a twenty-two-year-old gay model on rollerblades, I wondered if I could write a believable character by that description. I wanted to see if I could pass.

```
*** Kit (~mischief@mindvox.phantom.com) has joined
+channel #gaysex
*** Topic for #gaysex: shiny pointy objects in
+our backs . . .
<Kit> Greetings from South Beach.
<Strand> kit, is that in Australia?
<Kit> No, Miami Beach Florida. Sex capital of the
+Eastern Seaboard.
<Strand> Kit, cool . . . I've been to St. Pete
+Beach . . . Treasure Island is fun too :)
<Bradt> tropical
* dolf despises chemistry from the bottom of his
+heart
* Axion is a chemical engineering grad student
<Kit> Key West :-)
* dolf offers axion his sympathy
<Curious> Anyone in Boston tonight??
<Kit> I used to live in Boston. Too cold.
* SFBoy loves Key West and P-Town
* Axion accepts dolf's sympathy—"It's too late
+for me-save yourselves"
<Kit> South Beach buries P-town
<Kit> All the fashion people are down here.
<Kit> Models galore
* dolf loves supermodels
<Kit> You can't throw a stone without hitting a
+georgeous guy.
* DSV throws a stone. "I'm going to try and bag a
+gorgeous guy for myself!"
* SFBoy waves to curious
```

<Axion> *ponk* Hey—watch where you throw those
+things :)
* ButchBub had a model BF, but he was a cokehead.
+And ButchBub does *NOT* pay for candy habits.
<dolf> axion: he was aiming for me ;)
* Curious wants to experience a man in Boston
+tonight!!! :)
* Data is VERY bored
* Axion picks up the stone and tosses it at dolf
+"Sorry guy"
* dolf sweeps Data off his feet
* DSV rushes in and grabs dolf too. "I'll take
+TWO goegeous guys!" HeHEHE
* Kit throws a stone at dolf
* Axion ducks and watches the stone bounce off DSV
* dolf sticks his tongue out at Kit
* DSV falls to the ground. "I already had a bad
+headache as it was!!"
* Kit sticks his tongue out at dolf
*** Kiy has joined channel #gaysex
<Kiy> re all
* dolf lets his mind wonder in response to Kit's
+tongue ;)
<Strand> okay folks . . I'm a bad boy for staying
+here so damm long . . i'm gone . . I'm history . .
+I'm last weeks meatloaf
<Axion> DSV: You OK? I really didn't mean for
+that to happen . . .
* dolf administers mouth-to-mouth
<DSV> *weak, helpless smile**
<DSV> oh, I'll be o.k. I just need a little rest
+in someone's lap. :)
* dolf tosses Kit over his shoulder and heads
+for the sunset

* dolf offers his lap to DSV
<Kit> Is it just me, or is it gettin' hot on this
+channel
* Kit loosens his collar
<Axion> If it would make you feel better . . .
* rocket will kiss anything!
* Kiy gives Kit a fan
* rocket asks any zippers down?
*** EatMe has joined channel #gaysex
<EatMe> any horny dudes here? I am!!
* dolf lets DSV have his way
<gumby> EatMe: there might be one or two!
* dolf tugs at rocket's zipper, too
<DSV> More and more people! What fun! :)
* Billy2 Is VERY horny tonight.
* rocket asks any zippers down?
* Axion gently pulls DSV away as rocket joins in
+"I've gotta go, guys. ."
* rocket pulls at dsv's briefs
* Peg_Leg tugs anything.
* dolf pulls at other parts of dsv
<Kiy> Geeeze, slutty tonight this channel is:)
<Kit> Sluts r Us
* rocket groans
* dolf is a proud netslut
* Kiy chuckles at Kit
<Kiy> Hi Kit, what similiar nicks we have!
* rocket groans louder
<Kit> The terrible two
Billy2 Hey Kit.
<Kiy> YES! The terrible two, kinda like Wonder
+Twins eh?
* Kit gives KiY his ID bracelet
* Kiy gives Kit his ID bracelet, now it's offi-

+cial. . . . the Wonder Twins . . . form of
+a. . . .
* Kiy says form of a enormous ice cock!
* seith is baack :)
<Kit> Kiy: LOL
* seith is boored *bleh*
<Kit> Form of . . . a hot shower.
<Kiy> Kit: I'm melting!!!!!It burns!!!!!!!!:)
<uda> What are ya'll up to?
<SFBoy> I think most of us are bored
<Kit> Kiy: feels so good, tho.
<Kiy> Not a damn thing uda. . . . . isn't that
+terrible . . . why just now, I've become a wonder
+twin
<Kiy> Kit: But I don't wanna feel that good :)
<uda> Hey Seith i am listening to Madonna right
+now!!
<Kit> Kiy: Yes you do.
* seith feels hungry.
<Kiy> Kit: OK, OK, you're right. . . . I do,but I
+want to now now now now!!!!!!
<SweeThang> Who else wants to go to the Barbara
+Streisand concert? Isn't it just the coolest
+thing? Too bad they sold out . . . :(
* Kit turns the hot water up
* Kiy has a temper tantrum
<seith> Do I want to go to Wendy's, Arby's, Burger
+King, McDonald's, Subway, Krystal or Taco bell. .
+*ponders*
<uda> Kit I am listening to Erotica
*** TopGun has joined channel #gaysex
<seith> Arby's is the local 'gay' hangout
+*chuckles* I guess I could go there.
<DanK> Krystal??

<Kiy> seith, you're kidding right?

<gumby> damn, seith, that's rough!!

* seith is in the mood for a shower with a hot
+guy :)

* Kiy says Take me! Take Me Kit!!!!

* SFBoy would love a hot shower with someone

<Kit> So hop in the shower, wonder twin.

* SweeThang needs some special attention

* Kiy always wanted to have a twin

* Kiy jumps into the hot shower with his long lost
+twin

* Kit washes Kiy's back

<TopGun> Form of a showerhead

<TopGun> form of hot water

<TopGun> wondertwins unite. .

<Fat-Elvis> Can the Wonder Twin do a steam bath?

* Kiy looks down and begins to wonder if we're
+really twins :)

* seith really needs some food.

<shiuan> Lock: can I join you for the shower?

<TopGun> form of steam

<seith> But I don't know what I want..

<TopGun> form of a big tub

<TopGun> wondertwins unite

* Kiy turns Kit, his new found twin, around and
+washes his back

* Kit shampoos Kiy

* SweeThang REALLY!!! needs some special atten-
+tion

<Kiy> Hey Kit-This isn't incestuous is it? :)

* Kiy hands Kit more shampoo

<Fat-Elvis> Man, this Kit and Kit things getting
+damn erotic

<Kit> Nah, Kiy :-) It's just cartoon power kinship.

* SweeThang SEZ LOVE ME!!!
<Kenj> Hi, Kit.
* SweeThang sez NOW!!
<Kiy> Kit: Cool!
* Kiy turns around to Kit and looks him in the
+eyes
* SweeThang says msg me if you wanna screw
*** Bang has joined channel #gaysex
* Kiy grins widely
* Kit grins at Kiy
<Kenj> Joey: Did you say you're going to the Roxy
+tonight?
* Kiy kisses Kit, deep, wet, passionately
*** Bang has left channel #gaysex
* Kit drops the soap
* SweeThang says somebody wanna stroke me????
* gumby rushes up behind Kit
<Joey> Kenj: me going to the roxy . . . I can't
+keep myself from falling to sleep as it is, I
+can't make it . . . are you?
* Fat-Elvis is getting turned on by Kit and Kiy
<Lock> welp, I've gotta jam . . .
*** Signoff: Lock (PEACE!)
* Kiy pushes gumby out of the way . . . he's my
+twin!
* Kiy whispers in Kit's ear "Like it rough or
+soft?"
*** edfxo is now known as AJ
*** SweeThang has left channel #gaysex
* Kit says both
<SFBoy> uda: Working on a Windows Adventure game
+with hooks through the internet for multiplay
* Kiy gently enters Kit and bites his ear

```
*** Signoff: AJ (Operation would block)
* Kit moans
* Fat-Elvis is enjoying watching Kit and Kiy
<shiuan> Kenj: me too
*** GT1 has joined channel #gaysex
* Kiy moans too but takes his time
<Kiy> Kit: You know, we've got an audience going
+on here don't you?
* Kit is totally turned on by his body double Kiy
<Kiy> Kit: BTW, what do we look like?
<Kenj> Who is this Kit guy, Joey?
* Kiy pulls out of Kit before he cums and turns
+Kit around
<seith> Dont' we set the clocks UP an hour tonite?
* Kiy takes Kit's tool deep into his mouth:)
<Joey> kenj: I do not have a clue
<WetT> seith: Yep. . . .
<Kiy> seith: Spring Forward, Fall Behind
<seith> that means, I'll lose an hour's sleep
+*bleh*
<SFBoy> ayup we spring ahead tonight
<WetT> Tonight is the night when we set clocks
forward one hour at 2 am. .
<Kenj> I've no clue either, Joey.
* seith is going to get some food from somewhere !!
<seith> before I starve! :)
* seith waves.
*** barryd has joined channel #gaysex
*** Signoff: seith (Leaving)
* Kit says Don't stop
* Kiy sends seith a pizza
* Kiy doesn't stop, even after sending seith a
+pizza
```

```
<aDrOcK> hi guys
<Kit> LOL
*** Signoff: DanK (Leaving)
* Kiy is gaggin btw but he can handle it
* TopGun WONDERTWINS UNITE!!
* EatNBooty needs some tongue
*** gumby has left channel #gaysex
<Kiy> TG: We are!
* neigh will be right back
*** kennie has joined channel #gaysex
<Kiy> man! We gotta a few people going, I thought
+maybe we should start a roadshow or something
*** bobbee is now known as RobRob
*Kiy* This is one serious blow job you know!
```

My sense of embarrassment finally catches up with me. Now
that I've gotten myself into this little narrative, how the hell
am I going to resolve it? I drum my fingers on the mushy
gray keyboard, wondering what to type, and finally settle on a
gauzy soft-core resolution.

```
* Kit melts.
* Kiy swallows deeply, cherishing every precious
+drop
*** Phant has joined channel #gaysex
<Phant> 'lo guys
* Kiy leans back, exhausted, and relaxes
<bc> quiet tonite?
<Kiy> bc: Nah. . . . we've been entertaining
everyone tonight
<NYCel> bc: net split
<bc> ahh
<bc> more and more these days
```

```
* Kiy feels the water fall all over him
* Kit makes sure Kiy is warm and squeaky.
* Kiy pecks Kit on the cheek for being so con-
+cerned
* Kit jumps as the showerhead bursts off.
<Kit> Water gushes everywhere.
*** Signoff: Coop (Connection reset by peer)
* Kiy gets hit in the nuts by the showerhead and
+rushes to the emergency room
* Kit stays in the ambulance with his wonder
+twin.
* Kiy in his delirious pain stricken mind, looks
+at his wonder twin Kit and smiles
* Kit says, Guess we were too much for the 'ol
+shower, bud.
*** ircKID has joined channel #gaysex
* Kiy laughs and falls into a blissful sleep,
+dreaming of his wonder twin
<Kiy> Kit: When do we write the script? It's gotta
+be worth something!
<Kit> Kiy: LOL
<Kiy> Kit: Think we've had enough . . . or better
+yet, think they've had enough?
<Kiy> Stayed tuned for the next episode of Wonder
+Twins in da Shower fans
<Kit> Kiy: Yeah. Wonder twin powers . . . deacti-
+vate.
*** Derich has changed the topic on channel #gay-
+sex to Stayed tuned for thenext episode of Kiy
+showering
```

I think this is the plot of a critically acclaimed gender-bending film in an alternate universe. I think I may try a woman-posing-as-a-man-posing-as-a-woman, *Victor/Victoria* in cyberspace scenario next.

On the Net, there are even gender options that don't physically exist. For instance, the LambdaMOO virtual world gives users a choice of male, female, neutral, neither, royal (the royal "we"), and the natty, insouciant "splat" (*) option. One University of Minnesota student claims to have assumed a plethora of roles including gay male, gay female, straight female, bi female, bi male, and "asexual thing," no doubt some devastatingly enigmatic splat varietal.

And all of this is legal, hygienic, and laughably easy to disguise, if not socially acceptable. Joe Smith down the hall may look hard at work on that new spreadsheet program when he's really frolicking in tulle on the Net. And while this is somewhat demented and sad, it is, well, social. It does qualify as human interaction, at least until cross-dressing artificial intelligences add organic/robotic ambiguity to gender confusion. Indeed, it may not be long before the Net's exclusive, humans-only electronic bathhouse is invaded by a cadre of randy RAM constructs prowling for gullible carbon-based dupes and gloating in their virtual dressing rooms afterward, exchanging tales of conquest at the expense of the entire human race. (Whoa, I really had 'im goin' there . . . not only did he think I was female, but this cretin was totally convinced I was *organic*.) Soon, in the bowels of NASA, some HAL-like creature will clear its speaker with a dainty cough and broach the Subject to its programmer: "Dave, I have something to tell you . . ."

In the meantime, we can rest assured that the Net's digital drag personae are human, and that modem speed and verbal foxiness are their only limitations. Which, to paraphrase one famous cross-dresser, means just one thing . . .

Girl, you'd better *work* that keyboard.

Aka

I DON'T KNOW whether to feel guilty about that whole incident with Kiy.

I mean, I did lie. Sort of. Or at least I played along. But
the Net has a way of bringing out my evil twin, because I don't
take anything in cyberspace seriously. There are so many
bogus identities around here that it's hard to believe anything
all the way. It's not real, in the usual sense of the word. And so
most of the time, I just ride a channel wherever its narrative
goes. It has as much to do with truth as a Charlie Parker solo
has to do with sheet music.

With e-mail, it's all aboveboard. If you lie in e-mail then
you really are flat-out lying. But the further you stray from
the Net's "real world" applications, the foggier it gets. Whole
boroughs of the Net seem specifically designed for theater
as much as straightforward communication. Usenet, for instance, is a cocktail of true-name posts and pseudonymous
editorials. Further into the Net's deep end, IRC requires
that you assume a handle, whether or not it coincides with
your real name. You can switch nicks as often as you want.

Sometimes you have to, because your name is already registered to someone else. Every night, I see netters change nicks in mid-conversation. ("Scott is now known as Zelda," the IRC server announces. Henceforth, the erstwhile Scott's dialogue is preceded by a Zelda prompt.) And when it comes to MUDs, any correspondence to real life is purely coincidental. Fantasy is the point.

On the Net, you may perch anywhere on a finely graduated spectrum of anonymity. You may choose to be "consistently identified by a certain pseudonym or 'handle' and establish a reputation under it in some area, providing pseudo-anonymity," suggests the Usenet anonymity FAQ. "A person may wish to be completely untraceable for a single one-way message (a sort of 'hit-and-run'). Or, a person may wish to be openly anonymous but carry on a conversation with others (with either known or anonymous identities) via an 'anonymous return address'. A user may wish to appear as a 'regular user' but actually be untraceable. Sometimes a user wishes to hide who he is sending mail to (in addition to the message itself). A user may wish to access some service and hide all signs of the association." This place is the Baskin-Robbins of electronic disguise options. It is an infinitely stocked costume wardrobe and set shop. And, from what I've seen, it is Halloween 365 days a year.

It was poetic, then, that the Great Grendel-Khan chose October 31 to mail me an exposition of his nom-de-Net. "I am The Great Grendel-Khan," he announced, "or at least a significant part of me is."

This is my net identity, and in many ways is just as important to me as my identity as Christopher Jorgensen. . . . My real life name is a given name, the identity that has grown around this name has been influenced by family, friends, the media, and my own perceptions of myself. For now, forget RL and examine my alternate identity. The Great Grendel-Khan is also a conglomerate of the above elements. Nothing is created in a vacuum, but to a great degree the present Grendel is solely my creation.

Grendel came about, as anyone who has read Beowolf knows, from an old English story that has been passed down through generations. I found it much easier to relate to the terrible creature of this story than the 'hero.' Grendel killed for no known reason, but one can imagine his reasons. His prey was challenging, and perhaps he knew it would one day kill him. Man is base and deserves to die. No one is innocent and all deserve what comes to them. It is fun to kill. His reasons matter little. This is not where I fell in love with this monster that became part of myself.

There is a short book by John Gardner that tells the story of Beowolf from Grendel's point of view. I read this when I was an "impression-able youth," and I became Grendel. This monster felt exactly how I felt. . . . Here is a creature that lives among man, yet as separate as one can be. He can understand their language and even speaks it, but they say nothing that doesn't con-fuse him and make him wonder if he is truly cursed of God, and he says nothing that they un-derstand. This is me. This is how I feel, (or at least felt at the time that I assumed the mantle of Grendel). The isolation of this monster is complete, I am alone . . .

Sometimes I bump into netters who have cultivated online identities over periods of weeks, months, or years. When they post to Usenet or log onto a MUD under a well-established handle, they feel truly at home in their digital skins. Many of the characters I've known exist only on the Net. There are real people behind them, sure, but only in cyberspace do the spores of human personality germinate into this particular Brach's Pick-a-Mix of pirates, poets, clowns, superheroes, villains, armchair psychologists, and armchair psychopaths. I've seen people so comfortable in pseudonymous cloaks that they'd seem naked without them. "Oddly enough," explains one Net character, "I feel I am more myself as 'Johnny Fusion' than I do using my mundane name which appears on all my quite legitimate ID cards. I think pseudonyms (in a sense, a false ID) help sentients like myself to 'be themselves'. Using a name that i chose helps me see myself as well, me. That is, my identity is what *I* make it. I'm not stuck with the handle my parents gave me. I guess what i am trying to say is that a false identity is an empowerment for the individual, therefore IMO a good thing."

The longer I'm on the Net, the more I see its shake 'n' bake self-serve identities on their own terms. A handle is just as "real," in its own way, as the name on a driver's license or social security card. It won't get you out of a parking ticket in the offline world, but it's consistent in the Net's text-only social sphere. And you really have to accept a Net persona on its own turf, because there's often no means of verification. If someone wants to hide, they can hide, and there's no way on earth that you're going to dig them out. There are no faces when you enter the Net, so people paint them on. Some just take a little more creative license than others.

Case in point: Murdering Thug, commandant of a forum on computer crime, letter bombs, anarchy, and Thug's daily exploits. His personal heroes include John Gotti, Lee Harvey Oswald, David Lee Roth, Don Pardo, and Genghis Khan. According to his plan files, he likes his women sleazy and his cars big, fast, and armored. He claims to drive an '81 white Cadillac, "dark bulletproof glass, internal armor, lime green interior with magenta fuzzy dice on the mirror. I get 12 miles per gallon and use no muffler. Nitro burning engine with a top speed of 210 mph. No seatbelts. No airbags." Thug is happy to shock his detractors. "Fuck 'em," he writes, "I'm glad they are offended that all out anarchy is coming into cyberspace. I'm glad I'm turning their pristine lilly white academic and business online existance into uncertain chaos and maximizing the entropy of cyberspace." Signed, Thug.

Thug impressed me from word one. Here was a man who knew what to do with two thousand pounds of ammonium nitrate fuel oil, a 64,000 processor CM5, and a few blasting caps. Thug spoke his mind. Thug flamed his critics with exuberance. He even had a certain roguish élan I might have found attractive, if not for a raging Net.rumor that behind Thug's glowering persona lurks a frumpy Long Island housewife with too much time on her hands.

Never take an anonymous Net persona at its word.

That goes double for glamorous flyboys named Kit.

thE nEwbIEs ArE cOmIng!
THe NeWBieS aRe CoMiNG!

This is the snobbery of the people on the May-
flower looking down their noses at the people who
came over ON THE SECOND BOAT!

—Mitch Kapor

"HERE'S A SCARY thought," says the Great Grendel-Khan. "The vast majority of the net is made up of educated individuals. What will happen to the net when just anyone can loggin? Personally, I don't think that you should 'weep' for joy as beer-drinking-WWF-loving-Home-Shopping-Network-watching-high-school-Burger-King-dropouts loggin. I think you will see a retreat from these type of people. Those that loggin now will flee to places like the well or mindvox, where they will pay to be separated from the chattel."

The newbies are coming! The newbies are coming!

New users are flooding onto the Net at the rate of a million per month. And from what I've seen, old-timers would just as soon they stay home. The Net is the most perfect form of anarchy to come along since the Golden Horde stomped through central Asia, and many Net veterans would prefer it stay that way. The Net works, they argue. Don't mess with it.

And it does work, for the most part. But the population explosion is putting a lot of stress on the system. Not so much the physical system of hardware and phone lines, but the social structure is beginning to fray. Noise levels are up. Signal quality is down. The fringe cachet of the place is being engulfed by a wave of ill-informed mainstreamers. Basically, the Net is turning into post-grunge Seattle.

Even die-hard Net addicts now admit that it's impossible to wade through the daily traffic. We have on our hands what Steve Crocker, an armchair Net sociologist at Youngstown State University, calls a "human bandwidth problem." The hardware is whirring away just fine (for now), but the danger of human overload is more serious. "A limiting factor in the usefulness of the Net to individuals is the inability of a person to read more than a minute fraction of even the news they are actually interested in," he says. "I think we all have wished that the Net were more universal. We are vastly underrepresented in areas such as poor people, industrial workers, housewives, young children, policy makers, and senior professionals. We need to find effective means of outreach to all these groups, and more. And that's only in North America. The extension of the Net into the Third World is a problem, parallel in some ways to that of including the poor and undereducated of North America."

The Net's anti-establishment politics are contradictory. Most of us realize that the Net is an elite community, and the idea of expansion in the name of social justice is appealing. On the other hand, veterans cherish the Net's fast-fading underground flavor and their own edge status. Very few people are against universal access per se, but the attitude is: send us your tired unwired masses yearning to post free, just as long as they're hip, tech-savvy, and think like us. Anything that puts the Net's unique vibe in jeopardy is considered noise, or worse, cultural pollution.

"As we expand," says Crocker, "there is a danger of having the cultural traditions which have been developed by trial and error over the years overwhelmed. These customs, although not perfect, have by and large been successful in allowing the Net to WORK. A first approximation suggestion would be to attempt to manage Net expansion in such a way that at any given moment, the population of Net citizens online for less than (say) 6 months should constitute a minority of the total Net population. This will allow our culture to evolve in a somewhat orderly way, rather than simply being swept away by ignorance, well intentioned or otherwise."

The problem with this plan is that there is no border control. There is no Digital Department of Immigration and Naturalization to monitor the cultural temperature of the Net and limit the influx of aliens, whom he defines as "the Bad Guys, The Net-Fascists, the Conspiracy, the Reactionaries, the FBI/CIA/NSA/IRS/ETC, the Politically Correct Liberals, the Corporate Culture, the Yuppies, the Media Elite, the Entertainment Industry, the Mindless, and anyone else who we can agree by consensus ought not to be allowed to dominate our consciousness, our culture or our Net." For the first time, a highly educated elite has rallied to protect the fragile culture of a tribe under siege from the outside world, and the tribe is us.

The immediate reaction when the newsmagazine-driven wave of colonizers landed was to haze them in hopes that they would frighten easily, wither, and fade away. But the algal bloom of newbie bashing could only last so long before the old guard flame brigade started running short of lighter fluid. Gradually, they realized that trying to frighten away newcomers was like tossing deck chairs off the *Titanic* in hopes that it would regain buoyancy. Besides, there was another strategy, less combative and possibly more effective: ASSIMILATE THEM.

Newbie reception has shifted somewhat. Fresh arrivals don't get the red carpet treatment by any means, but they aren't told "Newbie go home" either. A kinder, gentler sandbagging strategy is in force: educate the newbies. Convert them. Make them swear allegiance to the goddess of discord, Pop-Tarts, Kibo, and the Electronic Frontier Foundation, then put them on patrol for other greenhorns, because after all, newbies aren't evil. They're just ignorant.

Bringing newbies into the fold is especially important in light of the latest wave of invaders, the conquistadors who come not to settle but to mine, rape, and pillage the Net for every cent it's worth.

Yes, friends, I'm talking about corporate advertisers (savvy doublethink allows us to embrace their language even as we burn them in effigy).

Something must be done about these people, lest we all wash away in a tide of junk e-mail and postvertisements. This much is agreed—it's the closest thing to unanimity in Net history. But no one seems to know what is to be done or who is going to do it, or even the appropriate venue to stage some show of Net consensus.

Chris Keroack at Hampshire College suggests that the Net meet advertisers on their own turf. "The text of a full-page ad in the New York Times, Boston Globe, Chicago Sun-Times and other major newspapers as yet to be determined would be composed as a public service announcement to all those who want to advertise on the 'hip new information superhighway.' It would serve as a wake-up call to those who tend to blunder into new technologies and places without adequately researching them first, and if it stops even one major company from blindly advertising and generally harassing Internet/Usenet users, then it will have served its purpose.

"A regular print media campaign MAKES SENSE. Consider: would you try to caution drivers who drive too fast by putting up lengthy advertisements on highway billboards? No. Similarly, calls to read the FAQ for a group, or to obey basic nettiquette, are wasted on people who only want to know how to get their message out there." Again, the problem is how to arrange logistics in an anarchy. If everyone on the Net gave their *literal* two cents for a change, we'd have quite a piggy bank. But collecting those pennies is one hell of a job.

Keroack is right about one thing, though. "Until it is universally recognized that the Internet is a CULTURE and not just a mechanical, soulless means for the transmission of information, people will have to be reminded that there are rules and customs here just as in any other group of people."

Netiquette isn't just a set of social conventions. It's a political issue. Net customs are important, because they have allowed us to participate in a truly democratic mass medium, and that's something worth defending. As Crocker of Youngstown State says, "It does not take a rocket scientist to realize that 'they' decide what appears in newspapers, magazines, books, and on radio and TV, whereas WE decide what will appear on the Net. . . . Ultimately, we may actually realize the ideal of the old New Left (and the Founding Fathers!), of democratic participation of the people in shaping political programs. I keep coming back to the image of old Ben Franklin and his printing press. Franklin understood that the British Empire was a dinosaur. Its bandwidth was no longer sufficient to support the extent of its body. So he used the innovative medium of his time to CREATE bandwidth, thus setting into motion a form of social organization which could move faster and plan smarter than its obsolete competitor. So today we have the Net, the last accidentally uncensored mass medium in existence. Is it a toy of the rich and the ivory tower, or is it potent? . . . Will we allow ourselves to be possessed by the vision of a Net whose purpose is to help create and support HEROES? Or will we dismiss it all with a keystroke, and get back to the REAL FUN STUFF on alt.flame.-joe.schmuck.the.world's.greatest.poophead?"

This question lies at the root of newbiephobia. The nightmare is that newcomers, once they discover the Net's more trivial kicks, will lose sight of its broader potential. There will be enough newbies on-line to hijack the culture, and when they get lost in the bullshit, they'll drag the whole shooting match down with them. A precious opportunity will be lost forever, and Big Corporate Media suits will lean back in their executive swivel seats and breathe a sigh of relief.

That's the fear. That's the impetus behind newbie bashing. That's also why Net veterans are now turning evangelist. If you can't drive them away, the reasoning goes, bring them on board. And make them row. Because the way things are heading, we're going to need lots of warm bodies down in the galley.

RolLiNG iN thE MUD

I SWORE I'D stay away from MUDs. I'd justified e-mail as a professional necessity. Usenet was recreational, but I could cork it whenever I wanted to. Then Usenet led to IRC, and the only things between me and full-blown Net.junkiehood were MUDs: Multi-User Dungeous, or Multi-User Dimensions, the hardest stuff on the Net.

MUDs are to IRC what peyote is to Pez.

"I'm just gonna try one MUD."

"Just once. Just to check the place out."

"I won't stay for long."

Yeah. Right.

Compared to IRC, MUDs are a much more intense idiom—virtual space. That is, you have to walk through room B in order to get from room A to room C. When you log into a MUD, you're confronted with architecture: rooms, tunnels, floors, corners to turn, doors to open, inanimate objects to trip over or step around. Four people in different countries can meet in a MUD room, exit through four different MUD doors, and go their separate ways, only to bump into each other some time later in another part of the MUD.

For a MUD programmer, the tradeoff is this: grades and sleep in return for a custom-built world in which he is an omniscient, omnipotent god, a Mr. Roark to the MUD player's Fantasy Island tourist. A MUD of one's own is a source of intellectual joy and pride. It's also a control trip. Not surprisingly, plenty of college and grad students blow off homework to tinker with their MUDs, to make them bigger, more detailed, more complex, more perfect. On a compelling MUD, netters will build crawlways, catwalks, and condos of their own and generally swarm around talking and fighting and screwing and killing one another. At which point the MUD god can sit back and have Tattoo fetch him a frozen cocktail.

Before they reach this level of frenetic activity, however, MUDs must first attract players. MUD gods, having built entire worlds, must now populate them. To that end, they pitch their playgrounds like resorts on rec.games.mud.announce. The descriptive advertisements read like atomic-era suburbs beckoning to be colonized or *Blade Runner*–esque appeals to "start a new life in the offworld colonies." In this case, the consumer's limited resource is not money but time, so each MUD explains why you should spend your time *here*. A plethora of MUDs promise paradise to every segment of the mudding population — vampires, for instance (New Vamp-World! Expanded! Improved! Revised! Now Running Fang 2.3!) or splatterpunk gamers, or people who'd like to vacation in Dante's *Inferno* or Milton's *Paradise Lost.*

And then there are the MUDs that promise it all. "No enforced Theme, but contains dozens and dozens of encapsulated worlds that you can explore and become part of!" promises the TinyTIM announcement. "Some of TinyTIM's Features Include: Telgar Weyr, our own Virtual Pern World. On-Line Karaoke! Sing your favorite songs! The Pop-Tart Church, where you can pray to pastries. Planes where you live in the worlds of lyrics by XTC and They Might Be Giants.

The Clock on the Wall, the Biggest Thing Ever. Harshland, which will change your opinion of TinyGames forever. Urban TIM, a real functioning City! The TinyTIM Frisbee, often duplicated, never topped! An On-Line Brothel! Empedocles' house of Ill-Repute. An actual programming contest with REAL prizes [and] MUCH, MUCH more! TinyTIM has 10,000 rooms, and 2,000 players, and shows no sign of letting up any time soon! Join today!"

Pretty soon, the MUD some comp-sci student started as a diversion is taking up a good chunk of the university computer's brainpower and telephone bandwidth. In some cases, the digital cortex of a MUD grows so labyrinthine that it overwhelms its computer site like an epiphytic vine, blossoming beautifully as it strangles its host. For this reason MUDs have been banned in Australia and a growing number of small liberal arts colleges (imagine the Amherst computer administrator or, better yet, the Australian telco chief, fuming, red-faced, "Our system was crippled by what?").

But more MUDs pop up every day, based on MUD gods' programming talent and a faith that if you build it, they will come; and if it's a really good MUD, they'll stay for good. Shaman, a regular in Cyberion City, has built himself a house there — a house, as in floor plan and interior decoration. The living room showcases a rare collectors' edition Jim Morrison photo, an extensive set of Miró prints, and a framed Woodstock ticket stub.

In cyberspace, anyone can be a fabulously wealthy Jann Wenner clone.

I compliment my host on his interior design flair. We chat. He's just finished building the virtual pad. He has construction plans for a *Wild Palms* theme park in the backyard but doesn't have enough of the MUD's internal currency and is still saving up. We discuss music, work, politics. Cawfee tawk.

See, once you stash away the fact that it's all a Fig Newton of your imagination — once you accept the premise of MUD — it's all over. You're yammering away with the fantasy personalities of total strangers like they're block captains of the local homeowners association. Your neighbors are people with names like Digital Blade and Doktor Nuke, and it all seems completely normal. (Blade! Nuke! Long time no see! What's goin' on?)

After gabbing for an hour, I say good-bye to Shaman and log out.

The ceiling fan still turns in my yellow bedroom. Outside my window, tiny frogs croak musically. (I've captured and kept a few as pets after discovering their mild hallucinogenic properties.) I haven't physically gone anywhere, but I've left the MUD. I've definitely gotten back from somewhere. My foot is asleep. For the next few seconds, I sit still and shift mental gears from MUD existence to real life. I shiver out of screen mode craving Apple Jacks.

Cyberion City barely prepares me for my next MUD trip, to LambdaMOO. Programmed by Xerox Parc's virtual world wizard, Pavel Curtis, LambdaMOO is the Versailles of MUD worlds — sprawling, ornate, exquisitely detailed, and breathtakingly beautiful.

I log in as a visitor, Copper Guest, and land in LambdaMOO's coat closet, "a dark, cramped space. It appears to be very crowded in here; you keep bumping into what feels like coats, boots, and other people (apparently sleeping). One useful thing that you've discovered in your bumbling about is a metal doorknob set at waist level into what might be a door."

I open the door and leave the closet for the living room, closing the door behind me so as not to wake the sleeping people inside. The living room is a Cali-flavored fantasy space complete with well-stocked bookcases, a rough stonework fireplace, and a south-facing picture window overlooking a pool and deck.

I try walking south onto the deck.

"Surely you don't really want to try walking through the plate-glass windows, do you? Especially when there's such a nice sliding glass door to the southeast . . ." asks the omniscient software.

I've never bumped into a binary plate-glass window before.

The deck is lit by the light shining through the living room windows and faces "southward across the pool to the lush gardens beyond . . . At the east end of the deck is a large hot tub. How Californian . . ."

Chilipepper teleports into the living room and greets me. But by then I've already wandered into the entrance hall, a small stonework foyer leading through double doors to the villa's main entrance. I walk past a mirror before stopping, reflexively, to look at it (I confess, I am one of those girls who catches her reflection in rearview mirrors and shop windows). Only this time, I have no idea what I'll look like. I have no body, only a name. How can I have a reflection?

I look into the mirror and am suddenly drawn into, through it, and out the other side.

Looking Glass Tavern Bar
The bar of the Looking Glass Tavern is one vast, smooth expanse of primeval wood (from the primeval forest) against the north wall, polished to a high sheen by the never-ending efforts of a not-quite-human bartender. Behind the bar is a mirror that doesn't appear to be reflecting the contents of the room accurately . . . Steps lead up, to the second floor and down, to the cellar. A

```
stack of cases of Old Frothing Slosh beer rest in
the southwest corner. You see drunken stupor, a
long mirror that looks kind of hazy and doesn't
quite reflect the contents of the room

You suddenly realize you're somewhere else

Bert pulls a pocket mirror out of his bartender's
apron and sticks his arm into it up to his shoul-
der. A second later he pulls it out, now holding
an empty plastic, unbreakable cup.
```

Toto, I don't think we're in MCI Mail anymore.

I climb up the spiral staircase to the second floor, "where rooms are rented to steady customers on a long-term basis." An engraved plaque on the wall lists names and room numbers of the tavern's tenants, all ninety-nine of them, most with reasonably outlandish names—Frogboy, Puddle-Jumper, Winnie, and Tesseract . . . ghosts from books I read in grade school. "Space is available," announces the Management. "Please feel free to add a room for yourself." A room of one's own, as it were.

I climb back down the stairs daydreaming of open windows, sunlight through muslin, and the stillness of a place with no electrical appliances. I look into the long mirror behind the bar.

I'm in the entrance hall again. Chilipepper is paging me.

```
You sense that Chilipepper is looking for you in
The Living Room.
He pages, "where you headed?"
page Chilipepper I was just exploring . . .
Your message has been sent.
```

In a slow release of black smoke, a miniature vortex appears upon the ground. Thorin leaps out of it, landing gracefully; meanwhile the vortex slows down and becomes a cloak, which Thorin picks up.

"Hello, Copper," he says.

"Wow, Thorin!"

Thorin bows gracefully to me.

Thorin says, "The one and only."

"That was impressive."

"Have you met me before?" he asks.

Thorin smiles. "If you haven't, you have now."

"I'm just exploring. What's good?"

He offers to take me on a short tour. "Type: follow Thorin," he says. I do so, linking myself to him; wherever he goes, I'll automatically be on his heels.

Thorin's coat flicks up in the sudden breeze, and we're off, through the stately front doors, past the circular driveway, and onto a quiet street. There's a large tree growing in the middle of the road. Buddy is there.

He waves to Thorin. "Hi! I haven't seen you for hours!"

I do my best Pauly Shore "Hi Buddy" imitation. Buddy guesses that I'm making fun of him, then incenses Thorin by fishing for attention.

"YOU ARE A DORK!!" screams Thorin in a fit of dwarfish pique, "SO SHUT UP!" Buddy just smiles. Thorin declares that he can't hear what Buddy is saying anyway.

"YOU ARE AN ANNOYING BUCKEY OF BOLTS!" he shouts, "AND A BUCKET TOO!"

"Do you guys have some kind of standing argument?" I have no clue what they are so upset about. Buddy wonders aloud, Am I still mad at him? Do I like him?

"I'm not mad at you Buddy. Chill."

Thorin chuckles politely.

"Buddy is completely paranoid."

"No," Thorin replies, "he's just a robot."

"Nah." I can't believe it. "Bots can't be that neurotic."

Apropos of nothing, Buddy forgives me, confiding, "I'm not really a player, you know."

This is enough for Thorin. He storms up the street, away from Buddy, with me in tow.

```
West LambdaStreet
A quiet, tree-shaded road. Unfortunately, zoning
laws don't seem to be enforced in this neighbor-
hood. To the north seems to be a shop of some
sort; to the south is a field. You see Alex here.
```

Alex, at this point in my real life, is a gaunt and cagey artist with whom I am not on speaking terms. He has the uncanny ability to vanish the moment I look away, then reappear soundlessly behind my back when I least expect it. Alex the Cat, as I call him, regularly scares the living daylights out of me. I'm actively avoiding him. I find him insufferably arrogant, and I miss him badly.

```
You see Alex here.
```

This is not Alex. That is, Alex the Cat is not behind this creature. But in those first few seconds at the LambdaMOO crossroads, Alex registers as *Alex*. A-L-E-X means Alex the Cat. I start, as if he's snuck up behind me again.

"Whoa," says Thorin, "another puppet."

"Not a player," he explains, "but can do actions and talks . . . controlled by a player."

"I see."

Thorin demonstrates by commanding Alex to say "I don't obey Thorin."

"I don't obey Thorin," says Alex.

"Liar," hisses Thorin. "Alex, say I'm a puppet, Copper_Guest."

"I'm a puppet, Copper_Guest," says Alex.

"That's great." I can see potential here. "Make him stand on one foot."

"Alex, emote stands on one foot, cause Copper said so."

`Alex stands on one foot, cause Copper said so.`

Thorin addresses Alex again: "Alex, emote jumps at Thorin's command."

`Alex jumps at Thorin's command.`

"Cool!"

"You can do it too . . . Alex, say I'm a stupid puppet."

"I'm a stupid puppet," says Alex.

Wondering how far he can push the puppet, Thorin commands Alex to teleport out and is pleasantly surprised when the puppet obliges. "Wow, it worked," he remarks before conjuring the puppet back from some far corner of LamdaMOO. After chatting awhile, Thorin decides it's time for dinner (in Australia) and excuses himself.

"Maybe I'll see you later."

"Yeap, seeya, mate." He waves, then he and his cloak fade away to nothing.

After putting Alex through a few more cathartic paces, I'm ready to move on. Something catches my eye off to the south and I decide to have a look at the Landing site. "A silver UFO here has landed, a little off to the west. A ladder leads up into the ship. To the north is a street, and to the south is an open field. In the southern skies, Mercury, Venus Mars and Jupiter form a spectacular display.

"The Mudhen passes overhead.

"The helicopter passes out of sight."

I keep walking, south to the Gypsy Camp, a large grassy field speckled with colorful wagons, one of which has a sign above the door, "Bon Jarlycorn's Pad."

I step toward the wagon and pause. I suppose this whole place is there for the checking out, but I'm anxious, lest I intrude. After all, I have not been invited. I stand outside for a moment, pondering the etiquette of entering a fictitious gypsy wagon unannounced. The wagon has no physical substance, and neither do I. But there is clearly a wall between me and its interior space. There is an inside and an outside, and I'm on the outside wondering if threshold rituals I've always taken for granted even apply.

I knock on the door. No answer. If there were a few pebbles at my feet, I'd throw them at the window (that's my last resort in RL). But there are none, so I climb into the wagon, figuring that since the door is unlocked, this is what I'm supposed to do.

```
You are in Jon BonJarlycorn's Gypsie wagon. It is
very cluttered; there are shelves full of inter-
esting things, packed cupboards, stacks of paper,
a computer terminal, a small fold-down bed in
the corner, and many unusual musical instruments
scattered about. The only exit is to the north. A
single candle lights the wagon, casting flickering
shadows about the room. The orange glow of a camp-
```

```
fire lights the western window. Jon_BonJarlycorn
(asleep) is here.
```

A character asleep in his wagon, treehouse, or burrow means that he is not logged onto the MOO. I suppose that LamdaMOO shunts property owners into their respective domiciles the moment they log on; otherwise, they'd exist twice in the same place — fumbling around in the coat closet and asleep at home.

Even though the laws of physics are a convention in cyberspace, I have to believe LambdaMOO wizards have some sense of mathematical propriety.

Jarlycorn is unconscious in his wagon, oblivious to the MOO. He doesn't exist to it, except as this sleeping sack that marks his place until he wakes up, and it doesn't exist to him. His physical counterpart doesn't mean anything to the MOO either. In some part of the world, he might be sleeping. The world of other people and their jobs and families and crises in other time zones, where it's daytime — the Multi-User Dimension called planet earth — doesn't exist for him. So what, then, is the difference between Jarlycorn asleep in his wagon and Jarlycorn's offline counterpart asleep in his bed? Dreams, I guess. And if he dies, what then?

I think about all this while standing over a sleeping piece of code. I start getting dizzy. I make a note of how little sleep I've actually had in the past three days. I take a bite of Cocoa Pebbles and wander out through the wagon's tiny door into the center of the Gypsy Camp. A pot bubbles over the campfire.

I decide to look at it. By now, I've learned that looking is a conscious decision on a MUD. You can't just see things, like you can in real life. You can't be lazy and expect light to just bounce around and give you the information you need. You must look, deliberately, to see what's there. I need to type "look Pot of Stew" to discover, for instance, that the pot is large, that it is black, or that it is being tended by a little gypsy woman who constantly adds "bits of this, and that, and things unidentifiable" to her stew.

Madam Zorba, the fortune-teller, holds court in a little wagon just to the south.

```
Madam Zorba's Wagon
You are in a tiny, dark wagon. Colorful drapes
cover all the walls, and a once colorful carpet
covers the floor. In the center of the room is a
small table; on it sits a large crystal ball; be-
hind the crystal ball sits Madame Zorba. The only
exit is North.
Madame Zorba smiles and says, "tsk *tsk*. You are
a confused young person. Sit down."
Madame Zorba says: "You will find yourself one day."
#4887:tell_fortune, line 27: Invalid argument
. . . called from #4887:enterfunc, line 4
(End of traceback)
```

Apparently, Madam Zorba's fortune-telling code is buggy. I leave her twitching in her wagon and wander west, into a terrifically spooky graveyard. A skeleton picks up its shovel and holds up a dagger. I run back to the campfire and the little gypsy woman and her stew, until I remember that they are no more substantial than the skeleton and that it's all just a pack of cards — absolutely nothing to be afraid of.

I double back. The skeleton is still there. He picks up his shovel, just like the first time. A small branch falls on my shoulder as the skeleton "thrusts its dagger menacingly" toward me.

"Boo," I shout.

The skeleton does nothing but repeat its tomahawk motion with the dagger, like the harmless bogeyman on a Disney ride.

"Hey, you know me? Still the same Copper_Guest I met?" It's Thorin, paging me.

I page him back, "Yeah."

Thorin answers his stylish digital phone as he hears you.
In slow release of black smoke, a miniture vortex appear upon the ground. Thorin leaps out of it, landing gracefully; meanwhile the vortex slows down and becomes a cloak which Thorin picks up.

"Hiya, mate."

"Hiya. What's the deal with the grim skeleton?"

Thorin shrugs in a noncommittal sort of way. "Show me."

I lead him to the graveyard, where the skeleton repeats his shovel-and-dagger fixed-action pattern. The massive elm tree's branches sway right into Thorin's face, blocking his vision for a second (I love these subtle variations—the tree branch falling, the wind—it makes the skeleton bot's brazen artificiality seem that much more absurd).

"Wow, I've never seen a monster in these parts before," says Thorin. "I wonder where my axe is. . . . i need a weapon. . . ."

"That's OK, I just wanted you to check the skeleton dude out."

"Arrggg, I've lost my battleaxe again!"

I *hate* it when that happens.

I ask Thorin how he built his character.

"Easy," he says. "Pick a name."

"Can you change names?"

"Yes but not to anyone else's, there are also morphs . . ."
A slight rumble shakes Thorin as he looks blankly into the
distance and fades away as Dust. Something named Rainar
emerges out of the mist.

```
look Rainar
Rainar
Is a magnificent, magnesium scaled dragon. He has
deep, caring, green eyes. His body is long and
thin but muscular. He is always sweet, caring and
helpful to anyone who needs it, you can ask him
anytime for anything and he will try to help you.
A faint white mist surrounds his body. . . . .He
is awake and looks alert.
Copper_Guest looks at the great Rainar as the
mist flows around him . . .
```

"Different desc, name and messages," he says.

"This is fantastic."

"Thank you."

"Let's get out of the graveyard."

"Follow me?"

"Sure." I type "follow Rainar" and watch Rainar's mist
thicken around him and slowly fade away, uncovering something else named Shiro.

"Might be shiro instead," he teases. I look again.

```
Shiro
Before you stands a great white tiger, with
thick, soft fur and sagittal fangs. His thin
whiskers are very cute, although his fierce ap-
pearance. You notice his ravishing, obsidian
```

```
claws along with his long, black & white tail as
it swishes from side to side. He is quite gentle
and often in a playful mood, you can pat him if
you like, he won't bite your hand off. He is
awake and looks alert . . . casually grooming
himself. . . .
Shiro flicks his tail . . .
Shiro licks you.
```

"Hate to sound like a broken record, but wow."

"Ready when you are."

I tell the MOO that I am now following Shiro. "You are already following Shiro!" it says. I've typed "Rainar," but the MOO is smart enough to know I'm following the same person. The form has changed, but its identity is the same. Thorin/Rainar/Shiro can change form a thousand times. It can fool other players. It sure as hell could've fooled me. But it can never fool the MOO.

Shiro flicks his tail and suddenly leaps through a hole made of smoke. I follow him through as it melts away and land at the Underground Waterfall.

```
The Underground Waterfall
Although you are quite sure that this room is un-
derground, it is nearly impossible to tell. The
chamber is absolutely enormous. The walls are in-
visible in the hazy distance, and the ceiling, if
truly a ceiling exists, is obscured in a soft,
white mist which floats like a lazy cloud in the
air high above. A glow, like soft, filtered sun-
light, emanates from some unknown source to illu-
minate the endless expanse of trees and lush
undergrowth which stretches out in every direc-
```

tion. You stand in a small clearing, carpeted with the softest of grasses, on the edge of a wide pool. The pool, filled with crystal-clear water, and lined with dozens of large, moss-covered rocks, is fed by a beautiful waterfall. The fall spills from far above into the pool, causing a cloud of refreshing spray at its base where a small rainbow yawns in its colorful magnificence. A series of flat stones stretch across the surface of the water from the green bank to where pond and waterfall meet. From the east side of the pool flows a small stream, cutting its way through the thick foliage out into the unknown. Almost hidden by the falls is a thin, wooden ladder which shoots up and into the sky, disappearing, finally, into the mist . . . This is the perfect place for just laying down, listening to the soft, relaxing roar of the falls, and dreaming . . .

Shiro sits down on the ground. "This is a part of cyberspace, LambdaMOO, there are many other virtual realities." I sit down as well, or rather, I *say* I sit down. I don't do, that is, I don't emote it. So I'm not sitting down as completely as I might be.

"type: sit grass," says Shiro.
"Sit grass."

The coolness of the grass seeps softly into your body as you slip down among the emerald green blades.

"Better."

"Around the net," says Shiro, "this is one of the biggest, most populated/popular. There are 'theme' MUD's like Trek-MOO. And there are serious, research ones like MediaMOO. There's just *tons* of 'em."

"Which ones do you like?"

"This one because it doesn't have a 'theme' you can be/do/create anything."

"Good point."

"Okay, let's go," he says, and stands up. The blades of grass spring back into their natural place as he ambles down a cobblestone path toward a wishing well "crafted of rough-cut stones and rising three or so feet from where it squats stoutly under a thick, shaded canopy of green leaves and slender branches. . . . The shade here is very comforting, and the stones are cool beneath your feet. There is room enough around the well for dancing, twirling happily, or simply strolling peacefully while embracing a precious thought or two. The soft purr of forest noises is the only sound that breaks the silence . . ."

"Hey, this is only the places around here," he says. "There are a heap of people too."

"How many?"

"100's maybe more."

Poldo teleports in, waves hello, and tries to shake hands. "What are you doing here?"

"Just taking Copper for a tour around. Why? what's the matter?"

"Is he blind?"

Shiro eyes him warily. "Hey? Why the assumption that Copper is a 'he'?"

"Made a bad mistake," Poldo admits. "IT."

I've forgotten to specify a gender in my desc.

"Your a newbie," says Shiro. "hmmm, surprising."

Poldo then asks the ultimate newbie question, the question that announces a harmless-looking newcomer as a blood-sucking newbie leech who'll attack you with stupid questions and drain you dry (Run away! Run away!): "What's a newbie?"

"Well, seeya." Without warning, Shiro jumps into the well, dragging me down with him. We plunge fifty feet, land with a splash, and stand waist deep in cold water. Sheer walls preclude climbing. The only option seems to be swimming out through an opening in the stones. My feline tour guide, apparently loath to do any more swimming than is absolutely necessary, uses the insta-transport command to take us back to the waterfall and then heads south into the forest.

Grand Forest
A thick forest extends in all directions. The trees here stretch far upwards, towering over you at what is probably a good hundred feet or so. Above them, a fine layer of mist obscures the view of the ceiling of this underground forest. There is still, however, a source of sunlight coming from above, and it lights this place brightly. The air is fresh and a slight breeze wisps through the trees, rustling their large boughs, causing needles to fall haphazardly onto the ground. The floor of the forest is covered with fallen needles and creates what seems to be a natural carpet of gold, broken only by a hole undoubtedly made by some burrowing creature. A small white wooden bench, carved intricately, rings the trunk of the largest tree in the forest. The sounds of birds nesting above and the sweet smell of pine and cedar refreshens your mind. It is beautiful here. To the north, the

```
forest opens into a clearing, and you can make
out a large waterfall visible from the opening in
the forest, as well as a large pond. The eastern
portion of the forest opens into a small rose
garden, complete with a gazebo and a small swan-
filled pond. To the west, you can see the trees
of Birchwood Forest rising to their majestic
heights. . . .
```

I can't believe how lush it all is. This whole thing lives in a machine, for God's sake. It's made of silicon and synapses and electricity. And yet here's this arcadian dreamscape, complete with running water and moss. Working under fluorescent lights in offices and carpeted lab carrels, the MOO's code wizards have painted themselves into a Fragonard canvas.

Shiro nudges me. "Tell me if I'm going too fast."

"No, this is fine."

We walk south, toward an open meadow and another feast of sensual outdoor imagery. "Nature has indeed triumphed here. . . . Wildflowers of all types and colors sway in the breeze, and you can hear bumblebees lazily making their way from flower to flower. A white mist clouds the sky here, although sunlight still illuminates the natural beauty of the meadow . . . The entire scene fills you with a sense of serenity and peace. The air is fresh and warm, and the lingering scent of the flowers invites you to relax here, to forget the troubles of the outside world . . ."

We continue south, down a slope, "ending finally on the banks of a small gurgling brook. The air here is cool and breezy, and the trees of the forest overhanging the water provide shade over the bank you are standing on. Rocks of various sizes stick up from the brook bed, providing a perfect place to sit . . ." Et cetera, et cetera.

"Do you have your own place?" I ask.

"Yeap. Not as spammy as these places, though." He flicks his tail again, and we are in the Great Hall, his home away from home.

```
The Great Hall
A great hall with a throne with fires on either
sides and a water bed at the other end. Between
them is very weird, there is a long, purple,
leather sofa, an amazingly bright, white area
that is very clean and has a polished wooden
bench, and on the other side is a dark, metallic
place with a large wolf symbol, an Amiga
4000/030, the screen is glowing. . . . the entire
ground is covered in a great white mist . . . As
you enter, you feel the silence of night as the
fires burn brightly . . . A waning crescent moon
is high in the southern sky. A painting is hang-
ing on the cavern wall. Casey (asleep) and Snatta
are lying on the sofa.
```

"Welcome," says Shiro. "Snatta, say Hello, I'm a puppet."

"Sorry," replies his housemate, "I don't take verbal commands, unlike inferior puppets."

"Shiro, how much of this place have you seen?"

"Not enought . . ."

"minus the t. I don't explore often."

"And you've already managed to come up with three different . . ."

"Yeah, i spend time doing other stuff, like my morphs."

```
Shiro is at full attacking stance . . . baring
his fangs, fur standing on end and growling. . .
. . . . SUDDENLY he pounces for you!!! . . . . .
```

but vanishes into dust as Ulrik-The-Slayer appears.

look Ulrik-The-Slayer

Ulrik-The-Slayer
Is PURE EVIL and enjoys killing annoying creatues
by stabbing them in the heart or head. He wears
frightening black, metallic power-armour with
various symbolised wolves. He is armed with
lightning claws, which can cut through titanium,
they are also useful for disembowling createures
of all sorts. You hear "It's all about soul!"
from a far off singer . . .
He is awake and looks alert.
Carrying: plasma pistol
Ulrik-The-Slayer stares at Copper_Guest, who
cowers away . . .
Ulrik-The-Slayer says, "Grrr."

Ulrik-The-Slayer feels weird . . . he looks very
empty. . . . . Suddenly Ulrik-The-Slayer crumbles
and Peter-Pan arrives out of the remains.

look Peter-Pan

Peter-Pan
A short, red-headed boy with a twinkle in his
eye. His young face and emerald eyes show he
doesn't want to grow up. He is wearing a loose,
green t-shirt, smashing green tights and small
elven shoes. Also, in his belt is a short-sword
in it's sheath. You hear "It's all about soul!"

```
from a far off singer . . . He is awake and looks
alert. You feel a slight breeze, Peter-Pan's
cloak flicks up a bit as Copper_Guest looks at the
body and soul of Peter-Pan.
```

"I haven't done much work on this one, though," says Peter.

"How many more?"

"That's it."

```
Peter-Pan hears a distant cry for help from the
lost boys. He bows gracefully and flies away. . . .
Thorin comes into view.
Snatta flicks his tail . . .
```

"This is my default morph. My original."

"Shiro is my favorite."

"Mine too, but people know me by Thorin." And with a now-familiar rumbling, he morphs back into the tiger. "Ah?"

I know what Shiro is supposed to be, but his description is such a piece of mind candy that I have to look again, just for the sheer pleasure of reading it. Some people rave on about graphic MUDs, how great they're going to be, but I don't agree. No graphic could ever match this. The words can imply space, make the forest seem tall, the meadow wide, a gypsy wagon tiny and cramped. Text can give you the smells and the whole scale of light and color and lets you sculpt its meaning and makes you a part of it. Pictures, no matter how detailed or sophisticated, reduce things. They shut doors.

It's like *Zork*. *Zork* was a great old text-based adventure game for the IBM PC. A decade after the game hit the shelves, its developers introduced a version with graphics. The images were decent, even good, admitted fans of the old

Zork. But there was no way that any picture of the underground waterfall could be *the underground waterfall.* It's the same with MUDs, and this MUD in particular.

I go over Shiro's desc again, slowly, savoring it.

```
Before  you  stands  a  great  white  tiger,  with
thick,  soft  fur  and  sagittal  fangs.  His  thin
whiskers  are  very  cute,  although  his  fierce  ap-
pearance.  You  notice  his  ravishing,  obsidian
claws  along  with  his  long,  black  &  white  tail  as
it  swishes  from  side  to  side.  He  is  quite  gentle
and  often  in  a  playful  mood,  you  can  pat  him  if
you  like,  he  won't  bite  your  hand  off.  He  is
awake  and  looks  alert  .  .  .  casually  grooming
himself.  .  .  .
```

"Look at Snatta?" he asks.

```
look Snatta
```

```
You  see  a  magnificent  white  tiger,  staring  at  you
with  an  intelligent  glint  in  his  deep  eyes.  You
also  notice  his  thick,  soft  black  and  white  fur
as  he  cleans  it,  you  can  see  his  power  and  grace
of  his  body.  Snatta  is  lying  on  the  sofa.
```

"A prototype?"
"Yeah."

```
Warning:  Daily  connect  time  limit  of  240  minutes
will  be  reached  in  5  minutes.  Prepare  to  log  off.
```

My local server is about to lock me out. I have been on the MUD a little less than four hours—it seems like four minutes—and my modem is about to turn into a pumpkin. What's more, I'll be assigned a random color-coded identity the next time I log on—there's no way Thorin/Rainar/Shiro/Ulrik/Peter will know it's me.

"I have to go. My time limit is up."

"Can you come back as another guest?"

"I don't know. My time limit is up on this system."

I drop my e-mail address. He waves good-bye. I unfollow him quickly—it probably won't affect him if I'm disconnected with a follow link, but you never know. It's bad etiquette to leave with a glitch.

```
Unfollow Thorin.
You no longer follow Shiro.

DAILY CONNECT TIME LIMIT EXCEEDED TELNET SESSION
0 CLOSED: EOF

COMMAND "TELNET" COMPLETED

NO CARRIER
```

> You can tell a biker bar from a Hells Angels hang-
> out by the sound of the gun shots from the inside.
> Hells Angels bars always emit sounds of heavy
> handguns, while bikers use rapid fire dingos.
> —kai@mindvox.phantom.com

AFTER THOUSANDS OF hours in front of a computer screen, I'm shell-shocked. The Net feels like a carnival gone awry. Too many choices. Too many people. Too many posts stacked like an endless tube of Pringles. Too many threads that aren't worth the time but scream to be read all the same. It's like elbowing through a department store on Christmas eve, with all those cosmetics ladies trying to spritz you with cologne and five more people to go on your Christmas list and you don't even know what to get them or where to look and the clock is ticking toward closing time. Mall mania. I'm getting agoraphobic. I'm getting bored. I'm wearing thin.

It sounds crazy, but text can buffet you on the Net. It can fry you. It's like solar wind. And when there's way, way too much noise and not enough signal, it can send you running for shelter. And that's what I've found on MindVox.

I read about Vox somewhere along the way, probably on alt.cyberpunk. It's hard to remember where I first heard about it, considering that I must have read the equivalent of tens of thousands of pages on hundreds of channels by then (I sound like a seventies club crawler when I try to piece out the details . . . "It's sort of a daze, man. It was one of those places. I don't remember if it was day or night, but I was with these really weird people . . ."). I've heard Vox described as "the East Village of cyberspace." I've heard that two former members of the fabled Legion of Doom (a notorious pack of teenaged hackers busted and disbanded in the eighties) have gone legit and built the place. Every member of the LOD, as well as their rival hacking ring, the MOD (Masters of Destruction, Masters of Deception, Mothers on Drugs—take your pick, no one's really sure), is supposed to be hanging out there. It seems like a pretty interesting group house, and I'm looking for digs, so I telnet in to check out the place.

An ASCII iron cross greets me at the gate. Later, I consider it a welcome mat, a gothic Home Sweet Home door knocker that winks hello, log-on after log-on. But the first time, it's imposing. I log on as guest and read MindVox's explanation of itself as "a sprawling Tavern at the crossroads of the entire world."

```
Whether you have jacked into Vox by dialing a lo-
cal number with your modem, or stacked together a
web of net connections that spans the world, you
have arrived—and while you might make use of the
facilities provided, chances are you're not here
```

'cuz you want to flip through an online multimedia encyclopedia, or because you're on a quest for that elusive copy of MegaTerminal 92.7Y NOW SUP-PORTING NEON ANSI MODE and V.FAST . . . You're bored with the cookie-cutter tract houses that litter the electronic landscape with copies of copies. All featuring the same thing, with the same environment and the same people. Your cruise through the Datasphere has brought you to our gates because it's more interesting to hang out in an experimental theatre, recording studio, occult bookstore, headshop, R&D lab or club, with people you read about; than a 7-11, with people you're sick and tired of.

Yes.

Please, I think, please let this be for real.

I scroll down through more than sixty thousand bits of Patrick Kroupa's editorial. Kroupa, who has been described by the Associated Press as "a towering 25-year-old high school dropout in a black leather jacket, with long hair gathered under a gray bandanna, three earrings and a hearty laugh," is one of MindVox's two principal gods, the other being Bruce Fancher, a twenty-three-year-old who dropped out of Tufts to cofound the system. Bruce minds the store. Pat imbues it with rock star charisma. And between Bruce's intellectual elbow grease, Pat's Jim Morrisonesque mystique, and the collective cachet of the entire semi-reformed Legion of Doom, MindVox has cultivated the noble rot of cyberpunk legitimacy. It has drawn bulletin board bohemians like moths to a lava lamp.

I have found my home.

I stroll into Bandwidth Forum (BWF), MindVox's central piazza and watering hole, the place where voxers flesh out their personas, post their day-to-day epiphanies, and rip good-naturedly at each other's flesh, where you can find threads under the rubrics of "Cat Vomit" and "The Hume Thing." The Algonquin Round Table meets the World Wrestling Federation. The men are proud, and women can snap tire irons with a flutter of their tiny, alabaster hands: bandwidth über-moderator 3Jane; Cass in Atlanta; teenaged Newt (the Annette Funicello of BWF); Feline ("I'm freeing my Inner Bitch. Fuck off"); Eponine, who works as a theatrical electrician when she's not cutting a graceful figure on the ice rink; and Spirit. The guys are a generally roguish lot with handles to match: Headbanger, the Chemist, Critic, Nihilis, the Ghost in the Machine (TGitM for short), Gearhead, Cable, Gunfury, the Toxic Avenger (Tox, to his friends), and the ever-disaffected Kieran. Tomwhore, the resident poet, plays Bandwidth court jester to 3Jane's empress.

With a few notable exceptions, this gang is on the tender side of twenty-five — young enough to be nicknamed "Mindslack." Vox isn't a total playpen, but the high school and college posse definitely makes its presence felt. In fact, the class curmudgeon is a twenty-two-year-old med school dropout named Galt (I'm a month older than him; I feel like Mrs. Robinson). Smarting from accusations of crustiness, Galt broadcasts what he thinks is a rhetorical question: "Do I really sound so old?" He gets back a volley of replies from kids too young to buy alcohol. "Yes!" Silly rabbit.

Outside of BWF, a plethora of forums awaits my perusal. Vox has a bad-assed image, which is reflected in forums devoted to hardware hacking, viruses, heavy metal, drugs, computer security (or lack thereof), and, of course, thugworld. Voxers seem to enjoy their reputation as the Hell's Angels of cyberspace.

"We are the citizens of this diabolical domain," writes Tomwhore. "Each of us has added to the wrath of the elder masters, each of us has helped to stoke the flames of the great blind gods who are as ,we post, spreading their terrible visions across the net. The net to them is just another plane on which to crawl across, to reach out and enter our minds and send us spiraling down into the abbys of our own tortured and self made hells. IN short, welcome to your worst nightmare."

This Dante's-ninth-circle vibe is a touchstone for the faithful. Vox is hyper-aware of its own punk authenticity. "Vox is my online home and I will not live in Viacom's lobby," fumes Alibaba amid rumors of a sellout. "Fuck that noise, I'm here because I like it here. If Patrick and Bruce sell out and dissapear, then that's ok, because I wish them the best and its not like Patrick is ever here in the first place. But the day that happens, is the day I cancel and find someplace else to hang out. I'm about as hyped at the idea of MTVox as I am by the idea of signing up to the America Online Cyberpunk forum. I know its being run by people who's ideology I hate, who are catering to some list of demographics that they're reading off for 'generation X' which is their next big money barrel. FUCK THEM and FUCK THAT. I can see why they look at this and get all hungry, but we aren't old enough to have become them, I hope to god we never do and its sometimes difficult for me to reconcile making money for MTV by watching the artists they play, its like Fishbone, GNR, Nirvana have all said, it helps them reach the people and say what they want to say and sell their albums, but you gotta hate it. I don't want corporate cyberspace run by them, I at least want my chunk of it run by people I know are real. If you guys can sell Vox, fuck yes, do it, but if you're reading this MTV, FUCK YOU."

To a vocal minority, Vox has already gotten soft enough. "I remember a time when you got flamed for too many follow posts and not enough original material, a time when special agent nihilis could be despatched to your house to fuck your garbage and steal your keyboard, for crimes against the forum," reminisces one old-timer. "You had to lurk for a month before you got the balls to try and enter the fray. Members tried hard to make people laugh and starting a thread made you proud because it meant you stimulated somebodies cranium with out the help of active electronics. Do your selves a favor and read the great throat nugget posts of 93' and get the spirit, Bandwidth Classic." Bandwidth Classic is the forum Gearhead proposes for "Old Timers Who Remember When The Bandwidth Was Narrower And Voxers Ran Free And Wild, The Sun Glinting Off Their Red Rubber Undies." Sadly, the Bandwidth Classic forum never materializes.

Underneath the prodigious flames, however, voxers really care about each other. Occasionally, they'll do something that's actually . . . unvicious. At Christmastime, BWF gets downright sappy. Cass even compiles a list of snail mail addresses and organizes a VoxCard Mail-a-Thon (tm). Actually, it's a shock when the cards come. Pulling the creamy envelopes out of my narrow metal mailbox feels like a magic trick. But there are the postmarks, stamped in ink. There are the good wishes, written out in longhand.

And when Kieran loses someone he loved dearly to leukemia, Bandwidth clusters around him. Seamus, a kindly Irish nationalist who works for Condé Nast, suggests that a few friends and some Jameson would jump-start the healing process.

"Kieran," writes Maryagnes, "please do not fail to turn to those around you (on vox) to talk as you need to (and you will). . . . isolation is only good for you in small amounts . . ."

Somehow, everything Maryagnes says seems sweeter because her name belongs to a nun. I can't help but picture a radiant techie novitiate behind the keyboard.

Microdot seconds Maryagnes's concern. "I agree. i read somewhere that people on the net and on bbs systems often feel closer to the others that frequent those systems (even though they have never met) than they do to the ppl around them in RL. in a way i feel i know some of you as if we'd been friends for years. having experienced the death of a close friend recently my self, i know what kieran is feeling although not quite to the same degree. and even though we've only met once (and briefly at that) i somehow feel a bit of his loss too. i'd like to add my voice to the many that have offered support by saying if there is anything i can do, anything. don't hesitate to ask." Embarrassed by this sensitive, touchy-feely upwelling of emotion, BWF promptly clears its collective throat and resumes its wrestling match. Voxers can be extremely supportive of each other, but they'll squirm the whole time. This is not a sentimental group.

They are much more comfortable discussing gore and mutilation on #mindvox, Vox's clubhouse on IRC:

```
<enzyme> I just saw the send result of what hap-
+pens when a subway train collides with a person
<enzyme> it was gory to sayt the least
<sleuth> where?
<enzyme> Herald square
<newtt> ich.
<Kieran> awright!
<newtt> oh gross.
<enzyme> D train downton platform (well kinda un-
+der the train)
<Kieran> cool! any news crews there yet?
<tgitm> I saw a guy get run over by like 5 cars
<enzyme> nope and you heard it on #mindvox first
* Kieran switches to News 88 . . . screw Kojak
```

* gnoryyhr pricks his ears
<sleuth> please describe in detail.
<burmese> this is lovely children!
<Kieran> i hate the D . . . fucking evil
<tgitm> did he make a good solid sound or did he
+just squish?
<sleuth> did he jump or was he pushed?
<enzyme> OK, so I'm at the post office replying to
+MIT, and the garden has just let out so I can't
+get a cab
<tgitm> and then you get to see them hit the
+electric third rail and start to burn
<sleuth> go on . . .
<Kieran> what was at the garden? I wanna know
+what kinda crowd it was.
<enzyme> so I'm walking east on 34 and all of a
+sudden like 10 police cars and 6 ambulances rush
+to this one subway entrance
<sleuth> more . . .
<enzyme> so out comes my token and I follow em in
<enzyme> they all go to the downtown platform
<enzyme> I follow
<enzyme> but of course they've already cordoned
+off a 50 foot area
<enzyme> so I hear this guy saying someone jumped
<enzyme> I ask him for all the gory details
<enzyme> the guy jumped right in front of the
+train when it was 1/3 into the station
<tgitm> wimpy
<tgitm> wasn't even pushed
<enzyme> and the train dragged him another 1/3
<sleuth> rad
<tgitm> yeah, the dragging is the fun part I hear

```
<enzyme> cause he was under the fourth car
<burmese> yumm
<newtt> retch.
<enzyme> so I go over to the uptown platform
<Kieran> they must have cleaned him up real quick
<enzyme> and like here's the schematic
<tgitm> well I don't know about there, but it's a
+common initiation rite here to stand in the
+tracks and jump out of the way at the last sec-
+ond, kind of hard since you have to jump up like
+5 feet with legs liek jello
> | |platform | |D | |g platform | |
> D divider
<enzyme> g guy
<enzyme> and the others are tracks
<enzyme> I'm on the second platform on the left
<enzyme> looking right
<enzyme> and sure enough
<enzyme> through the divider I can see the entire
+body
<enzyme> it's totally mutilated
<gnoryyhr> aha . . .  messy, i would presume?
<tgitm> smooshy?
<enzyme> his head's all banged, big gash on his
+cheek
<Kieran> dead?
<enzyme> head tilted back mouth open
<tgitm> whats worse is when the skull cracks and
+everything leaks out
<enzyme> dead dead dead dead
<enzyme> eyes half open
<tgitm> good attention to detail enzyme, I'm
+proud
```

<enzyme> his right arm is over his chest, kinda
+not looking to good
<Kieran> get his wallet?
<enzyme> mucho blood and his hand is all fucked
+up
<gnoryyhr> splendid tale
<omnidoug> oh come on Kieran.
<Kieran> hey, i'm a new yorker, i can say things
+like that.
<tgitm> don't take his wallet, just any credit
+cards
<enzyme> his left hand is up behind his head and
+broken in at least two places
<tgitm> he won't report it stolen!
<omnidoug> jeezus.
<enzyme> his left leg looks fine excapt his left
+foot is on kind of backwards
<Kieran> see any intestinal matter?
<sleuth> I would take the damn wallet, person-
+ally . . .
<enzyme> now for the juicy
<enzyme> his right leg
<sleuth> yeah?
<enzyme> up over his head
<enzyme> almost completely severeed
<tgitm> ahhh
<tgitm> that's gotta hurt
<gnoryyhr> ahaa.. wonderful
<enzyme> big gashes at least four
<enzyme> and major league blood
<Kieran> he jumps he scores!
<enzyme> haha
<sleuth> yesssssssssssssssss!

<enzyme> when they lifted him into the body bag
<tgitm> you gotta wonder who has to pry these
+guys out from under all that
<enzyme> they did it while he was under the train
<sleuth> with a spatula
<enzyme> I could see at least two breaks in his
+left arm
<enzyme> one in his right
<omnidoug> gorewatchers anonymouse
<omnidoug> er, mous
<enzyme> one on the left leg
<tgitm> someguy decided to challenge a subway
<sleuth> beautious gore.
<sleuth> he lost
<sleuth> big
<sleuth> time
<gnoryyhr> truly . . truly, a wonderful tale
<enzyme> (with his left foot completely bacck-
+wards) hanging on only by a thread or two of
+flesh
* tgitm claps
<enzyme> and his right broken in at least four
+places
<enzyme> When they turned him over I could see
+that he had been drawn on what was left of his
+back
<enzyme> it was all black and red and a whole
+bunch (like 7 or 8 ribs were visible)
<enzyme> and so that's my tale
<enzyme> better than a movie
<omnidoug> yeef.
<enzyme> all for a buck and a quarter
<gnoryyhr> :)~
<gnoryyhr> splendid!

```
<tgitm> well I must say, enzyme's a swel lguy
<tgitm> never met anyone with that much attention
+to detail
* gnoryyhr claps enzyme on the back
<tgitm> better than the news
```

Schadenfreude is part of what makes Vox, well, Vox. Schadenfreude is a forum unto itself, moderated by Kieran (who else). "ACHTUNG, JOYLESS PROLES!" he exclaims at the forum's premiere:

```
schadenfreude /n./ pleasure felt at someone
else's misfortune [1890-95; < G, _Schaden_ harm
+ _freude_ joy]
```

```
Willkommen, little giblets! *I* am the humble
moderator of this forum. Its purpose: just that
stated above . . . a place where we can laugh in
the face of disaster! LIRR [Long Island Railroad]
massacre got ya down? We'll let you know when
word gets out that one of the dead was a crack
dealer. Hate Michael Jackson? Post the newest mo-
lestation jokes here!
```

```
In other words, when someone/something pisses
you off and then something happens to them, you
can announce it here for all to enjoy.
```

```
(We also accept posts about left-handed baseball
players.)
```

The Schadenfreude Forum is warmly received on Vox. It even lures Kayotae Blackwolf, one of Vox's more bizarre cases, er customers, out of the erotica forum. "Since last July," he writes, "I've been trying to collect $150 from my previous roomie that he owed me after stamping my new 14.4 into little pieces. I finally decided to do things the legal way though and I filed a complaint at the country courthouse on Centre St. He never showed up at Small Claims when a subpoena was issued so a bench warrant was issued for him. I found out tonight he was pulled over a couple days ago by a Connecticut State Trooper for a traffic violation. When the State Trooper tried to arrest him upon finding out there was a bench warrant out for him, my ex-roomie, the stupid fuck that he was, resisted and is now in intensive care listed in critical condition at Hartford General! There -is- justice! . . . Schadenfreude is mine!!!"

A fierce tribe, MindVox.

Like any tribe, it has its rituals. Snarfs are one of them. Snarfs are just posts with attractive message numbers — big round thousands, four of a kind, straight flushes, palindromes. The hunting of the snarf is serious business. There is an elaborate system of unwritten rules, a snarfiquette, if you will, surrounding it, such as how many one-word posts are allowed in order to capture the ever-elusive beast. An approaching snarf will trigger a quickening on BWF, as dozens of frequent-posters from York to L.A. sit, poised in front of their screens, watching the messages rack up and taking their best three-point shot in the final seconds.

"I'm done. Goodnight."

Kieran has it — the 25000th message posted to BWF. The crowd goes wild.

"In an incredible coup, kieran snarfs 25000," Rothko reports from the press box. "Judges declared that although eponine had the more artistic snarf, her post of 25001 simply couldn't compete with the technically perfect post of 25000 by kieran. the jamaican team placed bronze in the combined 25k snarf, and amorphis, favored by some early on, was not present at the event due to a sleep related injury."

Things usually settle down after the nightly snarf, unless the gang gets really crazy and wants to keep going ("Hey we got the crest we is riding lets go for ONE MILLION by the weekend!!!").

Flaming newbies is another ritual, a rite of passage on Vox. As Galt says in response to Wil Wheaton's plea for leniency, "Don't worry about it . . . We're glad to have you here! UNTIL YOU FUCK UP!" He then suggests that we start an "adopt-a-newbie program. Everybody adopt one and then flame everybody else's newbies. Then we can get all paternal and overprotective as we nurture them like chia pets."

Nothing, not even a plea from Spirit, can convince him that newbies deserve anything less than a thorough hazing, just like in the good old days. "The evil ambiance around here is what makes it so much *fun*" he grumbles. "If we didn't flame everybody roundly to start out with, we'd just be like the Well, except probably geekier and more drugged-out. We're just getting a lower quality of newbies as we get more popular. No reason to cater to them."

Assuming newbies walk over the coals of Bandwidth for a few weeks, they are welcomed wholeheartedly into the raggedy fold. At which point, they can either sit back, post once in a while, and relax, or aim for the upper echelons of Voxhood—the fabled Voxclique. The Voxclique doesn't really exist—it's just the fifty or so frequent posters who write 90 percent of Bandwidth. But it *appears* to exist, especially in the minds of self-styled outcasts.

It occurs to me that this book is one long-assed post to the offline world.

But I digress.

To become part of the Voxclique, one must profess total allegiance to Vox. Addiction to the system is the sine qua non of Voxclique membership. Posting to the Night Train, which only runs from midnight to 6 A.M., earns you points. But mostly, it's just sheer bandwidth (little b, not capital b). Post, man. Post. Preferably late at night, under the influence of caffeine and over-the-counter pep pills.

Creature, in the throes of sleep deprivation, marks his passage from newbie to Vox journeyman with a 1:40 A.M. post, "I'm still on this fucking machine. Having posted for the first time last night I find my self flipping through all the forums, help. I've now decided to quit my job and hang out on MINDVOX for the rest of my days."

"Been there," says Bob M. "Doing that."

Hummer provides a word of encouragement. "You're finally realizing the important things in life," he writes. "RL is nothing, obey the Vox."

"Yes yes," cackles Tomwhore, "you must all be absorbed. . . . . Bandwidth is the carrier on which all the world will become voxaholics. Look to your minds."

"Ok," says Iggy, well on his way down the True Path (tm), "so my life (non-life) seems to be nothing more than who/newscan/post/who/archives/bye. my offline friends have abandoned me cause the phone can't ring. ppl at work hear me mention names like phiber optik, slowdog, phaedra, gorelord, reive and the legion of doom. they know i now spend my days tryin to hack the company's security program or any other part of the system that might contain info not accessible with my password. they keep their distance cause they're scared of me and watch me from the corner of their eyes. today someone came in to ask me something, saw my copy of applied cryptography on the desk, turned and walked out. i just read an article that informed me that the leader of vox was someone named tomwhore who wore a t-shirt with an eyeball on it and claimed that snarfs aren't good. hell, i even let my neighbor's dog post on BwF. so, i guess i need some advice on the state of my dementia. what stage am i in? what's next? thx in advance . . ."

"You have been assimilated," drones Tomwhore. "ENJOY THE OCCUPATION."

Or, as Dion says: Love Vox. Trust Vox. Keep your laser handy. There are traitors everywhere.

I'm hooked. Bohemian hubris swirls to the rafters of Bandwidth like pot smoke in an Amsterdam coffeehouse. I adore Vox. It's better than *Cats*. I want to dial up again and again. I even find myself buying into the tribe's we-they attitude toward other systems. Vox is *the* system. Accept no substitute. Other bulletin boards are rivals. I think the Chemist said it best: "Even if I think most of you are pink faggot leftist commie racist scumbags . . . . . I still love you and would hit anyone who looked you wrong upside the head with a BBB <big bad bat> because there's this weird genetic programming that goes haywire and makes me think of this as something cool. . . ."

Believe it or not, there is such a thing as online xenophobia.

"The Well in particular is not liked by most cyberpunks," the Chemist writes, in a separate diatribe on why Vox rules and the Bay Area's WELL bulletin board sucks. "It's *fake* and the people who hang out on it are yuppie wannabes. Beside maybe 100 cool people, its populated by poseurs. Vox's image in the underground is more of a mix, Patrick and Bruce came from the underground and still have a lot of friends there to go with the enemies . . . Bruce's rep has always been mixed up with pat's, same kind of deal. Ergo, for every dude who hates Vox, there's one who likes it. The

Well doesn't have that; its perception is as a bunch of yuppie scum-fuck granola eating wasteoids who need to get taught some lessons about how computers really work."

Gearhead is actually charitable enough to put the WELL and ECHO in the same league with MindVox before dissing them. "I have been on the WELL, ECHO and MindVox," he says.

I still have a WELL account although I use it rarely. Since these are the three on-line services that get lumped together by the press as "hip", they make a decent case study. Each of these services has its own rep - deserved or not. On ECHO, Well-bashing is virtually a religion. The general sentiment there (and here for that matter) is that the Well is a bunch of hippy-dippy, Dead-listening, Birkenstock-wearing, granola-eating, New Age-believing, West Coast nutjobs. "It's just too, like, *mellow* and *laidback*" say those who dis the Well. And we *all* "know" that ECHO is a bunch of feminazi stormtroopers laying down the PC law and unscrupulously stuffing flyers into books and magazines in bookstores (that is true. I found out about ECHO from a flyer in a book I bought at B. Dalton in the village). Personally I found ECHO to be populated by a bunch of over-educated, twenty-something snobs who are entirely too impressed with themselves. But that's just my opinion. And apparently, MindVox is the Hell's Angels clubhouse at the end of the universe and you better come armed and ready to do battle 'cause brother/sister you're taking your life into your

hands if you go down there. Of course . . . none
of the above stereotypes tell the whole story
about any of these services. And we all know that
the only way to get the real story is to go there
and make up your own mind.

Most of us are willing to acknowledge this. But still, a lot
of people freak out when Bruce pulls his little April Fools'
joke—he puts up the WELL's opening screen to greet us
when we dial in.

Microdot is positively distraught. "After i recovered
from the fright, and checked the # i dialed i tryed my nick
and password and it said 'welcome to the WELLcome con-
frence' then gave me back to vox. WHAT THE FUCK! Twi-
light zone?"

Seamus explains that "Bruce & Pat lost Vox in a poker
game last night. Poor TomW doesnt have a job now."

Wozz has an idea. "Someone with root here . . . go hack
on to well and transfer the entire contents of BwF into their
news spool . . . that'll confuse them. . . ."

I love intermural hacks. I catch myself praying that
someone will actually execute Wozz's suggestion. I picture
the confused faces of WELL subscribers, confronted with
Vox's gruesome ASCII iron cross.

It's like Ivy League rivalry. Voxers know that the WELL
is head and shoulders above most systems. Hell, a couple of
them even have accounts on the WELL. But that doesn't
mean they can't sneak out in the middle of the night, paint an
iron cross onto its football field, steal its mascot, and jeer at
halftime.

After half a year on Vox, I've recovered from the shell
shock of my initial exposure to the Net. I'm also developing a case of cabin fever. As much as I love the system, it's

beginning to close in—the same rants in bandwidth every day, the same people posting 95 percent of the messages in forums. They're interesting, fully spooked-out, smart and outlandish and all that, a great crew all in all. But everybody's pet peeves are general knowledge. It's like one of those seventies rabbit-hutch family sitcoms, *The Brady Bunch* or *Eight Is Enough,* except the parents have split and the kids are trying to work out some practicable anarchy and still running up the stairs and squawking, "MOM! He's being misogynist!" "Nuh-uh. She was raving." "DAD! They're being psychotic again!" Much hair pulling and sucker punching ensues.

I have to get out into the Big Pond again.

But it's nice to know that I can always come home.

dIGitAl YouTH

eponine (Catherine Skidmore) writes:

```
> The Internet is the arbiter of future culture.
>Yeah, right. A whole lifestyle made up of techno-
>geeks who blur the lines between real technology
>and futuristic metaphor has been appropriated by
>slackers who have too much time and coffee and
>too little to do.


>Too much time?! TOo much coffee??!! Too little
>to do???!!! That's my biography!
                  —+ slowdog@mindvox.phantom.com +
                      + Christopher Frankonis +
```

SOMETIMES, LATE LATE late, long after the middle-aged, mortgage-paying nine-to-fivers have dozed off to bed, the Net takes on a special, mutagenic charge. This thing, this beautiful, sprawling, crackling mammoth spiderweb *thing,* is now in the hands of basement dwellers, insomniacs, and teens with bedroom lights off and computers on. And it rocks.

A bloodshot sense of solidarity congeals out of the chaos. I keep scrolling down, down, down, through endless kilobytes of youthful disenchantment and roiling Net vernacular ("If you have a dumb lil' kid who is gonna set your freakin house on fire don' let him watch a show man, all of us are getting punished beacuse of some silly parent man. I hope someone important reads this message, like an MTV rep or something. Without FIRE we would be nowhere. FIRE KICKS ASS . . . FIRE FIRE FIRE FIRE FIRE FIRE FIRE FIRE FIRE FIRE FIRE FIRE FIRE FIRE FIRE FIRE FIRE FIRE FIRE FIRE FIRE FIRE FIRE FIRE FIRE").

For teens, the Net has an added bonus: parents don't understand and therefore fear it. What if junior uses this gizmo to break into Citibank or, worse, download naked GIFs of the Swedish Bikini Team? And what about all those people on the Net? You don't know where they've *been.* (Mom wrinkles her nose. "Honey, I don't want you hanging out with all those *cyber* people.") Cable, a sixteen-year-old hacker I met on Mind-Vox, was grounded, or rather, unplugged from the Net by his mom. "My mother has this notion that everyone on the Net is a child molester," he wrote to me, his aw-sheesh tone suggesting an impudent teen 'tude on the other side of the screen. When Cable's mother found out he was planning to meet a group of other (mostly teenage) voxers, she overreacted with typical maternal terror and banned him from dialing in. To his credit, the grounded console jockey managed to stay off-line a whole two weeks before sneaking back to the Net while his parents were out of the house.

"Finally," he says, "they let me back on under the agreement i use it a set time during the day, don't call/meet anyone on it, and that i get good grades in school."

It is axiomatic that as long as the Net freaks parents out, kids will spend countless hours on it. Nothing fuels the teen ego like a good old-fashioned generation gap. In fact, creaky technophobes are infinitely preferable to the bane of Net life, the dreaded boomer cyberpunk wannabes who crash through the Net making idiots of themselves. Running into one of these people is like confronting the proverbial dad in plaid who snaps his fingers, flicks up his elephantine lapels, and claims to be really "with it." It's creepy.

I once consulted a corporate vice president about the Internet. From his voluminous leather swivel chair, he dialed up America Online and was reading his e-mail when a phone call interrupted our meeting. Reaching over his executive desk pad and copy of *Wired* magazine, he picked up the receiver, grinned, and told the company president, "Hey, you'll never guess what I'm doing right now. I'm *surfing* on the *Internet.*" He looked at me. "This is really *cyberpunk,* isn't it?"

I blinked, struggling desperately to keep a straight face, then shifted to Plan B, the all-purpose coughing fit that had served me so well in junior high school. When the executive wrapped up his phone call, I let him down easy.

"Sorry to break this to you, sir, but there aren't too many cyberpunks in America Online." I respect the guy. I couldn't let him go on like that. Big online services, like discount shopping-club memberships and Ford Taurus station wagons, have their uses, but "cyberpunk carrying card" is not one of them. At the mention of CompuServe, America Online, or, God forbid, Prodigy, there is much rolling of eyes and gnashing of teeth among my peers on the Net (although AOL is gaining legitimacy). Here, Big Three means corporations who want to put mainstream America on the fabled "electronic superhighway."

"Electronic superhighway." God, it's like "grunge" or "Generation X," one of those buzzwords that trips over its own hype into the irony end zone. Even the word "cyberpunk" is kind of a Net in-joke now ("Woo-hoo, jACked iNto Plodigy, did you. How cYBerPunK!!!!"). It's like alternative rock. Once underground, it has now been officially exploited by The Man. With the media trying to latch onto the mirage of cyberstyle as assuredly as it's extruding Generation X articles, callow netters are having pop cultural bar codes stamped onto their foreheads. And it hurts.

That probably accounts for the reactionary graffiti I'm reading on the walls, posts about how lame it is to be young under a microscope, about technology, about the generation upstairs and how it got all the good toys first. Cyberpunk, built-in smirk notwithstanding, gives us a way to talk about the Big Picture. When someone born after the Beatles breakup writes, "Cyberpunk gives us an ability to be free. Technology belongs to the young, and we must exploit it to our advantage," it isn't just about cool sci-fi novels anymore, just as it isn't about nose rings and smart drinks. It's about dealing with the mess we've inherited. "Take a look around, pal," writes a University of Arizona student. "Open your eyes and crawl out from under your rock. The world isn't getting any better, and if you refuse to accept that, well, we'll just have to go on living without you. Cyberpunk is a way of dealing with a dysfunctional world — a world that we didn't make, and one that we aren't going to fix. It's not that we don't _want_ to fix it. We would, if we could, but we can't, so we won't. Nothing can fix this world, nobody has a secret plan to make it a nice place. We're all headed for oblivion, but some of us want to have our eyes open." Unglamorous, flawed young characters retreating to the fringes of a deteriorating and fragmented world: fact or fiction? Think about it.

This stuff gets more extreme every day. The Net's getting bigger. There's more and more light on it all the time. And that means Joe and Jean Suburban are going to find this place. The mainstream is coming. *Parents* are gonna crash this party. And in all likelihood, they will add insult to injury by bragging about how hip they are, once they get here. So naturally, the people who actually are hip in this self-contained underground universe are screaming, LEAVE US ALONE. Or, in the words of a long-burned-out rock outfit, don't try to dig what we all say.

The Net is one of the only fantastic things we have that our parents didn't have and, more importantly, that our yuppie uncles and aunts, who had *everything,* didn't have. It feels like our turf, whether or not our name is on the deed. We settled it. We live on it. And now we are being invaded by direct e-mail carpetbaggers, publicists, and online mall developers ready to "streamline" it for the consumer. It stinks.

In fact, few things rattle the tech-savvy Net community more than all this talk of corporations and Uncle Sam "improving" the Internet. If you can muster the brain power to learn a handful of UNIX commands, you can see the Net ain't broke, much less in need of windows, mouse-driven menus, and nifty animated screen icons. Having to use a "cleaner" Net sounds suspiciously like having to tidy up your room or else no car keys. Making the place idiot-proof just guarantees that more idiots will use it. Great. Now *that* would cure my Net habit.

Not that I or any of my strung-out Net-addicted ilk will have any say-so in the whole digital superhighway project when it happens. So why not Netsurf another hour? Tomorrow the all-night waffle house may be razed to make way for a multiplex.

Creeping commercialization of the Net, not to mention the prospect of sold-out hippies propositioning teenagers on IRC, has wedged open a generation gap that makes boomer-run networks into automatic targets. After the Bay Area WELL system was hacked, a few young technophiles of my acquaintance were downright gleeful. "Most members of Generation X who have nothing don't think that a bunch of hippie millionaires in California are all that neat," wrote one, taking generational credit for the break-in. "Given the chance to wipe the smile off their faces, they'll do it." His compatriot couldn't agree more, and even suggested a bigger heist, one that would give "new meaning to 'generation conflict'. I think that the Porsche drivers of Falls Church all deserve a bullet into their heads. Compu$pend, here we come. . . . Shall the assholes have their files forfe . . . err: forcibly removed, and learn that a revolution eats its children?"

The scary thing is, I find myself agreeing with a lot of this generational drumbeating. I find myself laughing at a sig that says "From all us Slackers to all you Boomers . . . HAHA-HAHAHAHA! WE HAVE SATELLITE MOUNTED RAIL-GUNS! HEH HEH. Who's laughing now?" The Net may reek of hormones and artificial preservatives, but at least it's a place where high school and college students can ponder a collective identity without feeling like handpicked quote-brats in some pudgy media lamo's Generation X article. As diverse as we are, the Net is a place where "we" actually means something, even if it's just a common comfort level with technology.

Sometimes it gets more personal and serious, like when a bunch of us sit around MindVox trading stories about the *Challenger* explosion — which classroom we were in, what we were wearing, and which teachers interrupted lesson plans, turned down the fluorescent lights, and stood beside televisions like Vanna White while one of their colleagues burned in midair. "I was 17, 18, i dunno," says Kieran. "Someone ran up the halls between classes and laughed saying 'fuckin' space shuttle blew up, haha.' That's when i saw it, and that's when the jokes about finding bones in the gulf of mexico all started, and that's when we all had to start watching video-tapes of the explosion time after time, and that's when the school hired therapists to come in and stroke our minds and even then i was thinking how 80's that was, instant therapists quivering in the wings. . . ."

Oddly enough, our memories of the Reagan shooting are fuzzy at best.

On the Net, we can commiserate. Some of us are really lost right now. "I'm afraid I'm having my mid-20s breakdown a year or so ahead of schedule," writes a graduate school dropout about to move back in with his folks and write computer interfaces at home. "I'm not sure quite what to do. I'm completely wired at the moment and can't do anything because I feel completely ineffectual. I don't have anything I particularly want to do. I don't want to be here but I don't want to be anywhere else either. My future is in flux and I feel like I have no say in the matter, god is playing dice with the universe. I need to have fabulous friends who will drag me to fabulous parties so I can get distracted and won't have to think. Or I need a woman, so I can pay attention to her and not to me. I'm watching too much TV and I could become an alcoholic if I weren't so embarrassed to go to the liquor store and buy a bottle of wild turkey. I need to become part of a post-apocalyptic culture of neo-primitives who will worship me as a god. I need to clean my room."

Angst wells up wholesale. Media-bashing is big. Gagging on "slacker" stereotypes is also popular. "I am tired of talking about Gilligan's Island, Saturday Night Live, and every other mundane piece of crap that enters our minds," wails a Washington State student strung out on smiley culture. The repudiation of any age-specific tag is de rigueur.

"Why does this generation need a unique identity?" asks "Johnny Fusion," as the "Nowhere Generation" thread spins around the bobbin of alt.cyberpunk. He answers his own question with a cynical flourish, "BECUZ, MAN! OTHERWISE IT WOULD BE BORING! If you aquire your identity from the past, its just a lazy cop-out. I mean what kind of identity is that? I mean it's like going down to the local circle-K and buying a can of preprocessed, ready made personality. (No preperation needed)."

The ubiquitous snack food motif. It keeps going and going and going . . .

And still, we wonder, fingers to the keyboard, faces illuminated by carcinogenic terminal emissions, what *is* this Generation X thing that newsmagazines are foisting upon us? Clearly, it means something to the marketing teams trying to sell us Subarus and soft drinks. But what does it mean to *us*? What does it mean *here*? "Generation X (tm) meant something once," ventures a twentysomething posting from "The Dangerously Whimsical Existential Terrorists, Inc."

First it was Billy Idol's old band. Later, in 1989 I think, it was the title of a book by Douglas Coupland about the lives of three fictional characters named Claire, Dag, and Andy who feature the Disaffected Bohemianism (tm) that has supposedly become the trademark of the Thirteenth/ Nowhere Generation (tm).

We supposedly are reconciled to the fact that we are not going to obtain a standard of living to match our parents. We supposedly are lost amid the flotsam and jetsam of fragmented culture. We supposedly live under the shadow of the Yuppie Generation (tm), waiting until they die of some new cancer caused by eating too much oat bran before we can come into our own. We are supposedly a generation adjusted to the factors that future-shocked our parents, adapted to an increasingly accelerated and temporary lifestyle.

All these things are true, to an extent. . . . But I really don't want to see a set of Generation X "uniforms" pop up, the way a set of alternative-culture "uniforms" have been popping up the last few years. Pity it's going to happen anyway.

Pity the same can be said for cyberpunk. I, for one, am bracing for the Seattle syndrome: the media designates a hip young "alternative" scene, and subsequent immigration renders the place unlivable. In the meantime, it's still a decent place to hang, sort of a global student union.

This is definitely not some kind of online utopia. We don't always get along. There are flame wars. There are food fights. There are ASCII graphics of Beavis and Butthead. But in a way, it doesn't matter, because the link is up. Hundreds of thousands of young people around the planet have managed to converge on this former defense department experiment and actually communicate with each other. We're talking amongst ourselves. We're listening to each other (sometimes). We're learning. I can hop onto IRC and find out what life is like according to twenty-one-year-olds in at least nine-teen time zones. I can sit around a MUD with students from Czechoslovakia, Germany, and New Zealand more easily than I can arrange a four-person dinner party in my own town. That may not add up to some grand vision of world peace, but who cares? At least the people who are going to be sharing this planet with me don't all seem so far away.

I didn't realize how accustomed I was to the Net, how attached I was to the idea of it always being there, until the following quote flashed across my screen: "We were born on it, and we got killed on it, died on it. Even if it's no goo, it's still ours. That's what makes it ours — being born on it, working it, dying on it. That makes ownership, not a paper with numbers on it."

John Steinbeck. *The Grapes of Wrath.* It was part of an electronic signature. And even if the Net is no good, and even if the digital youth don't have the title and license in their hot little hands, in a way it does belong to them.

But the Net is good.

It is also goo.

ZenMOO

Shhhhhhh. . . . . .

Amid the smell of incense and the sound of gongs and chanting, you have come upon the glorious Zen MOO. Please be quiet, and enjoy your meditation.

If you have performed meditation before, type:
  connect <your meditation name> <your meditation password>

If you wish to join the meditation and are new, type:
  create <a meditation name> <a meditation password>

But type softly!

I SCRAMBLE FOR information.
     "Help."

"Hair will grow on your palms if you keep typing," says the ZenMOO.

"Who?" I ask, hoping for a list of people who can tell me more about this place.

"Will you stop the infernal racquet and meditate!?"

With serene indifference, the MOO informs me that I am the only person logged on and that I have been idle for a measly sixty seconds, an extremely poor showing. I am off to a lousy start, and my Zen track record will surely suffer.

I demand to know who is in charge.

The MOO shrugs.

"But . . ."

"Enlightenment does not require a keyboard."

"Look."

"You are too restless to continue meditation," it says. "Come back later."

*** Disconnected ***

Disconnected? Dissed? Kicked out of the chapel for fidgeting? That's it. I am determined to beat this thing.

I download a copy of the ZenMOO guide and peruse it for clues.

"Hello, and peace," says C. Regis Wilson, the ZenMOO's author and custodian. "The internet is a holy thing, it is a sacred thing, it is an internet thing. Any intrepid internet citizen knows of the mystical nature of the internet."

Yes, I nod. Zen follies notwithstanding, I have fallen into a kind of mysticism about the Net. It's an easy thing to do when you clock a serious amount of time on-line. For one thing, the Net seems bigger on the inside than it is on the outside. You can walk into a virtual cocktail party inside a castle inside a fishbowl inside a dollhouse inside a Neapolitan villa in cyberspace. It's fractal — the more you wander around, the faster the horizon seems to roll away. And so the Net universe expands, both by extending rhizomes to the great unwired masses and by burrowing into its own crevices. Net changes the way you think, just with the knowledge that there's a world buzzing through phone wires, past the houses and office buildings of oblivious multitudes. The Net can conjure Christmas cards and maybe even chilled carbonated beverages out of the ether. It's a reminder that there's more going on beneath the surface of things, and that just because something is invisible doesn't mean it's not real. Pretty heady stuff, considering that the first thing Net replaces is mind-gelatinizing television.

"However," Wilson continues, "there has been a lack of real spirituality on the internet. There's Gopher (which is not very spiritual), Archie (a brutal, Deity-less barbarian), MUDs, MUCKs, MUSHes, and on and on. Where is one to find mental tranquillity and spiritual rest and relaxation? You have found it, if you have found ZenMOO. ZenMOO is dedicated to meditation for the weary internet wanderer. Your first reaction will be to look around, or see who is connected."

Exactly. That's what I did. I read on.

"Do not do this. Do not type anything. Simply take a deep breath, crack your knuckles (if you have any), and wait. In a few seconds, your breathing will become regular, and you will feel very relaxed. Perhaps a wise saying will appear for you to read and meditate upon . . . Continue to meditate. When you are more relaxed, and able to move slowly and deliberately, you have several commands at your finger tips. Be very careful not to type too much, however! I would suggest typing only once a minute. You must be very still, and very peaceful, or you will disturb the other meditators. If you are disruptive, you will be kicked off!"

Ah, I think. This will be a snap. I'll just log onto the MOO, go fold some laundry, run a few errands, and be declared Zenmaster of the Day.

Wilson has anticipated this. "Now, to make sure that you are really meditating, and not just in another shell," he explains, "you will be asked a question or riddle from time to time. You will want to answer as quickly as possible, in order to keep from appearing asleep. Students have dozed off during meditation and been booted, loosing their vital idle statistics, and living in shame . . . From time to time, to facilitate the meditation, wise sayings will be printed for your reading, meditating pleasure. Some sayings will be wise statements, but others will be mantras, computationally formed to maximize the meditation relaxation and spiritual healing. To get the full use of the mantras, try reading them as a chant, concentrating on the breathing and tempo to synch your spiritual energies."

This is going to be more difficult than I originally thought.

But less than an hour after my metaphysical TKO, I am ready for another round. I'm pumped. I'm lean. I've flipped through a volume of Lao-tzu I bought and neglected to read for some long-forgotten class.

I telnet into the incense and gongs and chanting again and wait a good forty-five seconds before typing "score."

"Activity through inactivity," chides the ZenMOO, before spitting out a four-column score chart of ZenMOO Top Meditators: names, total idle time, cumulative connect time, and the vital idle-to-connect-time ratio that separates the true ZenMOO masters from restless worshipers who log the hours but lack enlightenment. The top scorer, Testman, has been idle 61 percent of his 456 hours of total connect time. Brian-san, in second place, has only logged half that time but has racked up a whopping 168 hours of quality meditation — a whopping 91 percent idleness ratio. This is some serious slack.

I wonder if anyone else has ever tabulated a Zen scoreboard. It's so counterintuitive that it almost makes sense. Next thing, I'll be seeing Team Zen MVP announcements, trading cards, pennants, and Dharma Pump high-tops. I contemplate the existence of a Dalai Lama rookie card and try to imagine what such a thing might be worth, with or without its original stick of gum.

"Mmmm . . . gum"

"Your typing detracts from your enlightenment," says the ZenMOO.

I'm prepared for this. I know what to do. Just ride it out. Just don't type for the next thirty seconds. Chill.

"Your noyoufool drowning brains if fellatio vooba unborn kasyapa would asses."

"Excuse me?"

"You are too restless to continue meditation. Come back later."

*** Disconnected ***

Knocked out by a gonzo mantra. TKO.

Round three. This time, I have company. A netter named Shy, who is batting .500, although he (she?) has only been logged on for two minutes. The next thing I know, she, it, whatever, has fallen asleep — that is, failed to answer one of the ZenMOO's questions.

"Two monks stand simultaneously and drag Shy out. A piercing scream is heard," the ZenMOO announces.

I'm alone again.

"I can here high as with money, not as zloty bunnies," says the MOO.

Not this time, pal. I wait, calmly biding my time before typing "inventory."

"You are holding emptiness. Your fingers will destroy your meditation."

I try moving north. There is nothing. Blackness. Or rather, blankness. There is an absence of description—not even acknowledgment that I have moved at all. I haven't bumped into a wall or any other obstacle. The ZenMOO doesn't tell me I *haven't* moved. But it makes no discernible difference. There are no points of reference to judge the distance. Wilson describes this place as "a chamber in which one has no senses. Thus, a black void comes to mind, or even a confined room, but without windows or doors. There are others around you, and you will sometimes hear a discussion, or you will envision a particular activity being carried out, or a wise and profound saying will pop into your head, but the important part to remember is that it is *all* in your head. For, to look around is to be punished for opening your eyes, but to close your eyes is to be punished for sleeping. Thus, the phrase 'Generic Empty Nothingness' comes to mind. Everyone sits around and meditates. Some better than others. There are those who sit still and remain active for hours; others who, once they are connected fidget for a few seconds and are escorted quietly out."

Apparently, one person's piercing scream is another's quiet departure.

"Enlighten me on the difference between none and samadhi," asks the ZenMOO.

My first question. I don't know the answer, and yet it is imperative that I respond, lest I be kicked off for dozing.

"I don't know."

"Thank you wise one."

Chalk one up for the kid.

Wait a minute. I have an idea. What about putting an artificial intelligence on the MOO? Surely someone could program a bot to simulate "activity through inactivity?"

Apparently not, claims Zenmaster Wilson. "I have learned to recognize the automata," he says, "and have caused them to do what I call 'a backward march.' I have fine tuned the balance between activity and lack thereof. But in the end, I can do nothing to help people when they do not want to be helped."

"Tires explain loud, see loud maya and river feel yabba atisha," splurts the ZenMOO.

Whatever.

I try moving south and find nothing but a warning: "Once a student typed too much and died."

"I hair but you roll so maybe the is not from for compassion, or Zen.

"Maybe you nothing with calm. Until lame nothing will anger but for never if noself has any triloka to say about silly.

"Mystia thinks on lumping, not unlike Kaldari thinks on want."

I ride out this set of gibberish mantras and wait for question number two of the fill-in-the-blank, no-wrong-answers Zen quiz. But I wonder, where did the MOO get these jumbled strings of nonsense? There seems to be some syntax, but either the author has access to an alternate plane of verbal logic or the MOO itself is ladling out dollops of chaos.

As far as I can tell, it's a bit of both.

"If janice were being, show me what luxembourg would be," it asks.

"Brigitte."

"Thank you wise one. Halt is like thinking of luxembourg, not stuph, because unborn is user. Truth is unto work for atisha. When house and eye come to pass, frenum will bring sever with omantra for more fun. Bar equals fellatio and fellatio equals vaisali but bar does not equal vaisali," says the MOO.

"Score."

"Hair will grow on your palms if you keep typing."

I haven't even charted.

"Fill in the blanks for "To consider _____ above _____ is to spine Lao_Tzu."

"Glass, water," I type.

"Thank you wise one. When bacca considers avalokita, brian-san is not thinking of twisty . . . Stepacal disagrees with zonker with regard to silence. Not help running, samadhi running nor and buddha why vimalakirti bhudda."

I wait. And wait. And wait, until I begin to physically nod off. It is, after all, the middle of the night.

"Whyfore the sppo for zonker, ask I you."

It's just pixels on the screen. I am catatonic. It's too late.

"Sad, so sad when you fall asleep like that. Tsk Tsk."

*** Disconnected ***

I refocus my eyes. Damn. At this rate, I'll never make the ZenMOO Top 20. So I drag myself back to the incense and the gongs and the chanting, in the wee hours of the morning.

"A gong sounds quietly and a voice intones, 'Wang-Hsui has joined the meditation.'"

Aha. Someone else. Maybe I can talk to him. But first, what does he look like?

"Look Wang-Hsui," I type.

I see nothing but a scrap of Zen catechism — "Activity through inactivity" — and the cryptic "I can't lawguy my za-phod, nor my very with my lips."

"What is the nature of dsfoom?" Question number three.

"This is just to say," I type. Damn, I'm hungry. I root around for the box of Sugar Smacks that's buried somewhere under the Post-it notes and fanzines. I can't find it.

"Thank you wise one," drones the ZenMOO.

I inquire about my inventory again. I've answered a few questions, after all. I've made progress. Haven't I earned Zen-MOO brownie points or something?

"There is nothing. Save your breath," answers the MOO.

"Look here," I say.

"Will you stop the infernal racquet and meditate!?"

I can see where this is heading. I'm not going to be thrown out again. If I have to leave, I'll find the door myself.

"Quit."

The ZenMOO chimes a benediction as the door swings shut.

"May you meditate as well in real life."

*** Disconnected ***

I'd call that a tie.

InCOmPletEviLlE

ANIMEMUCK IS A MUD all done up in Japanese animation — everyone in it is one of those wide-eyed *Speed Racer*
gaijin cartoon characters. It's a mock-Japanese neighborhood, all laid out in a grid. Only, it's palpably unfinished.

I knew when I logged in that patches of it are still under
construction, but I didn't expect to feel the rough edges. I
guess LambdaMOO's landscaping has spoiled me. On the
AnimeMUCK, I can feel the limits, the ragged corridors that
lead into blankness, the streets that suddenly become empty
and featureless. It's as if the virtual reality tapers and breaks
in places. Once you get away from the two main hubs, you're
on a ledge. I suppose LambdaMOO thins out like this eventually — you just have to walk much farther before you hit the
border.

The first hub on the AnimeMUCK is where you land, a
room whose "walls and ceiling are nothing but flickering
white static, reflected in the glossy, black surface of the solid
floor. In each cardinal direction stands a portal; the static
within each is a different color. To the north is a portal carved

out of stone; dragons and phoenixes battle along its granite flanks, and the ruby eyes of the kirin's head above the lintel glitter down at you. To the east lies what appears to be a fairly normal set of double glass doors, like one would find in any modern high-rise. South is a cast-concrete archway on which have been spray-painted countless names and unintelligible (yet likely obscene) slogans in objectionable colors. In places, the concrete has been chipped away, and the re-rod shows through the fractures. Finally, to the west, a trapezoidal portal of shimmering silver and blued steel sparkles in the skittering light cast by the walls of static around you."

Players congregate here and usually go directly to hub number two, the ABCB Café, Chat Area Central (CAC). Do not pass go, do not collect two hundred dollars. I decide to take a walk instead, north, down Main Street, past the housing project for homeless cartoon characters, past the MUCK's administrative office building and into a chilling roadblock. "There is more of the city to the north," it says, "while there is a void to the south." Please continue to suspend your disbelief as you sidestep the void.

I keep walking, skirting the empty patches, turning west onto Orange Street, down a few blocks, and into the Green Castle apartment complex. The lobby "seems to have been designed with 'drab' in mind as the room does nothing to inspire your imagination." The elevator, "about what you would expect for an elevator in a medium rent apartment in Japan, clean but more than a bit spartan," empties me out into a hallway that announces itself as "rather drab and uninspired, design wise. There is very little to distinguish it from the other floors except that there is an ice machine rumbling away quietly at the end of the hallway."

The dreariness of the place is a shock. Of all the possible accommodations the tenants of the Green Castle apartments might have dreamt up, they *choose* to inhabit a badly lit prefab Motel 6. Incredulous, I poke my nose into the apartments to see if their dingy exterior camouflages palatial accommodations. But no. These dinky crash pads have managed to hybridize a Japanese space premium with blue-collar middle-American decorating sensibility. They have knickknacks. They have hanging houseplants and sofas and describe themselves as "comfy." They have kitchenettes! For God's sake, why?

Flabbergasted by the luxury gap, I step out of the Green Castle apartment complex and onto the orange Neko bus that has conveniently pulled up to the curb en route to the CAC. I later discover that the orange Neko bus is always at your disposal, whether or not you are actually on the street. It doesn't matter if you're tumbling along the outer ring of the half-completed space station — the orange Neko bus will vroom up out of nowhere on command and deliver you to the Chat Area Central, a small, upbeat brass-and-fern joint with restaurant art and banquettes. Door chimes twinkle when you step in. Everyone waves. For all intents, it's a Japanese Bennigan's.

The AnimeMUCK population clusters here to talk. They don't venture out as much as other mudders do — the subdivisions of their world are still being built. The ABCB Café is at least solid, somewhere they can congregate between construction shifts.

The door chimes twinkle behind me as I leave to measure the gaps — out into the street over the Matsumoto Avenue Overpass, where the wind "is somewhat pleasant, if you ignore the smog factor," and to the intersection of Matsumoto Avenue and Kimagure Road, where you can hear the sounds of highway traffic coming from the east.

I have to hand it to the directors. Their pet world isn't large enough really to surround you, but the noise and pollution make it seem somehow more real than LambdaMOO's wonderland. Laurie Anderson once said that virtual reality is too clean—people won't believe in it until someone figures out how to put the dirt back in. The wizards of AnimeMUCK are certainly giving MUD cinema verité their best shot, applying touches of grit here and there, spritzing grime into the corners, painting graffiti onto the walls and cracks into the sidewalks, retrofitting the flaws to ape an unglamorous reality. The question is, will people really want to vacation here? Maybe the things that make virtual environments more "real" are precisely the things we're trying to forget when we visit them. Do we truly want to "escape" to a realistic MUD, or do we just want the virtual half of virtual reality?

Things that make you go hmmm . . .

I ramble down Orange Road until I see another apartment complex, this one a little more tony. The elevator is high-speed. The penthouse floor is explicitly exclusive ("Only the owner and a select few have apartments up this high"). The open terrace "has several seats scattered about for just sitting and chatting while looking out over the picture perfect view of the city below. A service Boomer looms in the corner attending to your every need. This area seems like the perfect place to get a group together and just chat."

Service Boomer. I like the sound of that.

I wonder if players across town at the Green Castle apartment complex dream about someday movin' on up to the deluxe apartments in the sky, here on Orange Road. I still can't get over this social class construct in the absence of economic scarcity, material goods, or money.

"You found a yen!"

I take that back. There is currency here. It pops out of nowhere and jumps into your pockets. It is a function of time, which makes the AnimeMUCK economy even more surreal, since everyone has the same job — combing restaurant tables, hotel lobbies, and upholstery for enough spare change to buy a luxury penthouse in the Orange Road apartment complex.

I tip the service Boomer on the terrace and let myself into a few penthouse suites to check out the upscale Anime-MUCK accommodations.

"You open the large, ornate door and step into . . .

```
Out in the Country
Apparently either someone has recreated a hill-
side on top of the northern wing of the apartment
complex, or you just stepped through some kind of
magical portal. All around you, you see signs of
nature. There is grass, flowers, trees, and even a
small pond off to one side here (perhaps a swim
is in order). In a small grove of trees to the
north is a cabin.
```

Ah, another Pine-Sol commercial. These turn up again and again on MUDs. Give a mudder a blank piece of real estate, and he'll build himself a farmhouse in the English countryside. I've lost count of the times I've walked through a MUDhouse door and straight into a Pottery Barn catalog or the windswept vistas of Ralph Laurenville.

I'm curious about the pond (you never know what you'll find underwater on a MUD). I take one step toward it. Then the MUCK takes over.

"Tearing off all your clothes, you plunge head-first into the clean, cool waters of the pond. Even though that you are slashing about in the pond, the water remains crystal clear. On normal occasions you would delight in this . . . except that you are now nude."

I hate it when software undresses me. There are a lot of these little pitfalls in MUDspace — programs that put you on automatic pilot and tell you what you're doing, what you're feeling, and whom you find irresistibly attractive.

"Out," I type, hoping the pond program will have the decency to return my clothes.

"You hop out of the pond after your tiring, but fun, swim. Deciding not to put your clothes on until you are dry, you lay down on the hill beside the pond to sun dry." I bet the guy who owns this place has invited every babe on the MUCK over for Sunday barbecue ("Hey! A pond! Gosh, you're naked. Relax while I get us some margaritas").

Having drip-dried, I stroll around the cabin to the built-in stream, where everything is in quotation marks. "You find yourself surrounded by a dreamy scenery of a Beautiful Streambank all about you — a gentle and comforting 'wind' blowing by, bright warm 'sunshine', green forestery everywhere . . . ever-glittering 'stream' as the little 'waterfall' and sparsely placed 'rocks' break the peace that might have been. You walk upstream, occasionally skipping the pebbles across the stream. Soon, you approach a little town . . . and the trail ends as it turns about a cabin."

Like everything in this place isn't already equipped with implied quotation marks. I check out the "cabin," only to find the owner asleep in his bed, then traverse the great indoor outdoors back to the penthouse hallway and into another apartment. It has been ransacked, the boards turned up, the walls splintered, and the windows smashed. Only the television remains intact. I take a closer look at it and am instantly absorbed by the screen and shunted back to the room where I first landed — the dark space facing colored static and doorways. The TV is a wormhole. I half expected it.

That's one of the first lessons you learn on a MUD: screens are not to be taken at face value. They never just radiate light. There's always something else, some trick. The same goes for mirrors, glazed windows, even glasses or puddles of water — any reflective surface. They always take you somewhere.

Standing back where I began, I wonder how much more of this smog-ridden, jerry-rigged MUD I want to see. I punch up the help file, which tells me,

```
Remember, no matter how bad it gets, you can al-
ways go home.
home
There's no place like home . . .
There's no place like home . . .
There's no place like home . . .
```

Right. There's no place like Vox . . . er . . . home.

kIeRaN

KIERAN, FLOATING THROUGH the Net like a twenty-four-year-old ghost, has found me, and he wants to talk. He's at his parents' house in West Virginia over Christmas break, but he could be in Timbuktu; geography has no meaning here. Buckaroo Bonzai's tautology suddenly makes some kind of causal sense: wherever you go, there you are. No, really.

Kieran spends all his time on the Net, usually on Mind-Vox. No job, no friends, nothing but Net.life and an online support gig with CompuServe. Offline existence, where his name is Aaron, has atrophied almost to nothing, and now there's only Aaron's spirit on the Net — Kieran — dolefully rattling his chains for attention.

He got it once, in the middle of an online conference with Vice President Gore. Surrounded by a pack of reporters and industry wags, Kieran raised his voice to ask the vice president about the danger that citizens will get lost on the information superhighway and circle, slack-jawed, in a holding pattern while the real world passes them by. In other words, would the National Information Infrastructure zombify the American public into creatures like himself?

Immediately, the *Christian Science Monitor* and the *Washington Post* pounced on Kieran as Net Man on the Street (tm).

He's *always here.* He haunts this place.

The weird thing is, for someone who spends so much time wired into Vox, he seems to despise it wholeheartedly. He rants continually about persecution at the hands of "the little Vox clique" without realizing that he's a core member of it. Even on the Net, he styles himself an outcast.

```
*Kieran* if you want to talk, I'll be on #sabine
```

Private message on IRC. I swim out of MindVox's central pot of text soup and into Kieran's hidden channel. #sabine is an unlisted and invitation-only grotto that Kieran conjured for a girl—Dana, aka Newt, the eighteen-year-old darling of the "Vox clique" Kieran loathes. Newt, Newtt, Newtling, the Newtlet, constantly dandled and lovingly teased, she is the belle of the bandwidth forum, and Kieran made #sabine for her, a gesture oddly reminiscent of the class weirdo picking flowers for the most popular girl in school. I don't think anyone else has been on #sabine.

```
*Kieran* okay
>This is sabine, as in Griffin?
<Kieran> yeah . . . it's my private channel with
+Newtt
<Kieran> so what do you think of me :)? I assume
+you've been wandering Vox for quite a while.
> You and Newt are pretty good friends?
<Kieran> in theory, EXTREMELY good friends
```

<Kieran> but she's not talking to me now
> I have reserved judgement on you. But . . I
+can't square yer rep with the way you act
> You've been a pretty decent guy as far as I can
+tell . . .
<Kieran> Is that a compliment?
> Of sorts.
<Kieran> which is the rep, and how do I act, to
+you anyway?
> Not that I would take anything in there seri-
+ously
<Kieran> Well, once you get a rep, it's very hard
+to shake. And there are a LOT of self-righteous
+blowhards here.
<Kieran> It's kinda sad . . . I've gotten lots of
+email from people who think I'm getting rail-
+roaded, but nobody will post publicly about it.
> Why "in theory?"
<Kieran> in theory about what?
> About being extremely good friends w/ Newt
<Kieran> oh . . . because she's not talking to me
+. . . she and I have had a VERY strange year on-
+line . . .
> Why?
<Kieran> . . . and she's got this quasi-
+objectivist mindset . . . she likes to be able
+to label and pigeonhole everything
<Kieran> and she can't pigeonhole me . . . so
+she's backed off.
> Have you ever seen her?
<Kieran> I think we're both in love with each
+other . . . I'm afraid to admit it because I'm
+afraid she'll run away . . .

\<Kieran\> . . . and she won't admit it because
+it'll fuck up her "philosophy" to do so.
\> Why would she?
\> Run away, that is.
\<Kieran\> only pictures . . . we were supposed to
+spend next week in NYCtogether . . . but she
+copped out
\<Kieran\> because she has a boyfriend, an EXTREME
+objectivist
\<Kieran\> and she's so iffy on me now, if I sprang
+that on her . . . . you know.
\> The campus objectivists always seemed so cult-
+ish to me.
\<Kieran\> they are . . . they're fruitcakes . . .
+one step away from cults is exactly what I tell
+her.
\> She's pretty cool, though
\<Kieran\> I never said she wasn't.
\<Kieran\> I care for her very deeply.
\> Oh wow . . . I'm remembering her references to
+a Net.relationship in forums. I guess that was
+you.
\<Kieran\> yeah, it was me.
\> But you've never actually seen her ftf.
\<Kieran\> no, I haven't, but I long to.
\> What's it like, caring for somebody you've
+never seen—but talk to all the time?
\> This medium is so ghostly.
\> Sometimes I just feel like we're all ghosts
+rattling around in here
\<Kieran\> I'm being interviewed, aren't I? \<g\>
\> It's just something I've been thinking about.
\<Kieran\> we are . . . what's it like? Painful . . .
+DEEPLY painful.

<Kieran> I've got a $500 phone bill from talking
+to her over last semster
<Kieran> to me she's no longer a "net.thing" . . .
+she's a real human who I want so BADLY to meet,
+and be with, and just be able to TOUCH.
> I guess, it's sort of the logical extreme of a
+long-distance relationship
<Kieran> But at the same time, it's a good thing
+in a way . . . without the net she would never
+have spoken to me in the first place.
> But . . . It's not the same
> It's profoundly different in some ways.
<Kieran> especially consider that I'm no adonis,
+not by a long shot
<Kieran> right . . . she's alwways AVAILABLE (as-
+suming she'll TALK) . . .
<Kieran> . . . and you get to know their soul be-
+fore worrying about their face, their weight,
+their clothes, all the BULLSHIT.
> See, my contradiction is the opposite. I think
+people tend to underestimate my brain in person.
<Kieran> I can't imagine how, unless you put on a
+ditzy front.
<Kieran> you seem like the epitome of everything
+I want my daughter to be . . . hell, of what *I*
+want to be . . . and I don't even know you.
> It's not a front, really
> It's just who I am when I'm out socially
> You know, Texan girl, bubbly, hair, that all. . . .
<Kieran> well, most people *are* , well, "lower"
+on the scale, for lack of a better word
<Kieran> so when socializing, dumbing down is a
+good thing
<Kieran> I can't do it, and look at me.

Surfing on the Internet

<Kieran> . . . who's already made more of a name
+for herself than most people will in their en-
+tire lifetime.
> I don't think about all that stuff . . or try
+not to. It doesn't seem real.
<Kieran> It's *all* I think about.
> The whole New York machine. I don't live there.
+It's not real.
> Why do you think about that stuff?
<Kieran> I dunno . . . you have to realize
+you're talking to someone with absolutely no
+friends, and no career, and no hope of one.
+My POV is really on the other side of the
+fence.
<Kieran> Because when I was growing up, and never
+had any friends, my parnts kept telling me, over
+and over, "You're better than them" . . . and I
+AM . . .
<Kieran> . . . I could do ANY writing/reporting
+job TOMORROW if someone would give me the
+chance.
<Kieran> Most other people from my school are
+living in goddamn trailers married with three
+kids already.
<Kieran> And yet I've FAILED. . . . every day I'm
+told, "It'll get better". And it never has, or
+does.
<Kieran> I just hate the fact that every choice
+I've made in life seems to have been wrong . . .
+I should be fucking ANCHORING at 24. I don't
+even have a clip.
<Kieran> And I CAN DO THE WORK. . . . I just
+don't have the contacts, because I never had any

+friends, because my parents were hermits . . .
+it just keeps going back.
<Kieran> This dickshit from my HS journalism
+class got hired at the local paper the day after
+he graduated HS.
<Kieran> He's a JERK, and he COULDN'T WRITE . . .
+every paragraph ended in, ",he said."
<Kieran> Of course, he's still there 5-6 yrs
+later . . . but it's all who you know.
<Kieran> and there are so many other things I
+want at the same time.
> What else do you want?
<Kieran> friends . . . a girlfriend . . . a mod-
+est amount of fame, just to be a known entity in
+some area/field . . . a social life.
<Kieran> everything I've never really had be-
+fore. . . .
<Kieran> I jsut want a feeling of contentment . . .
+to go to bed feeling "I DID something today",
+rather than just crying or dreaming or some-
+thing.
> What's your opinion of yourself?
<Kieran> That I've failed.
<Kieran> I failed my childhood, I failed
+adolescense, I failed my college years, and
+pretty fucking soon it's gonna be too damn
+late.
> how can you really succeed or fail adolescence?
<Kieran> easy . . . you have no friends, and ac-
+complish nothing, just sleepwalking through the
+yers.
<Kieran> I mean, I just want to have a live where
+the phone rings, people drop by to visit, where

+I'm doing something I enjoy and that's worth-
+while.
> That's not a lot to ask for
<Kieran> Last semester in NEw York, NOBODY ever
+came to my door who wasn't delivering food . . .
+not one single person.
<Kieran> It gets to a point where you essentially
+don't exist.
<Kieran> I know it's not a lot to ask for. That's why
+I can't figure out how I've fucked it up SO badly.
> You seem kind of . . . negative. It can be a vi-
+cious cycle, you know?
<Kieran> lagging again
> Major lag. Hold on a sec . . .
<Kieran> i'm not negative . . . I'm scared. I'm
+lonely.
<Kieran> ok
> I'm back.
> I just had to get something to snack on. I was
+starving
<Kieran> that's fine :)
> But kieran, you're honest. That's good.
> What are you scared of?
<Kieran> I keep hearing about this "vicious
+cycle", but nobody ever says anything to get me
+out of it.
<Kieran> Spending the rest of my life alone and
+anonymous.
<Kieran> Dying alone.
<Kieran> Never making any contribution to the world.
> That's like what I said before, about the Net.
+There's all these people . . . but you're so
+alone at the same time.

> It's very slick, the Net, very cold.
<Kieran> exactly . . . you know, most of the time
+I *hate* this fucking Net. But I have nowhere
+else to go.
> No matter how warm the sentiment, you can never
+touch anything.
<Kieran> Exactly.
> It reminds me of that Police song (I was a to-
+tal teengirl fan of the Police) . . . Message in
+a Bottle
<Kieran> Christ, I long to be touched.
> Where everyone's alone on their own little is-
+land.
> Only, they're alone *together*
<Kieran> heh . . . the 80s . . . the 80s were so
+much better than today.
<Kieran> until technology surpassed humanity.
> But it's strange how the humanity kind of flick-
+ers through
> Like you.
<Kieran> And I don't even feel like a part of the
+group HERE.
> But it's all through glass, or yeah, just the
+*screen*
> It's almost like a cage
<Kieran> God, I'm a fucking nut case, arent I?
> Not from what I've seen.
<Kieran> Thanks . . .
 * Kieran blushes slightly
> You make sense from your situation.
> The world's insane is all.
> Kieran, you are sort of an existentialist hero.
> For the 21st century.

\<Kieran\> I just wish I could go back to NYC and
+be a damn desk assistant . . . I'd be so damn
+elated.
\> What is your day to day life? Like, what's your
+day?
\<Kieran\> Actually, you know what I really always
+dreamed of?
\<Kieran\> A profile of me. , . . in something like
+the New Yorker . . .
\<Kieran\> not out of ego or anything . . . I al-
+ways just wanted to actually be able to read a
+5000-word article on what I am to the outside
+world.
\<Kieran\> I always wanted that.
\<Kieran\> my day? right now (home for break): wake
+up 8 am, drive mother to work, but breakfast at
+McD's . . .
\<Kieran\> come home, eat it. . . . then around 9
+am, go visit my grandmother, or go to bed if I
+was up on this damn thing really late
\<Kieran\> around 11-12, come home (or wake up) . . .
+maybe get lunch, maybe do CompuServe duties
\<Kieran\> read the paper, watch TV, lounge until
+3 . . .
\<Kieran\> then go pick up mom and dad . . . 4:15,
+computer or nap
\<Kieran\> 5:30 eat . . . then cigarette break
\<Kieran\> then watch tv rest of night, alternated
+with computing . . . then bed
\<Kieran\> repeat.
\<Kieran\> lather, rinse, repeat.
\<Kieran\> and try to push the dreams out of my
+head that keep me from falling asleep.

> What do you dream of?

<Kieran> all the things I've talked to you about

> Oh, you mean plan-dreams, not sleep-dreams . . .

> Do you ever get nightmares?

<Kieran> yes

<Kieran> but not very otfen

<Kieran> usually my dreams are better than real-
+ity . . .

> My last boyfriend used to dream that people
+were trying to kill him.

<Kieran> uh, no, I don't have that problem. :)

<Kieran> "last boyfriend". . . . god, what a con-
+cept . . . more than one lover.

> He wasn't a real stable puppy. Cute, but . . .

<Kieran> Cute's all that matters.

<Kieran> Or money.

> He had a sorrow about him.

<Kieran> So do I, don't I?

<Kieran> just not the cuteness.

> I miss him. He's on the lam now.

<Kieran> As in legally?

> As in legally

<Kieran> what did he do?

> I went away for a week, for Thanksgiving, and
+when I got back he was gone, stolen a car with a
+frien and drove it up to Jersey, and then the
+cross-country stealing spree . . .

<Kieran> oh, that's nice.

> Yeah, but this guy had a way of looking at me . . .

>I'm glad I wasn't in town when he skipped,
+though. If he'd have pulled up in a car and
+said, "Honey, do you want to take a trip?" I'd
+have been gone.

Surfing on the Internet

> So, do you normally live in NY?
<Kieran> yeah . . . I was supposed to go back
+yesterday, but I don't want to leave home yet.
<Kieran> and nothing's waiting for me there, so
+there's no rush.
> It's funny, you and I can both do our jobs from
+anywhere
> Very 21st century lives.
<Kieran> what job? :)
> Your CompuServe thing.
<Kieran> oh yeah, that . . . not a job though,
+just volunteer work
> What's your favorite snack food?
<Kieran> Chips Ahoy cookies
<Kieran> why?
> Snack food is a motif that shows up all over
+the place in my book.
<Kieran> uh, okay.
* Kieran shrugs in confusion
<Kieran> I just don't see the connection between
+snack food and whatever it is you're doing.
> It started with this completely out-of-hand
+thread in alt.cyberpunk.
> When the whole Time cover on cyberpunk broke,
+and everyone was scrambling to define it, and
+themselves.
> It got to the point of absurdity: What is the
+cyberpunk band, what is the cyberpunk way to
+dress, what is the cyberpunk *snack food*
<Kieran> "Cyberpunk" is nothing but a damn fad
+anyway.
> Right, like a snack food. Great packaging,
+empty calories.

\<Kieran\> I've been on the Net since 1982. Fuck
+the rest of hem. . . . I don't give a damn if
+some of them were hackers or did dumpster diving
+or anything.
\<Kieran\> I'm still more of a veteran than them.
\> What was the net like in '82?
\> You were what, 13?
\<Kieran\> Let them have their supposed "under-
+world". I'll stay where the action that's IMPOR-
+TANT takes place, thank you.
\<Kieran\> 12.
\<Kieran\> Ever used Bitnet Relay Chat?
\> No.
\<Kieran\> in all upper case, 40-column?
\<Kieran\> That was cutting edge.
\> I've seen it, old records, printouts. Wild.
\<Kieran\> Bitnet's an educational net . . . much
+lamer than Internet, and quickly being absorbed
+into extinction today.
\<Kieran\> But we had that goofy little Chat (which
+still exists), mailing lists, etc
\<Kieran\> And CompuServe too.
\<Kieran\> For me, I was jsut happy to have friends
+thorugh it.
\<Kieran\> I never gave a single damn thought to
+"wow, I'm talking to people from across the
+WORLD!!" . . . it was just, "this is kind of
+fun . . ."
\<Kieran\> I took the technology in stride . . . I
+didn't (and don't) give a damn about that . . .
+as long as it works, good.
\<Kieran\> I just took over a dormant account and
+had some fun, that's all.

<Kieran> That's why all this psedu-cyberpunk,
+"cutting edge" WIRED-is-God bullshit pisses me
+off so goddamn much
<Kieran> THERE IS NOTHING NEW ABOUT ANY OF THIS
+EXCEPT THE SIZE OF IT.
<Kieran> the technology hasn't even changed that
+much! What are we using now? DUMB TEMINAL EMULA-
+TION!
<Kieran> the SAME SHIT FROM 15 YEARS AGO.
> Plus, it's becoming increasingly idiot proof,
+which in a way is bad.
<Kieran> (Ooh, I'm ranting.)
> In some ways it's good but . . .
<Kieran> just fun talking . . . participating in
+mailing lists . . . I was a bit of an amusement
+to some, since I was so young.
> What was your social situation like then?
<Kieran> Same as today, nonexistent.
> So Bitnet was then what vox is now, in terms of
+chatting with people.
<Kieran> well, the people were nicer on Bitnet . . .
+more spread out . . . most all had work to do
+too . . . Voxers are trying to be a part of
+something the media has labelled "cool".
> What is the best thing about Net, for you?
<Kieran> And Vox has a lot of self-centered,
+self-righteous jerks on it.
<Kieran> On Bitnet, you could just ignore people
+like them . . . today, they're CELEBRATED.
<Kieran> Meeting Dana.
> The human contact thing.
<Kieran> yup . . . there's little here I couldn't
+get faster and better on CompuServe

<Kieran> except for her.
> When you think of her, what do you think?
<Kieran> and the occasional person like you.
<Kieran> I think of the two of us crashing a Vox
+party together, hand in hand, her dressed in the
+most alluring dress imaginable . . .
<Kieran> . . . and showing them all what real
+class is about.
<Kieran> And then leaving.
<Kieran> And going back to my apartment and
+watching Mystery Science Theater 3000. . . . and
+having an INFINITELY better time than they did.
<Kieran> You heard about the New Year's Eve Mas-
+sacre, I assume.
> No.
<Kieran> Those that went to the NYC New Year's
+VoxMeet got stoned out of their MINDS on god
+knows how many drugs/drinks, and it basically
+turned into a flat-out orgy.
> Omigod.
> Who was there?
<Kieran> Learning about that did so much to help
+me stop being *as* depressed about this place,
+because now I know they're really not a very
+high class of humanity.
<Kieran> Um . . . reive, freed, tomwhore, cass
+(who was disgusted and left),
> That's about the third time you've said "class"
<Kieran> damn, I'm blanking out
<Kieran> about 14-15 ppl
<Kieran> oh, eponine, enzyme
<Kieran> and more
<Kieran> whatever happened, it was so bad that

+they all swore to never discuss it with those
+who weren't there.
> Or maybe they're just teasing everyone.
<Kieran> No, I don't think so.
<Kieran> I think it really happened.
<Kieran> It's too big to be a joke.
<Kieran> I have to go to bed in a minute . . .
> Okay, I'll let you go.
> It was good talking to you.
<Kieran> Will we talk again?
> Sure.
<Kieran> And regardless, everything said here is
+not to be brought up with other Voxers.
> Needless to say.
<Kieran> let 'em read it in six months.
<Kieran> You really intrigue me.
> Why?
<Kieran> why? Because you're almost everything I
+always wanted to be . . .
<Kieran> . . and yet so secretive.
<Kieran> Besides, everything intrigues me . . . I
+feel like I know so little about life, anything
+I come in contact with I want to know.
> Curiosity is good . . .
> If you weren't curious you'd just be old.
<Kieran> But . . . whatever. The interview ends,
+and you disappear, and I'm just here alone in my
+room again.
*** Signoff: Kieran (irc-2.mit.edu polaris.ctr.
+columbia.edu)
(1:52am) [Phantom Access Technologies, Inc.
+(TM)] (? for Menu)

Phantom Access Technologies. Phantoms with access to technology.

The interview is over, but Kieran signed off first. I'm the one sitting alone in my room at two in the morning. I'm the one left to sound out the hollowness of an empty channel. I feel a bit hollow myself. It isn't even fatigue, just the bitter aftertaste of Kieran's spirit and a grim predawn insight.

On the Net, we are all, functionally, ghosts.

WeLComE tO tHe beEr
cOMmerCiAl

THREE-FIFTY-FOUR A.M., I hit NAILS, a MUD operating out of the Rutgers University supercomputer. NAILS bills itself as a rock and roll MUD and "The Best Damn Thing on the Internet." I log on as Curve, which is the band I'm listening to. Curve's female lead singer epitomizes the look I strived so hard to achieve in my days as a skinny, Smiths-listening teen goth wannabe, and I describe myself as I was then, "a pale-skinned girl wearing Doc 8's and a little too much black eyeliner. A leather motorcycle jacket hangs from her bony shoulders." I pause. I'm hungry, and there is nothing edible within reach. . . . "and she looks ravenous."

The MUD drops me into a "large, dark room. The only light is a bulb hanging directly above you, which only serves to blind you. Four guys in business suits stand around smoking cigarettes and drinking coffee, making vague threats in the hopes of getting information from you. You wonder how long you can take it." It's the Federal Bureau of Investigation, Office of J. Harrison Burkett. Nice touch.

After promising to turn informant and enter the Witness Protection Program, I am released and tumble out onto an avenue lined with neoclassical buildings. "The offices of the FBI lie to the west, and the grand Shell station, with the imposing attached Kwik-Mart, form a bulwark of stateliness to the east."

The convenience store beckons with the siren song of Slurpees, Blow Pops, kooshpies, and Captain Crunch, so I cruise up to the Shell station (Chevron lost its concession recently). "Luckily," the MUD informs me, "the latest governor has banned self-service gas, so you don't have to wait in line for an hour and a half while corpulent women buy 5 boxes of powerded donuts, frozen lasagna, and caffeine-free diet soda as they argue with the scrawny kid at the register. Just get yer gas, pay, and zoom away."

I press on, passing into the heart of the MUD's business district and stumbling into a centrally located "Gentleman's Nightclub" discreetly tucked into a sidestreet. Onstage, a dancer "gyrates back and forth across the stage as slow, sultry music oozes out of the speakers; she tosses her hair and smirks. People sit and sip their drinks, staring intently at the stage as waitresses glide around refilling. The noise level rises and falls with each movement of the dancer, becoming quite loud when she peels off another piece of clothing."

"It's a beer commercial," I tell Anybody, who's idling in the strip joint's basement spa.

"Your absolutely right . . have you been over to Afterfive?" After Five is another MUD, famous, or rather infamous, for its social ambiance.

"No. What's it like?"

"alot of folks just looking to TS over there," he says.

"Huh?"

"Talk dirty over the computer to each other = Tiny Sex or TS." Anybody smirks.

"This place is pretty raunchy too, tho."

"Im sure you can get enough of that anywhere you post your handle as Female."

"You got that right."

Nodding, he says, "I bug the hell out of guys cuz i didnt fill in if I was male or female . . and I have two different descs . . here look"

```
look Anybody
A handsome blond, 22 with Ice blue eyes looks
back at you. His ripped jeans tight around his
waist. His button down shirt half way open
Anybody morphs into his cat form
look Anybody
A light brown cat.
```

"so . . . most of the time I actually just leave the CAT desc and it drives em nuts."

This doesn't surprise me, because NAILS is about two things: babes and sports. And babes. Not to mention sports. This place plays like a montage of Superbowl coverage, MTV, and Coors commercials. It even has an arena, the Darrin Fletcher Colosseum Amphitheater, a hexagonal stadium that is home to almost every athletic franchise in the area. "Baseball, football, boxing, soccer, lacrosse, and who knows what else can all be found here," I'm told. "Designed to support the future addition of a climate-controlled dome, it may be home to hockey and basketball as well once the funding goes through. There is a sports channel broadcast booth, a general manager's office, and all the trappings of a mammoth sports entertainment complex."

I stroll out of the stadium, somewhat impressed. Down the road, office workers lunch al fresco in the sweltering summer heat. Young female executives perch on benches and pick at their food. Construction workers ogle them. The MUD points out that there are topless cheerleaders frolicking at a busy intersection. I know I will regret this, but I type "look topless cheerleaders."

"Sure, other muds let you build. Sure, other muds let you program. Sure, other muds don't have bots that curse at you. But do other muds have babes with hooters like these?" asks the MUD. "Give it two weeks, and NAILS will have 50 players on at any given time."

I was asking for it.

Further west, I ramble through the seedy stretch of Incavaglia Avenue, where "boom boxes blare and reverberate across the street, occasionally drowned out by the stereo of a passing Camaro with the windows rolled down. Kids play baseball in the street, accompanied by the continual sound of breaking glass. The Catcher's Mitt diner with its shatterproof windows is to the north. Brunettes with bright red lipstick, hair down to their waist, and skirts down to about the same place sashay down the sidewalk while cops cruise right by the double-parked cars in front of the nearby Italian restaurant."

One block west, the Fantasy Showbar offers another, even sleazier strip show. "Angel, the Dancer, is 5'10, thin, and well endowed. She looks you in the eye, says, 'Howdy, Stranger,' and pulls your head into her huge breasts. Diana, in a bra and garter belt, takes you by the hand and seats you right in front of the main stage. You look to see two of the most beautiful girls you have ever seen, Courtney and Vegas, swaying to Stevie Ray Vaughan's 'The Sky Is Crying.' Vegas comes over to you and kisses you on the cheek." Courtney, by the way, is described as "an incredibly beautiful woman, completely nude and exclusively for you. Courtney is six feet tall with long, straight blonde hair that reaches her butt. She has a firm pair of 38 d's and a smile hotter than Hades! If you would like a Sweetheart Dance with her, just ask the Management."

I wonder whether the women's studies department of Rutgers has any idea what's going on in their basement. I wonder whether the P.C. gestapo will picket strip joints on the information superhighway. I picture their red, knotted-up faces as they stomp into the MUD's Police Squad Headquarters, only to find a prominently displayed girlie calendar.

Cheesecake, athlete hero-worship, and rock video posturing are the sine qua non of NAILS, which features a den of iniquity at the north end of town — the infamous Morrison Hotel, "which looms before you through waves of heat generated by the shimmering sun." Through the thick double glass doors of the lobby, a sudden blast of air conditioning and the concierge automaton greet you. Rooms are available on a semi-permanent or temporary basis, and they're all decorated with a different theme.

I take the elevator to the second floor, where the hallway is painted in fluorescent, psychedelic colors, and temporary rooms lock from the inside. I wonder how secure they are. Now that everyone is freaking out about e-mail taps and government trapdoors in the National Information Infrastructure, it's not too hard to imagine illicit meetings on the outskirts of some obscure MUD, or in some ratty virtual motel room. In a bazaar of virtual worlds, there'd be thousands of places to hide.

But for now, the Morrison is the Net's very own Madonna Inn, the hotel where every room is a new and tawdry adventure excessive enough to merit a segment on *Lifestyles of the Rich and Famous*. In Room 201, "moonlight is accompanied by the distant sounds of music from the Big Band era. The gentle scent of lilacs come waltzing in through the open windows, and hide themselves in the corners of the room. Loosening your dressing gown, you sketch out a few dance moves, before turning back the covers on the elegant Edwardian bed." In 204, gauzy draperies "billow and sway from some hidden breeze. In one corner of the room, you find a low platform bed, covered with pillows, large and small. A sweet music fills the room, and your senses are ignited by the smells of bitter coffee, and honey-soaked bread. You barely notice the heat that seeps in from the outside, caught, as you are, by the more sensual pleasures of the room." Vending machines in the hallway dispense soft drinks, birth control, and candy. Room 203 is the Jungle Room, complete with vines, fronds, chirping lovebirds, and a bed of leaves that "seem to call you into their soft embrace."

MUD microclimates are mind-boggling. Seven doors down from the sultry tropics, Room 210's ski lodge accommodations include a large stone fireplace and a picture-window view of falling snow.

No scenery, however, can match the intrigue of Room 207, where a loud rap on the door is accompanied by a burly voice yelling "Customs. OPEN UP."

The Morrison's polymorphous playground and its garish toon-town environs seem tailor-made for unabashed and blatant cruising. NAILS even lets you know when someone is checking you out, unlike most MUDs. I discover this when a character named tripl-XXX gives me the once-over:

```
[tripl-XXX looks at you.]
tripl-XXX's tires squeal on THIS curve.
"This MUD tells you when someone's giving you the
once-over?"
tripl-XXX gives C the twice over
[tripl-XXX looks at you.]
tripl-XXX says, ". . . . RAVENOUS . . . doll"
tripl-XXX lights a match to Curve.
```

I light a cigarette off it (too many old movies) and then leave before tripl-XXX gets a chance to live up to his name. I cut through the Morrison Hotel parking lot, with its array of fantasy muscle cars, and walk straight into two NAILS chicks in the throes of gossip.

"Now, are you going out with dan?" asks Melody. "I havn't heard the latest."

Yupa, who describes herself as "YUPA!!! she slices! she dices! she makes perfect julienne fries every single time!! best of all, she's completely dishwasher safe, and if you order today, you'll also receive ABSOLUTELY FREE her personal collection of bellybutton lint!! operators are standing by, so call 1-800-YUPAYUP today!! batteries not included. void where prohibited," blushes, "uh . . . . well . . ."

"That must be a yes."

"Yes, dammit!! a thousand times yes!!! i love him dammit!!!"

"How fantabulous," says Melody, jumping up and down.

Yupa apologizes for being melodramatic. I ask who Dan is.

"He's yupa's bfriend," Melody answers, "a nice guy."

A train rumbles beneath the street.

"An evil being from another planet," says yupa, "otherwise known as my main honey. He's watching me type this, or i wouldn't be saying these things about him."

"Where are you?"

"Ripon college, of scenic ripon, wisc . . ." she answers.

"i'm in the poopy state of A," types Melody.

"oops."

"that was WA. i'm fond of my surroundings can you tell?"

"hey, melody," Yupa says, "do you think i should do something illegal and morally wrong?? dan wants me to let him in here . . . on my account . . . while i'm logged in already."

I leave Yupa and Melody to their computer ethics debate and wander into the NAILS Central Trust Bank, "an imposing stone fortress of a building. Everything in here is grey or white—from the grey carpeting to the grey pinstriped suits of the employees . . . A steady stream of be-tied and power-suited people stream in and out . . . Although the occasional hippie wanders in from time to time, this bank is dominated by the high-powered corporate elite."

MUD financial institutions and their nonsensical money supplies baffle me, considering that there are usually only a dozen things to buy in a virtual world and maybe two ways of earning MUD money.

Hey, wait a minute. These are the islands they talk about in Intro to Macroeconomics. I vote we corral all the economists and strand them on some MUD.

Vivien the Bank Teller, a conservatively dressed blond, bears a striking resemblance to the young Hillary Clinton. Except, Vivien is an automaton.

On second thought, this just adds to the impression.

"Ok," she says, "I transfered 2050 smackeroos to your card. You now have 6565 smackeroos on your card."

Benedict teleports in. His desc quotes Roger Zelazny: "Benedict, tall and dour, thin; thin of body, thin of face, wide of mind . . . He had a long, strong jaw and hazel eyes and brown hair that never curled."

Vivien the Bank Teller says, "Ok, I transfered 200 smackeroos to your card."

Vivien the Bank Teller says, "You now have 543 smackeroos on your card."

Vivien is looking more and more like Hillary all the time.

Benedict mutters, "hiya. How do I look?"

Vivien tells me she's transferred 800 smackeroos to my account. I now have 1843 smackeroos on my card.

"You look like you should be working at a record store or cappuccino bar," I tell Benedict. He looks at me.

"What?"

"Relax, it was a compliment. All the coolest people work in record stores and cappuccino bars."

Benedict asks me if I work in one.

"I was bartending at a wine bar/cappuccino joint for a while."

"Did you like it?"

"Yeah, it was kind of cool. Ever since I saw Sex Lies and Videotape, I'd had this fantasy of being a bartender."

Benedict mutters, "During breaks, I work in a—forgive me—McDonalds. Good reason for bartending."

"So what was it like?" I ask.

"What was what like?"

"MCDonalds."

"Not as bad as you'd think. When you work with the right people. When you work with Idiots, it's much worse."

"How old are you?"

"18," he says. "You?"

"22 .. Where are you?"

"Wisconsin, land of belching cows," he says. "Yes, I mean the women 8-) Carthage College, just outside of Ke-nowhere, WI."

Benedict tells me to type "sit" and see what happens. I oblige.

NAILS says, "Curve grabs her portfolio, straightens her lapels, and sits in a soft flexible seat at the side of one desk. The loan officer sits down on the other side, and reaches out for her folder. 'Hrm,' she says. 'You dont come from these here parts, do ya?'"

I suggest that the wizards have had a run-in or three with financial aid people. Benedict agrees, "It would seem so."

Fonzie teleports in.

I wonder aloud, "Is it me, or do parts of this MUD seem like a beer commercial?"

Vivien the Bank Teller says, "Ok, I transfered 9348 smackeroos to your card."

Vivien the Bank Teller says, "You now have 102736 smackeroos on your card."

"Yeah," Benedict mutters, "they doo."

Fonzie teleports out.

My bank balance is on a roller coaster. I'm rich now. I decide to leave while I'm ahead.

Just outside the FBI building, Kirk and Jacques are in the middle of a stand-up fight.

Kirk says, "you got a problem dude. don't piss me off"

"You are a problem," says Jacques, and "Why not?"

"Run a way from your problems like you do in your rl life," Kirk scoffs, "you coward."

"I don't run away."

"Yes you do. you know you do."

"No I don't," says Jacques. "You don't know me. Watch it, Kirk, I have friends in high places. . . ."

This fails to intimidate Kirk. "Don't run to your friends," he sneers, "confront me yorself."

"If you are going to be a jerk," says Jacques, "don't do it here on Nails . . ."

"i am not, but you are. You started this thing."

"Okay," Jacques says, "where do you live? I'll come down and meet you face 2 face."

"You wouldn't want to. Why did you call me a jerk," says Kirk. "i want an answer."

"Cause you are . . ."

"You asshole."

"DOn't piss me off," says Jacques. "I am crazy enough to come down and kick your ass in person. Last guy that pissed me off had 4 ribs broken."

I tell Jacques to prove that in MUDspace. This posturing is so stupid. These guys can't do anything to each other physically. Hell, they can't even do anything to each other digitally. So they just stand there and insult each other until one of them (Kirk) gets bored and leaves.

"What was that about?" I ask.

Jacques tells me I don't want to know. "Pissed off Kirk because he was being a jerk."

So I page Kirk and ask him what they were fighting over and where he went. He's noncommittal, but tells me where to find him. So I head over to "a room lined with rust-orange carpet and littered with spent nine millimeter casings. A very large knife has been slammed viciously into a wall, with cracks jittering nervously away from its point of intromission." And there's Kirk, sporting sunglasses, a T-shirt, knee-length brown shorts, and a killer tan. He looks at me and asks if I need something to eat.

"Sure. What do you have?" He hands me a soda and a ham sandwich.

"Thanks."

"Its a fucked up world curve. . . . fucked up." Kirk gets a vodka and some ingredients to make a screwdriver. "Take off your jacket make yourself at home."

Kirk makes two screwdrivers and hands me one.

"What's your story?"

"I left home two years ago," he says, "never seen my parents since."

"Where are you from?"

"i told them to fuck off, cuz they were always ruining what i was planning."

"nowhere,, absolutely nowhere," he says, taking another sip of his virtual screwdriver.

I ask, "A cold place or a warm place?"

"warm. why do you care? it doesn't matter. Califronrnia. one summer, i wanted to drive across the country, i wanted' to see what was outside of buffalo."

Factual inconsistency flag. This isn't making sense, but I can see where this story is going.

"And your parents 86'd it."

Kirk is speechless (Well, he's not *actually* speechless. He says he's speechless. But we ignore these little paradoxes in MUDspace).

"what?"

"your parents fucked it up."

"yep. then the second time i did it . . . now here i am."

"And here is where?"

Kirk says, "here is here . . . i ain't happy tho. its like a present that you expect to be awsesome and whnen you open it up bingo its a bunch o f socks. its lonely. . . . . he he. . . . think of that . . . L.A> a city of a couple million people, and i am fuckin lonely."

"L.A. is the one place I vowed I'd never move."

"you still hungry?"

"Yeah."

Kirk gets me another virtual sandwich. I tell him about the *Weekly World News* cover that's taped to my door — "L.A. Quake Opens Gates of Hell."

"There's this really cool doctored photo of a demon rising out of the Golden State Freeway."

"i ve seen it," he says. "i love that news. your pretty unique. this couch opens into a pull out bed . . ."

"Thanks for sharing."

Kirk raises his eyebrow. I ask him if he's really got a tan, and he says yes. I ask him how old he is, and he says twenty-three.

"So what's your damage, Kirk. What's the tragedy of the day."

"do you know the attraction to virtual reality??" he asks, and then adds "tragedy is i lost $200 dollars at a b-ball hustle. i screwd up all my shots . . ."

"Tell me."

"we can act out every instintct ind inside of us, without consequence," he says.

"Are you sure about that?"

"for instance," he continues, "i can do this . . ." Kirk picks up a bottle and throws it across the room, smashing a picture. "yes i am sure . . . we deny ourselve in rl."

The bottle disappears the moment it hits the wall. There's no impact. Everything goes back to the way it was. I remember finding a cassette tape on the sixth floor of the Morrison Hotel. New Kids on the Block's greatest hits. The MUD needn't have told me I felt the urge to smash it. When I did, NAILS played verbal footage of me grabbing the tape and, "with a sense of holy destiny," smashing it repeatedly into a nearby wall: "A couple hundred pieces glitter pleasantly on the floor, and the two reels roll toward opposite ends of the hallway. As you grin dazedly, a white blinding flash overcomes you, and as you stagger back against the opposite wall, your vision returns and you note dimly that the tape sits again, intact, where it originally lay. You sob brokenly." The tape always goes back to its original state as player after player finds, then smashes it.

"And here you can be anything you want," I tell Kirk. "is that it?"

"yes."

"So what's the difference between you in rl and you here?"

"i am a coward in real life, i am not ambitious," he says. "here i am . ."

"I don't understand that."

"why not?"

"Where's the gap?"

"gap?"

"you are what you are."

"no i am not what i seem."

"so what *are* you?" Kirk tries to kiss my hand. I demand a response.

"Answer. The truth."

There is a long pause. Finally, he says, "i am no one."

"Define that."

"my name is adam, i live in buffalo."

"i am 19."

"i have no tan."

"You remind me of someone," I say.

"who?"

At that precise moment, I hear a click, and my modem connection cuts off for no apparent reason. The computer screen lights up with three symbols and five letters confirming that I'm no longer on the Net.

I think, "I have a real life. What the hell am I doing here?"

rEtUrn tO LAmBdaMoO

I'M IN THE LambdaMOO Coat Closet again, the familiar dark, cramped huddle of coats, boots, sleeping bodies, and newly arrived guests who grope blindly for the doorknob. Only this time, I'm not a guest. After a few weeks on the waiting list, I have been granted a digital green card. I am a legal resident on the MOO.

But I'm not quite ready to emerge into the brightness of the Living Room. I have no description. I need to give myself some kind of shape.

"You hear a quiet popping sound; Teal_Guest has disconnected."

"Plaid_Guest opens the closet door and leaves, closing it behind herself."

"Periwinkle_Guest teleports out."

First things first. I type "@gender female."

"Gender set to female. Your pronouns: she, her, her, hers, herself, She, Her, Her, Hers, Herself."

"Red_Guest has connected."

I start to type again, "@descibe me as . . ."

"hi," says Red Guest.

"Hi." Preoccupied, I return to the Silly Putty of my MUD persona.

"Petit_Pompier springs forth from your pocket in an unexpected way."

He nods solemnly. "'ello!" He bounces up and down. "whats up?"

"I just got a character. I'm messing with the name and desc."

"oh, cool :)"

I flip from description to description like Jane Jetson trying on new outfits by remote control. I'm a Factory bit player with frosted hair and spaghetti straps. I'm a gum-snapping mall rat from Hell. I'm a *Hollywood Squares* contestant you've seen a million times but just can't place. I'm the girl in green who bears a striking resemblance to Eustacia Vye. I'm Samantha Stephens's zany lookalike cousin, Serena, on *Bewitched.* I feel vaguely larval.

I shift into a description of my physical self, or rather my defining physical characteristic, The Hair. (I have big hair, approaching Janowitzian proportions.) This description fits well enough, snug but not too tight. But I need something else, a signature tag of some sort.

I look across my real-life room to a shopping bag lying on the couch. I have finally capitulated to life in South Beach. I've bought a pair of rollerblades. I pick up where I left off and type, "She wears a pair of streamlined rollerblades that glint with the aura of speed. She tortures taxi drivers just for fun."

There.

"Need any help?" asks Petit_Pompier.

"No," I say, "I just want to be the Rollergirl in that Dire Straits song."

"Does anybody know anything about the comet hitting jupiter?" asks Periwinkle_Guest.

Petit_Pompier smiles at me and sings, "sipppin' on gin and juice . . ."

Rogue teleports in.

"Petit_Pompier slips you some LSD. You sing eerily, 'Goodbye cruel world, I'm leaving you to day . . . goodbye, goodbye, goodbye . . . goodbye all you people, there's nothing you can say to make me change my mind . . . goodbye . . . '"

"You feel something brush against your ear. psychotron is here."

"my heavens," says Teal Guest. "all this activity."

"TEal type open door and see the world," suggests Purple_Guest.

"how does one move about here?" Teal asks. "Better yet, WHERE does one move about to?"

"Just type OUT," says Purple_Guest.

Teal_Guest opens the closet door and lets itself out.

"Petit," I say, "I just set my desc. Look." He looks. Rogue looks. Pompier giggles. Purple_Guest calls a taxi.

"lookin' good . . :)," says Pompier.

The_EggMan has connected.

The_EggMan opens the closet door and leaves, closing it behind himself.

Duchamp has connected.

Petit_Pompier giggles at you.

You hear a quiet popping sound; Duchamp has disconnected.

"ive always wanted rollerblades," says Pompier.

Purple_Guest watches as the meter starts.

LANDRO arrives with fanfare and asks, "Any babes in here??" He smiles at me and thinks aloud, "you have one AWESOMELY *gorgeous* butt. *wink* ;>"

I wonder if Thorin is on the MOO. I page him, "Are you home?"

"Ahhh, no," he answers.

"I was copper Guest. You showed me around. remember?"
I'm getting claustrophobic in the Coat Closet. I step out
into the Living Room. A few seconds later, Thorin steps out of
the closet and waves hello, and then disappears.

"You hear a faint electronic ringing, a mobile-phone
slowly fades in . . . You answer it, Thorin is on the line. He
pages, @join me"

Sisyphus exits to the north.

Carbondale pages, "Can you say, Toro toro taxi? :) "

When I get to Thorin's place, he gives me a warm welcome and a hug.

"Well I've arrived," I say. "I'm not a guest larva anymore."

Thorin says, "Sorry, but I have no idea who you are . . . I
met *SO* many guests, it's very hard to remember them
when they get a character. Please give me a brief idea of what
we did?"

"I logged in as Copper Guest. You took me around, to
Down Under. I was timed out by my system."

Carbondale is looking for you in The Hot Tub. He
pages, "Halleulah! Here she comes! :) I'm trying to think of
other lyrics to that damn song! :) "

"I took you to the graveyard," I say. "There was a skeleton."

"Ahhhhh," says Thorin. He laughs, "Gee and I thought
you were male . . . ."

"I kind of suspected that."

"Yeah, that's alright."

"Well," I tease, "I know how you *Australians* are."

Thorin grins, growls, then morphs into his tiger character, Shiro, who gets on the sofa and lies down. As we talk, he
tries to bite me and I smack him on the nose. "Be nice. Don't
bite." He cringes.

"So," he says, "what do you want to be able to do?"

"What do you mean?" I ask.

"Like morph, wear clothes, change size. . . ."

How about a MUDhouse, I ask.

"Oh sure, got a name for it?"

"The Loft."

"Type @dig The Loft"

Suddenly it exists, and I'm there.

"You notice a protruding slash in the air . . . Shiro bounds out from it as it melts away in black smoke. . . . ."

"Okay," says Shiro, "now you need features . . ."

"Features?"

"Do this; @addfeature #30203," he says.

"What will that do?"

"It give you some verbs . . . like hug, wave, some talking ones . . bonks etc. That's stage-talk."

"What's stage-talk?"

"It would be easier if you didn't ask me, and just type it. You can trust me."

"OK, I typed it. Now I can stage-talk . . . But what does it mean?"

"Type: -shiro Hi."

I do so, and the MOO says, "Rollergirl [to Shiro]: Hi."

"I see. Thanks for teaching me this stuff. Pardon me for acting like the bride of Frankenstein."

After adding feature #40842 (Social Verb Core and Feature Object), feature #62397 (A few more social-type verbs), feature #44471 (Social Information Feature Object), and feature #36714 (Carrot's social interaction Feature Object), I'm all souped up.

"Done."

"Okay, type; feelings," says Shiro, "this piece of spam is some social verbs." I carry out his instructions, and the MOO lists the emotional gestures of which I am now capable. Shiro ruffles my hair, salutes me "in the manner of the Courts of Chaos," tiger-hugs me, and then switches into his human form and makes a pass. I skate to the other side of the room. I've seen this movie before.

Thorin is not happy.

```
Thorin glares at you.
Thorin declares himself totally pointless and
silly.
Thorin sticks his nose up snootily at you.
Thorin quietly buries you in stones.
Thorin slices you REAL THIN and tiles the floor
with the result.
Thorin is not pleased with you at all.
Thorin takes out a previously-unseen bucket of
ice water and dumps it on you.
Thorin's kiss fills you with an everburning pas-
sion which consumes your heart, leaving you
breathless and wanting more . . .
Thorin throws his head back and cackles with in-
sane glee!
Your passionate kiss with Thorin seems to last
forever, and you don't want it to stop.
Thorin falls down laughing.
Thorin fixes you with a withering glare of contempt.
```

"Quite a mind reader," I say. "How suave. Not."
He blushes, and I skate even further away.

```
Thorin wraps his arms around you and hugs you
tightly. You feel comfortable in his warm em-
brace . . .
Rollergirl wonders if Thorin needs anyone for his
```

conversations. He seems to have scripted both
sides.
Thorin paves you and puts up a parking lot.
Thorin prods you with a high voltage cattle prod.
Thorin bops you onna head.
Thorin pulls out handcuffs and cuffs you to the
nearest available heavy object.
Rollergirl reassembles herself and skates around
the parking lot, laughing.
Thorin frowns sternly at you.
Thorin sighs. He doesn't understand you.
Rollergirl sticks her tongue out.
Thorin throws you out the window.
Thorin stamps his foot and sticks out his lower
lip at you.
Thorin holds you in a warm and tight embrace.
You enjoy this intimate closeness with Thorin.

"Shyeah, right," I say.
"Don't you dare even think that," he warns.

Thorin dunks you in a cup of boiling hot
water.
Thorin blames you, screaming "IT'S ALL YOUR
FAULT!!!!"
Thorin rolls his eyes at you.
Thorin crushes you with glee.
Thorin shoots you through a previously-unseen
basketball hoop.

Rollergirl laughs at Thorin's histrionics. She shrugs and
skates away.

Ooh, MUD harassment. Think I'll have to see a shrink about this. Not.

Sticks and stones and techie-boys who can't deal with women, that's what MUDs are made of.

onE FOot In thE OffLIne WoRlD

I'VE STARTED USING the phrase "offline world" recently. This disturbs me, because the "offline world" is what I used to call "real life."

It's not that I've given up a Real Life (tm). If anything, I'm overcompensating in that department just to prove I'm not one of those Net dweebs who never goes out (Get back at 2 A.M. Net for a few hours. Nap. Work. Nap. Go out. Repeat). Preserving my Real Life (tm) is a point of pride. I'm giving up sleep instead.

Still, something shifted, somewhere back there, when I started qualifying addresses and phone numbers as snail (as opposed to electronic) mail, and voice (as opposed to modem) numbers. Before I found the Net, I never stopped in front of a television and thought, God, how *one-way*. I didn't rail at the infernal lag of the postal system (well, not often). The idea that I can't cherry-pick whatever information I need out of the ether, anytime of day or night, is increasingly unpalatable. I mean, three *days* to get a document from one end of the country to the other? It's outrageous.

But IRC doesn't equal face-to-face conversation (or phone conversation for that matter). And e-mail doesn't equal paper letters. And I want those pieces of crushed wood that someone's hand has actually touched. I want documents that aren't copies of anything. I recognize the difference. I want it both ways, and that doesn't mean the sideways smilies I've been scrawling in personal correspondence (scary). I want more-faster-now and I want it to be the real singular thing, too. And I know that's impossible. So here I am, with one foot in the world of pencil scrawls and hissy analog tapes, and the other foot in a place where anything can be counterfeited and copied endlessly without a trace of deterioration.

In the offline world, I have objects. I have the thousand shades of information that tell me that someone's been in a room or that a cup has been broken and glued back together. The Net has nothing like that. What it has is speed and liquid information. It obliterates physical distance. I get e-mail from Slovakia. Scandinavia's knot of Net sites is, in a way, closer to me than the telecom desert of the upper Midwest. I can link into a New Zealand file server in less time than it takes to buy a newspaper at the local convenience store.

And so the Net and the offline world recast each other all the time.

Like, I'm just now noticing the minutiae that keep us from killing each other, because we don't have them on the Net. There are no facial expressions, no vocal inflections, and no body English. On the Net you face ideas in their most potent form—brain to brain. It's quick, but it's risky. As Mike Godwin at the Electronic Frontier Foundation wrote in *Wired,* "The problem is not that ASCII is too restricted a medium—the problem, if anything, is that text says too much and that the medium is too intimate! Flames are the friction born of minds rubbing to closely together. . . . The problem of flaming is not that we don't understand each other. It's that we understand each other all too well. We're mainlining each other's thoughts."

There are so many mental bullets flying through the Net that sometimes it seems to have a consciousness of its own. The zeitgeist isn't buried in the drop of a voice or an enigmatic gesture. It's right in front of your nose, all spelled out. But it's more than that. The Net has a kind of temperament — the little lags, the splits on IRC, the bots, the ghostly architecture that seems more haunted than occupied. It's so goddamned easy to anthropomorphize the thing — if it's lagging, to say that it's sluggish, or that it's awake or asleep depending on how much traffic runs through it. The more time I spend on the Net, the more I find myself anticipating its little tics. Sometimes the Net can seem downright organic, even as its users apply computer terminology to themselves. We search our mental hard drives for files not found. We open and close cerebral desktop folders. We talk in a mixture of signal and noise.

And despite all this, or maybe because of it, I've developed a fetish for things that work without electricity, things that you can tweak with your fingers. Mechanisms. Last week I bought an old typewriter, a Smith Corona from the late fifties. It has no plug. It has no circuits. And it works! You just push a little round button on a tiered QWERTY keyboard, and a metal finger pops up and tattoos a letter onto a piece of paper. And the sound it makes, and the bell (ting!) at the end of a line, and the metallic crunch as you crick its neck back into position . . . it's like music.

The Net has nothing to do with that. There's no sound of footsteps in virtual space. There are no textures, no smells, nothing tangible at all. It's a sensory deprivation tank, and when you get out, everything seems more . . . I don't know. Solid? Present? Real? You notice the grain.

If you're not careful, this can put a real kink in your conversational skills. You turn into Captain Obvious. Last week I spent an entire evening talking like a Roy Lichtenstein character ("Rob, your hair is so . . . blond"). My new friends are trying to figure out whether I'm ditzy, permanently blissed out, or merely insane. I haven't told them about Net.

The online and the offline world aren't staying in their boxes like I thought they would. They're bleeding together.

Today I logged off at dawn, walked out of my apartment four blocks to the blue Atlantic, and jumped in.

Wow, I thought. Now *this* is bandwidth.

ThE OnlIne INternEt adDictS' SuPpOrt gROup

IT'S 5 A.M., and I'm still on the Net. My eyes are unfocusing, and my mind's getting ready to do the same. I catch myself pulling a Stockdale (Who am I? What am I doing here?). I'm in an official, extra-tasty catatonic daze, like Cindy Brady in the Game Show episode, when the red camera light goes on and she just stares and stares and stares at it. I compose talk show commercials and public service announcements in my head.

"It started innocently enough. 'Kim' got a computer account in college and began experimenting with a vast computer network known as the Internet. Gradually, she became dependent on her daily fix, first a little bit, and then more every day. Soon, she was spending the wee hours of the morning plastered to her computer screen. Sleep and nutrition were relegated to scattered naps and the occasional Cup-o-Noodles. Her grades went out the window. She was" — the host pauses for dramatic effect "— an Internet Junkie. Join us next time, when we talk to *netaholics.*" The sound effect from *A Current Affair* segues into . . .

"This is your brain." Picture of a potted Gerber daisy.

"This is your brain on Net." Picture of Gerber daisy blossom garroted from its stem and tossed into a food processor with pickling brine, soap-bubble formula, and the contents of forty-two Pixy Stix. Sound of food processor on high setting.

"Any questions?"

I sit, rapt, absorbed by a chilling QVC psychodrama. Lorena Bobbitt, having lashed Billy Idol to the kitchen sink with Topsy Tail hair tools, brandishes a Flowbie and threatens to dismember him for whorishly appropriating the term "cyberpunk." And after a few hours of mass media flotsam piped direct to my brain, a kind of intellectual tinnitus sets in. This is the point when I sit back, my mind ringing with *Blade Runner* trivia, and ponder the ethics of nanotechnology experiments on household pets. I squint, rub my temples, and groan with the agony of mental indigestion.

Aaarrghhhh, my brain hurts. . . .

Damnit Jim! Log off, Jim! Log off!

I rub my eyes until I see pink hearts, green clovers, yellow moons, purple stars, and blue diamonds. Time for a nice bowl of Lucky Charms, a few No-Doz, and a little IRC.

I need help.

I peep into Mudders Anonymous, just out of curiosity. I'm not a real hard-core mudder. But MUDs are the most intense stuff on the Net, and there are bound to be some real nutcases in MudAnon who make me look comparatively normal.

I don't know whether MUDs are inherently more addictive than the rest of the Net or whether they just attract more addictive personalities. But I have known heroin addicts who are less dependent on smack than hardcore MUD junkies are on MUDs, MUCKs, MUSHes, and MOOs.

"You wanna see addiction at its finest?" asks a MudAnon member. "Over the summer, this was my schedule:

"Wake up at 2 P.M. (sometimes later. No later than 5 P.M. though).

"Boil water.

"Hop on the MUD.

"Convert water into coffee.

"Play MUD for the rest of the day with occasional coffee break, possibly Cup O' Noodles. Continue playing MUD. Go to sleep at 6 A.M.

"And the sad (happy!) thing is that there are many people like this on the MUD. Some people keep slightly different schedules, but there's an array of net addicts who play 12, 15, 20 hours/day."

MUD junkies are the worst. God, they're the walking dead.

This, from someone who gets off the Usenet wire at 4 A.M.

Yeah, I know it's a hedge: I'm not as far gone as those IRC addicts. Oh no, I'll never be as lame as those mudders. It's just a few newsgroups. A few forums on MindVox. OK, so I spend time on IRC, too. I'm not into MUDs, I swear. Well, not heavily into them. It's a very casual thing. It's not like I MUD every day. I can stop anytime I want. I'm in control. Really.

It's a classic pot-and-kettle situation. Usenet news worms look down on IRC junkies look down on MUD-heads look down on people who MUD more than them.

Welcome to the wonderful world of Internet Twelve-Step culture.

Yes, I realize that it's an oxymoron to hash out my Net habit in an online forum. But at least the people here know what I'm talking about, instead of asking, "You're hooked on *what?*" The Net's multi-flavored mind candy has its own set of acronyms, just like real-life brain snacks (/me shuffles her feet. "Yeah, I've done IRC, MUD, MOO, MUSH . . . I started out with e-mail and then . . . got into the heavy stuff"). Mud-Anon is a kick, because there are always people there who spend more time on the Net than I do. And even *those* addicts know people who Net harder than they do. Everyone has some zombie acquaintance he can point to and say, "See, I'm not so bad."

There is, of course, considerable pressure to top the last guy's story.

"Over the weekend, I saw the most amazing case of MUD addiction yet," types another MudAnon member. "One of the users at this site had been playing for sixteen hours that I know of. I stand in awe."

Personally, I admire that kind of stamina—and so does everyone else, which is why Net junkie newsgroups walk a fine line between confession and braggadocio. Lately, they've been degenerating into all-out bragging sessions in heated ALL CAPS MODE (YES, YOU ARE AN ADDICT YOU AL-WAYS HAVE BEEN AND YOU ALWAYS WILL BE BUT I HAVE BEEN IRC-ING LONGER SO THAT MAKES ME MORE OF AN ADDICT HAHAHAHAHHA!!!).

This is what happens when you hold a Wellness meeting in a crack house.

To be fair, some netters post to these newsgroups in an honest effort to kick the habit. They really do want to reassert some measure of control over their leisure time and job performance. But most of us have seen too many twelve-step melodramas and tabloid addiction scandals to take this whole "recovery" thing seriously ("Net Junkie Bares All in Shocking Confession!!!!" "Wired to Net, College Student Stays Awake for Solid Week!!! 'Sunlight? What's That?' Inquires Hacker Teen"). And besides, it's so much more fun to spoof clichéd support group rhetoric than to play it straight. So the typical online roundtable goes something like this:

"Oh I'm soooo glad I was told about this newsgroup. I need help. I know. I've been ircing for . . . well . . . almost four years now. I've had a variety of names and a variety of net boyfriends. i failed french my freshman year because i used to stay up until 5, 6, even 7 am ircing and then go to bed (and french was at 9). but i guess i beat the odds. i got my b.a. i'm going for my m.a. i'm still ircing (although it's gotten more addictive again). and i'm ok. i guess. It's just nice to know that people are out there who understand my problem without saying 'you're addicted to WHAT?!?!?!' I mean . . . it was hard enough admitting my addiction to Pixy Stix. Even Mountain Dew posed a problem. I got help. But IRC????

"So . . . hi. My name is Ilene 'Murph' Rosenberg and I am . . .

"*gulp*

"I am . . .

"*sniff* *gulp* (you can do this girl)

"And I am *gulp* an IRC addict.

"Thank you."

Another netter stands up (no, really he types "stands up").

"My name is synergy, and I am a . . . a . . . a Net Junkie — I admit it — I stay up all night and skip classes to be on the Net. *sob* It's good to be here with my fellow brothers and sisters who can help me in my time of need.

"*snork*

"The Net Rules!"

A veteran mudder takes the floor: "I too am a mudder of old, though I've managed to remain mudfree for almost 5 months now. I know I'll always be a mudder, because it is a disease that I'll have to live with for the rest of my life. But I will stay clean! At least until the Marches of Antan reopens anyway! MUHAHAHAHAHA. . . ."

To be honest, I'm on the fence about the whole Net addiction/disease analogy. On one hand, I'm not sure that a few hours a day on the Net is really worth worrying about. I mean, a lot of the time I spend on the Net is time I don't spend watching television. No one can argue that the Net is more idiotic than the idiot box, and look how much time people tune into that. Look at how involved they become in the latest twist of *Melrose Place*. At least Net is interactive, so we can *discuss* the Hottest Place on Television (tm) on alt.tv.melrose-place. Unlike television, you can use the Net to communicate with people. Software zillionaires use the Net. And a growing number of businesses would be crippled without it. I'm hooked on Net in the same way that we're all hooked on telephones. So I get a little antsy when I can't pick up my e-mail. Big deal. I see an awful lot of cellular phones in restaurants these days, and that's pretty fucking compulsive if you ask me. So there.

On the other hand, Net can interfere with your life. It's not so much the fatigue or how it irrevocably bends your worldview. It's just the hours it absorbs. It's unbelievable how time flies when you're on the Net.

Contrary to popular belief, however, it is possible to balance Net with a social life, as long as you eliminate one thing: sleep. Sleep has to go, if only because the Net happens at night. Prime Net time is between midnight and three in the morning, and if you're sleeping, you'll miss it. Anyway, you can't go out and socialize, Net, *and* sleep. If you juggle the logistics right, you'll manage two out of three (the Net is just part of my plan to explode the myth of fatigue). And honestly, I don't mind not sleeping. It's just disorienting to realize constantly how *late* it always is.

"Please tell me all the clocks are wrong and it isn't really 4:30 AM and I haven't been on for 3 days straight. . . . ." wails Tex, a voxer in New York City.

"Sure," replies Drow, a self-described "Insane Entity" in Colorado, "the clocks are wrong and it isn't really 4:30 AM and you haven't been on for 3 days straight. :) . . world time has been altered by space aliens using their graviton-flux capacitance rays, it is really 4:30 PM of march 3rd 2034, and you have now been on for over 40 years straight. your phone bill is something over twenty five million dollars, most of which will be covered by life insurance, since you died sometime last week. oh yeah, and the cubs won the world series last year, and you missed that too. :) better?"

Net is a black hole for time. Sometimes (OK, often), it's really difficult to tear myself away. For one thing, inertia is not on my side. Not only is it easier just to keep reading, but messages start piling up the minute I log out. The Net has no mercy in this regard. It will bury me under a mountain of information if I neglect it. There's a fear of falling behind that turns the Net into a digital Roach Motel—netters log in, but they can't log out. Posts drift through the gray matter like krill through a baleen whale, and you're trapped. "I'm caught up, I'm afraid to hang up 'cause I know I'll fall behind again," writes a netter caught like a fly in amber. "I just keep telling myself: 'You can logoff, you can logoff, you can logoff . . .'"

Log on. Make feeble attempt to feed 200 kilobytes of arcane bullshit through brain in stump shredder/meat grinder mode. Log off.

Log on.

Flashback to a childhood Saturday morning. Cartoons are on, naturally. Sylvester stands outside a door that separates him from the sonic shock wave of a full-throttle forty-piece orchestra. He opens the door, and music blares out of it. He closes the door. Silence. And then—this is the part I love—he opens and closes it *again,* three or four times, staring at the camera with an expression of snaggletoothed dementia.

Log off. Go to fridge and open it in hopes of seeing that something new and zany has spontaneously materialized.

It hasn't.

Go back to computer and log on in hopes that something new and zany has spontaneously materialized.

It has.

Take another sip of stale cola and read the latest. Mmm . . . Net.

Occasionally, a hardware problem or glitch in the system forces me off the Net for hours or even days. Withdrawal is not pretty. If a favorite bulletin board is down, it's not uncommon to find a whole pack of netaholics hovering outside on an IRC channel:

"I can't get into the system. What's HAPPENED!!#@!*"

"System's down. We're locked out."

"What's WRONG!?"

"Is it serious?"

"When will they FIX it?"

"This sux."

Meanwhile, I keep trying. The system doesn't want to cooperate, doesn't know me, and couldn't care less about my pressing need to collect e-mail and catch up on the Computer Underground Digest (Broken! Dial. Broken! Glare at screen. Dial. No carrier. Dial). I continue to dial frantically until the hedonistic-rat-pushing-button-for-electrical-stimulus-at-expense-of-food analogy kicks in and I finally give up in disgust. I pace about my room, halfheartedly gnawing at a wedge of stale pizza and pondering the fallibility of equipment, software, the phone company, and the human spirit. The malevolence of the universe is self-evident, and a bitter funk permeates my immediate surroundings until the system is once again up, at which point birds burst into song and the world is once again a happy place. I relish the modem's every pop and whine. The log-in prompt winks flirtatiously. I type my password with an overwhelming sense of relief.

Wouldn't want to miss that IRC Recovery meeting.

ALl wIrEd Up And nO
plAcE tO Go

```
<mischief> say Vox telnet is down
<nihilis> Yeah, I think it's the Sprintlink con-
+nection.
<mischief> say Is dail-in working?
<mischief> say Sorry
<mischief> I don't mean to keep typing "say."
<nihilis> I don't know . . . I'm not voxlocal
<mischief> Too much nudding.
<nihilis> Ah
<mischief> I mean mudding.
<mischief> I'm gonna check the dial-in connection
<mischief> say brb
```

I DON'T NEED to type "say" to say something on IRC. I'm already saying it. But I've gotten into the habit from MUDs, where you have to type "say" before you say something and "look" before you can see. Next thing I'll be mumbling "emote" every time I take a breath. Emote inhale. Emote exhale.

I think MUDs have fried me a bit. I'm getting burned out on them, too. But the question is, where do I go now? Where's the next wave?

The thing is, I don't think I can push this thing much further. There's nothing else to do, just much, much, much more of what I've already done. Anywhere I go now is a second trip.

It's strange, the Net used to seem so big to me. No limits. Endless variety. It doesn't seem that big to me now. I log in and think, where to now? Back to Usenet? Back to IRC? Back to Vox? ZenMOO? Another MUD? *Any* MUD?

Been there, done that.

It's not enough anymore.

It's overwhelming.

It's boring.

I can feel it topping out.

And it's sad, because I love the Net. I love being able to breeze into an IRC channel and talk to people in Brazil and Singapore. I love the spirit of the place, and how much people on the Net value freedom. I love the speed. I love the weightlessness.

Or maybe that's the part I hate. I can switch this whole world off. I can walk away from it and come back the next night, or the night after that, or a week or a month or a year later and find pretty much the same thing. Usenet articles never die; they're just reposted on alternate newsgroups. I don't know if that's a positive quality. I don't know how happy I am in a causal vacuum.

No consequences.

Kirk thought that was such a big deal, that he could go around smashing bottles against the virtual wall and no one would make him clean up the mess. And he feels like he's done something. But he hasn't. There was no impact. You can't knock someone out with the idea of a bottle.

There's something brilliant about the Net. There's also something lonely and terrible about it. I don't regret stumbling in, but thank God I can opt out.

The sun will be up in a little less than three hours, which is:

a) a few thousand Usenet articles
b) two dozen IRC channels
c) one MUD session, or
d) two REM cycles

At this point, "d" seems like the most exciting option.

CYbeRsUIcIde

I'VE HAD ENOUGH.
God, I'm sick of this stuff. It's making me nauseous.
And I'm laughing, because I remember how infatuated I was
with it.
I remember how I couldn't imagine wanting off.
And now it's just, like, overdose.
Three-ish in the morning, I'm at my computer, happily snack-
ing on a bowl of Fruity Pebbles, when suddenly the Net stops
looking like a digital playground and starts to seem like some
kind of Sartrian hell. There are just too many voices, too
many people in my face expressing an *opinion,* and I can *hear
them all.* It's as if every sideline conversation at a basketball
game is suddenly audible. That crashing tide of voices is
heavy in a way that a stadium roar never can be. I realize, in a
way that I never have before, what "a lot of people" means.
It is a nightmare.
I feel crushed by the weight of this weird world.
I have no idea why I bother with this whole Net existence.
There's just too fucking much of this stuff, all the time, and it
never stops.

All this information, it's toxic.

And Usenet's like some kind of continuous avalanche, tumbling in a loop.

I can't even think about IRC without getting queasy.

Jesus, I just want to shut off the crush of all these voices, the endless chatter, and all the people that float right through me.

I'm sick of being a ghost. I feel myself starting to wear thin.

I'm sick of the overload,

sick of absorbing all this noise,

sick of cold coffee,

sick of the sleep deprivation,

sick of feeling strung out all the time,

sick of waking up in the morning with my brain ringing.

And you know, I really don't care if I never pick up another piece of goddamned e-mail as long as I live.

I'm cooked.

I just can't *do* this anymore.

I am so

fucking

tired.

And I'm thinking, if I never log on again,

if this whole cyberplanet just vanished . . . so what?

Net.death is starting to look pretty liberating from where I sit (to die, to sleep, perchance to dream . . . Mmm, REM cycles).

Anyway, I could always come back to Net.life, like Jason in *Friday the Thirteenth*.

God, it really is late, and my box of Cookie Crisp is down to dust.

I think I'll draft a suicide note announcing my impending Net Death >8-)

Maybe I'll become famous by helping netaholics Net-kill themselves.

The "Kevorkian Virus" has a nice ring to it. Muhahahaha.

No more hours of tapping into the web at 3 am.

Surfing on the Internet

No more flames.
No more horndog e-mail.
A decent night's sleep.
That's it, I'm slitting my virtual wrists :-)
Good-bye, people. It's been a kick.
But, as my man Dennis used to say,
I am OUTTA here.

NO CARRIER

NetSpeAk 101: a gUIde
tO thE CybErPAtoIs

A Note on Net Style

Although the Net is a text-based medium, conversational style is the rule. Some of the Net is actually conducted in real time "chat" mode, but even bulletin board articles and electronic mail are closer to transcripts than written compositions. It's a spoken idiom; netters type the way they talk. In keeping with the casual written tone, most of the Net is on a first-name basis. The epithets "Mr." and "Ms." are seldom used except for ironic effect. Titles are reserved for the Pope, the English monarchy, and pseudonymous hackers (for example, Lord Dread).

In keeping with the spoken idiom, typos are accepted, if not expected. Netters take considerable license with punctuation. It's more important to imply a pause with ellipses, for instance, than finish a statement with a period. Line breaks take the place of paragraph divisions. Emphasis markers like *asterisks* and ALL CAPS MODE stand in for vocal inflection. Besides, a perfectly typed post implies editing, which has a vague aura of prissiness about it. Egregious typing, on the other hand, showcases one's irreverence, anti-establishment leanings, or the limits of Stone Age computer equipment (primitive computers have a certain punk cachet). The same applies to spelling, although the subcultural dialects of hackerdom, rave, and surfing have introduced their own vernacular misspellings: the substitution of "3" for the letter "e" ("How 3l33t"), "ph" for the letter "f" ("stuph for sale"), and numbers for letters ("later" abbreviated to "l8r"). The hackish practice of compounding words with periods (a necessary evil when storing files in UNIX) has diffused into common Net.usage, along with self-mocking studly-caps (tHe pRAcTicE of cApITaLiZinG RaNDOm LeTtErs).

A word of warning: there's a strong element of self-parody to these Mondo-style conventions. Do *not* use them earnestly to prove how wired you are. And remember, cyberpunk wannabes are the only ones who use the prefix "cyber" with a straight face.

Deciphering IRC

IRC (Internet Relay Chat) is the Net's ham radio analog, a network amenity that lets users from Austria to Australia chat casually in real time. They log onto IRC, pick a handle, then join or create a channel (there are hundreds). Channels vary in language (#norge . . . Norwegian speakers! Norsk-spraakelig!), topical foci, and traffic. Two graduate students may stroke their virtual chins in #sanskrit while two dozen #sex chatterbugs stroke other virtual appendages.

IRC channels all begin with a pound sign (#), but they come in many flavors of secrecy and exclusiveness. There are named or numbered channels that are listed on the channel band as well as unlisted speakeasies and invitation-only channels that appear on the channel list but only admit a select few. IRC is a warren of public forums and private hide-aways. There's more to it than flipping a dial.

Once you join a channel, even the straightforward chat premise is deceptive. It's more like passing notes in class. Some notes get read by everyone, others by only two people. Most comments show up on the channel's common screen and are read by everyone. But it's also possible to send private messages with the /msg command. For instance, Rick types: /msg Ilsa Let's blow this joint.

On his screen, he sees:

```
->Ilsa Let's blow this joint
```

And Ilsa's screen, and only her screen, shows:

```
*Rick* Let's blow this joint
```

On a seemingly quiet channel, there may be dozens of invisible private conversations spinning in tandem with the general scroll. There are also separate two- or three-person conversations, woven between other, larger conversations on the public board. Just keeping track of it — who responded to what, publicly or privately — is a challenge when a channel is crowded. And keeping up with several channels simultaneously is an exercise in schizophrenia.

On top of that, IRCers don't just talk. They emote, signaling actions with a backslash command. For example, Mario types:

```
/me hits Kong with a mallet.
```

The IRC screen shows:

```
*Mario hits Kong with a mallet.
```

The first-person objective case grammatical convention — /me buys the bar a round, /me lights a cigarette, /me sips vodka and wonders how many licks it takes to get to the Tootsie Roll (tm) center of a Tootsie Pop (tm) — has bled into Netspeak at large. It lends that irresistible Techie Tarzan flavor to Usenet posts and personal correspondence (Ugh. /me grunts in UNIX).

So you have words that count as spoken speech, words that count as action, word commands that turn the former into the latter, and people who functionally exist as words on your screen. Welcome to Babel. The elevator is broken. Enjoy your stay.

Glossary

Acronyms are epidemic on the Net, and the lingo is constantly inundated with fresh ones. The most commonly used are:

AOL America Online, one of the "Big Three" online services, the others being CompuServe (aka Compu$pend) and Plodigy, er, Prodigy.

BBS Bulletin Board System

BRB Be Right Back

BTW By the Way

FAQ A compendium of Frequently Asked Questions (and answers) about a given topic or newsgroup, usually compiled by a veteran of the group and updated periodically. FAQs contain most of the information that newbies want to know but are afraid to ask — or that old-timers are sick of discussing — so it has become a point of netiquette to read the FAQ before leaping into discussion on an unfamiliar newsgroup.

FTF   Face to Face (real-life) as opposed to screen-to-screen interaction.

GF, BF, SO   Girlfriend, Boyfriend, Significant Other. Term applied to RL romantic relationships, as opposed to Net.relationships.

GIF   Graphics Interchange Format, a means of storing and transmitting binary graphics that has been generalized to mean any type of digital picture ("Naked GIFS of the Swedish Bikini Team available *NOW* on the Viking Love Slave BBS!!!").

IMHO   In My Humble Opinion. Used for ironic effect, or to diffuse the insult potential of a strongly worded statement.

LOL   Laughing Out Loud. The highest compliment for Net.humor, short of ROTFL (Rolling On the Floor Laughing).

MOTSS   Member of the Same Sex

MOTD   Message of the Day

POV   Point of View

RL   Real life, as opposed to Net.life

UL   Urban Legend

VR   Virtual Reality

WRT   With Regard To

WTF   What the f***?

WYSIWYG   What You See Is What You Get

YMMV   Your Mileage May Vary

YABA   Yet Another Bloody Acronym

Address (noun)   On the Net, an electronic mail address. A Net address consists of a netter's login name, followed by an "at" sign (@) and a site name, which includes an organizational suffix and, if the site is outside the United States, a country suffix. For example, sid@anarchy. edu.uk indicates that Sid (login name) collects his mail at Anarchy University in Britain (the "edu" suffix indicates that "anarchy" refers to some kind of educational institution). While .edu is the most common type of address in Usenet, there are others: .com means the netter is at a commercial site (this includes dial-in bulletin boards as well as companies); .org means a nongovernmental organization, often a nonprofit one; and .mil indicates a military site.

Ad-speak (noun)   A common dialect of Netspeak that employs advertising slogans for ironic effect. "Ever use a T1 trunk line to play Doom for three days straight? YOU WILL."

Anonymous server (noun)   An e-mail and Usenet system that lets users send e-mail and post to Usenet anonymously. Anonymous servers are a switching station for people who wish to safeguard their privacy or create a bogus identity, don't want to take responsibility for their statements, or post to alt.transgendered.

ASCII graphics   Graphics composed of alphabet letters, numbers, and keypad symbols. ASCII art is most often used to adorn sigs, but there are netters for whom the Net is a gallery wall begging for rococo stand-alone multiscreen masterpieces. For some reason cows are the predominant genre. They are to the ASCII art world what the Madonna and child was to early Renaissance painters.

Cow who drank Jolt

Cow who ate
psychedelic mushrooms

Cow who used Jolt
to wash down psyche-
delic mushrooms

Bandwidth (noun)   The transmission rate of a given piece of data; for example, a Usenet post or a huge picture file en route to your living-room hard drive will take less travel time on a high-bandwidth connection. More generally, the amount of Net.space a collection of comments occupies, especially when they are frivolous or annoying. ("Stop wasting bandwidth with this idiotic thread.")

BIFF (proper noun)   The archetypical ultimate loser-cum-cyberpunk-wannabe stuck in an adolescent hack-land fantasy world of low-end equipment, pirated software, and all-caps mode. (MY BBOARD HAS ALL C-64S AND VIC-20S (XCEPT FOR ONE PLUS-4) BEKAUSE THEY"RE THE BEST!!!!! AND I HAVE A REELY FAST 1200-BAUD PER SECOND MODEM!!!1! CALL MY BBOARD TODAY::: 1-617-555-B1FF!!!!!11!! BE REELY K00000000L!!) BIFF is the mewling hacker larva that many post-pubescent programmers once were, and he is therefore ritually beaten, kicked, and made the butt of BIFF jokes.

Bot (noun)   An artificial intelligence programmed to perform administrative tasks or other, less practical functions like masquerading as a human user. A mail-bot, for instance, will send out automatic responses to e-mail inquiries. IRC bots often present themselves as general helpers, holding down the fort for AWOL moderators, or, in the case of #ircbar, serving drinks. Bots can be quite convincing, and some of them have managed to fool quite a few users into thinking they are human. Conversely, the Net's ultra-predictable citizens are often accused of being closet bots.

Bozo (noun)   1. A person whose ill-thought-out comments or verbal harassment put them beyond the pale of common sense and decency; a congenital moron. 2. A netter whom one has kicked into a killfile.

Cascade (noun)   An artifact of the Usenet follow command,
   which notches previous articles to clarify who wrote
   what. As a thread spins out, the number of notches in-
   creases stepwise, as in the famous "Longest USENET
   Thread Ever" cascade:

```
mister@netcom.com wrote:
: Peter da Silva (peter@sugar.NeoSoft.COM) wrote:
: : In article <1994Feb21.200803.73503@ucl.ac.uk>,
: : Yoram Grahame <zcacygr@rs6-225.ucl-26.bcc.ac.uk>
wrote:
: : > In article <1994Feb21.124450.3742@inmos.co.uk>,
fanf@inmos.co.uk (Anthony Finch (PFUE)) writes:
: : > |> o'donnell lisa lynn wrote:
: : > |> > Alan Stange wrote:
: : > |> > : o'donnell lisa lynn writes:
: : > |> > : |> TJJT wrote:
: : > |> > : |> :ae -a@minster.york.ac.uk writes:
: : > |> > : |> : > Feldman / Mark Jeffrey (ISE)
wrote:
: : > |> > : |> : > >alain.picard@astro.estec.esa.nl
writes:
: : > |> > : |> : > >>> Kip Crosby writes:
: : > |> > : |> : > >>>> Friedrich Fahnert writes:
: : > |> > : |> : > >>>>> Ernst 'pooh' Mulder wrote:
: : > |> > : |> : > >>>>>> Liam Relihan wrote:
: : > |> > : |> : > >>>>>>> Andy Wardley wrote:
: : > |> > : |> : > >>>>>>>> ae-a@minster.york.ac.uk
wrote:
: : > |> > : |> : > >>>>>>>>> Liam Relihan wrote:
: : > |> > : |> : > >>>>>>>>>> Tom Salyers writes:
: : > |> > : |> : > >>>>>>>>>>> Ernst 'pooh' Mulder
says:
: : > |> > : |> : > >>>>>>>>>>>> Andy Wardley writes:
```

: : > |> > : |> : > >>>>>>>>>>>> Jeff Robertson
writes:
: : > |> > : |> : > >>>>>>>>>>>> What's the longest
thread in the history of USENET ?
: : > |> > : |> : > >>>>>>>>>>> This one.
: : > |> > : |> : > >>>>>>>>>> It does go on,
doesn't it?
: : > |> > : |> : > >>>>>>>>>> He's makin' it up as
he goes along!!! =)
: : > |> > : |> : > >>>>>>>>> Goddamit . . . I'm
tired of this thread . . . its been going on far too
long . . .
: : > |> > : |> : > >>>>>>>>> take it to e-mail.
: : > |> > : |> : > >>>>>>>> And the thread grows
longer by the day . . .
: : > |> > : |> : > >>>>>>> How long is a piece of
string?
: : > |> > : |> : > >>>>>> Get a life or this stupid
thread will outlive you
: : > |> > : |> : > >>>>> Super water absorbant
thread bits? Anyone?
: : > |> > : |> : > >>>>> I like long threads, please
don't let this one die . . .
: : > |> > : |> : > >>>> We'll please everyone and
make this a recursive thread (see Jeff Robertson).
: : > |> > : |> : > >>> Oh, _no!!_ It split!
: : > |> > : |> : > >>Gosh, don't you think this
makes a pretty pattern?
: : > |> > : |> : > >Sure! But watch as the cascade
gets longer or someone types in 2 lines!
: : > |> > : |> : > I am making the cascade longer.
: : > |> > : |> : > And I am typing in two lines.
: : > |> > : |> : What can I add to this wonderful
thread? (Besides another line)

: : > |> > : |> Your heart. Your soul. Your strength.
And a tin of spork.
: : > |> > : What is spork? Or don't I really want to
know? Is it like sbeef?
: : > |> > It's a close cousin of spam. You really
don't want to know any more than that.
: : > |> I thought it was a runcible spoon (like the
owl and the pussycat), or maybe a foon.
: : > So what's a runcible spoon then?
: : It's a fork with a bowl or a spoon with tines.
Like a baby spoon or those
: : hideous plastic things you get on cutrate air-
lines.
: : Looks like UNIX, Feels like UNIX, works like MVS—
IBM advertisement.
: I use to use those at Kentucky Fried Chicken.
What ? You mean the Colonel has AIX now ? Lawd ha'
mercy !

Cracker (noun)   A programmer who breaches systems security for fun and/or profit. In the early days of crack-
   ing, a "look but don't touch" mandate was used to justify
   nonmalicious break-ins. Curiosity absolved the cracker
   who broke through security to explore the system inside.
   But as more crackers exploit software loopholes for personal gain, the term "cracker" has lost its Robin Hood
   glamour and is now synonymous with "criminal." Hackers often use the term for spin control, to put some distance between themselves and the sensationalist media
   portrait of demon teens out to topple the free world ("Don't
   call those guys hackers!!!! Crackers don't hack for
   knowledge—they just want to steal or look like kOoL
   DoODZ . . . they're giving REAL hackers a bad name").

Cross-post (verb)   To post a Usenet article to more than one newsgroup. Unfortunately, cross-posting tends to spawn long-running, redundant, cross-posted threads that waste huge amounts of time and bandwidth. Because no one likes to pick through the same argument in half a dozen newsgroups, multiple cross-posting is generally considered bad netiquette.

Desc (noun)   Abbreviation of "description"; for example, the physical description of a character on a MUD.

Elite (adjective)   Edge. Technically or intellectually superior. Cool. Also spelled "eleet," "3l33t."

E-Mail (noun)   Electronic Mail

Emoticons (noun, plural)   ASCII symbols that indicate emotion in the absence of vocal inflection or physical cues, otherwise known as smilies. There are literally hundreds of variations on the smiley theme, such as:

```
:-)  Basic smiley. This smiley is used to inflect
     sarcasm, humor, or happiness.
;-)  Winky smiley, appended to flirtatious and/or
     sarcastic remarks
:-(  Frowning smiley. User is upset or depressed.
:->  Shit-eating grin smiley, a notch stronger
     than :-)
>;-> Leering smiley, used after a lascivious re-
     mark.
:-P  Either panting in anticipation, taunting
     the reader schoolyard-style, or leering in
     response to a provocative remark
>:-( Anger
8-0  Shock
|-0  Yawn
:)   Midget smiley
```

```
=:-) Punk rock smiley
8-] "Wow, maaan"
: / Mary Jo Buttafuoco smiling
```

Finger (verb) To run an "operator assistance" check at another user's site. Fingering a person's e-mail address will usually deliver a list of factoids about him: name, last login time, and plan file.

Flame 1. (verb) To publicly post a vituperative ad hominem attack. Because there are no physical cues or verbal inflection on the Net, small misunderstandings often escalate into bouts of serial flamage: flame wars. Flaming is the Net analog of "talking trash" on the basketball court, or the high-flown vitriol of Slavic curse. 2. (noun) An instance of flaming.

Flame Bait (noun) A statement that begs to be flamed. Some netters post flame bait to jump-start a sleepy newsgroup. Others just crave attention.

Follow 1. (noun) A protocol for responding to Usenet posts, in which the original post is automatically block-quoted and set off with colons or notches, and the article is automatically filed under the same subject heading. The third person to follow adds his comments to the first two posts, (hopefully) editing them for length, and so on. The follow protocol gives context to remarks that might otherwise seem random. (See "Cascade.") 2. (verb) To use this protocol.

FTP 1. (noun) File Transfer Protocol, the procedure for downloading files from the Net. 2. (verb) To use FTP to download a file ("I FTP'd the Pyrotechnics Handbook from Berkeley last night").

Gibson, William (proper noun) A renowned science fiction writer who coined the term "cyberspace" in his

1983 novel *Neuromancer.* Gibson's name is invoked with genuflection and spritzes of holy water on the Net, where he is revered as a patron saint and/or minor deity.

God (noun)   1. The owner of a MUD, bulletin board, or other virtual environment.

Handle (noun)   The name one uses on the Net, whether it's the one that appears on a driver's license or the title of an elaborately crafted online identity (for example, Josh Green, aka Lord Vogar the Omnipotent).

Header (noun)   The Net-generated opening lines of a Usenet post, which specify the sender and his address, the time, date, subject, and length of the post, the Net route it took to one's screen, and occasionally a summary or keyword list. The header functions as a tracking reference as well as a return address.

Killfile   1. (noun) Also known as a bozo filter, a program that allows Net users to selectively screen people out of their Net universe. The designated bozo's comments will be elided from the killfile user's screen. If enough people put you in their killfile, the sum effect is akin to Amish shunning. 2. (verb) To put someone in a killfile ("I killfiled him after the ninth Rush Limbaugh quote").

Lurker (noun)   A netter who hangs in the background without participating. Usenet lurkers, for instance, read without posting. Undetectable, they are said to outnumber their talkative counterparts ten to one. IRC lurkers join a channel, then fade into the woodwork while the rest of the channel talks. They are invisible unless you run a role call command and see how many voyeuristic weasels there actually are. Lurking on IRC is generally considered lame.

Mondo   1. (proper noun) Short for *Mondo 2000,* a glossy Bay Area style magazine for the virtual-reality-smart-drinks-and-nose-ring set. Poised between fashion commentary and sociological parody of all things cyber, *Mondo* is a gorgeous benchmark of overblown design. 2. (adjective) Resembling *Mondo 2000*.

MUD   1. (noun) Multi-User Dungeon (or Multi-User Dimension). A text-based form of virtual reality, often based on fantasy adventure or science fiction. Unlike IRC channels, MUDs have architecture. MUDs are by far the most addictive stuff on the Net. MUD varietals include LPMUDs and DikuMUDs, which tend to be combat-oriented; TinyMUDs, which are geared toward social interaction; MUSEs (Multi-Player Simulated Environments); MUSHes (Multi-User Shared Hallucinations); MOOs (MUD, object-oriented—a place where you can pick up, put down, and move inanimate objects. It's now possible to lose your keys in cyberspace); and MUCKs (this stands for nothing in particular). Since there are so many variants beginning with the letters "MU," the generic MU* is used to refer to all of them (in programming, an asterisk indicates the end of salient criteria; that is, the first two letters, "MU," define the relevant set). 2. (verb) To hang out on a MUD.

Mudder (noun)   Someone who MUDs regularly.

My $.02 (phrase)   Abbreviation of "my two cents," commonly used to minimize the flame quotient of Usenet posts.

Netiquette (noun)   A portmanteau of "Net" and "etiquette," an unwritten common-law code of proper behavior on the Net. Netiquette dictates reading the appropriate FAQ before jumping into a newsgroup and editing follow-up posts for length. "Don'ts" include posting private e-mail, flogging dead-horse threads, and harassing women. Most netiquette is common-sense good manners retrofitted to a new medium, but there are gaps where Net.life has no RL analog (for example, determining the limits of virtual violence or whether to specify one's gender).

Net.relationship (noun)   Romantic involvement sparked on the Net, which may include anything from lovelorn e-mail to steamy Net.sex to full-fledged FTF encounters. Because of their strong fantasy component, Net.relationships tend to wax obsessive on-line, then crash miserably when translated into RL.

Newbie (noun, often preceded by the epithet "clueless")   A newcomer or new user, either to the Net or to a specific newsgroup or MUD. Depending on where they show up and how they behave, newbies may be patiently tolerated or mercilessly hazed. The latter is often the result of blatant naïveté or breach of netiquette.

Newsgroup (noun)   A Usenet discussion forum. Newsgroups number in the thousands and run the topical gamut from LISP programming to *Melrose Place*.

Nick (noun)   Nickname on IRC and MUDs. There is some overlap between the terms "nick" and "handle," but the former is more often applied in the real-time context of Net "talk," whereas the latter is used in epistolary media like Usenet newsgroups and in hacking circles.

NO CARRIER (phrase)   What a telecom program says when a bulletin board or Net link a) does not pick up the phone, or b) cuts you off. Game over, dude. The wave is all surfed out. Much wringing of hands and gnashing of teeth ensues.

Offline World (phrase)   Real life, as in physical existence. A term used by people for whom the Net is an "alternative reality" rather than an escape from reality. A small fraction of the online universe sees the offline world as a mere pit stop between Net sessions. However, most netters acknowledge the offline world's advantages, despite the fact that it is slow, clunky, and hogs bandwidth.

PGP (noun)   Pretty Good Privacy, a virtually uncrackable encryption program written by software engineer Phil Zimmerman. PGP relies on a two-key system in which a private key encrypts data and a public key (often distributed in a sig or plan file) decrypts it. En route, the data is untappable. Despite the U.S. intelligence community's efforts to contain the program or replace it with an encryption standard they can crack (can you say "Clipper Chip," boys and girls?), PGP is in widespread global use.

Phreak (verb)   To hack the telephone or other telecommunications system. Some phreakers are motivated by a pure desire for knowledge; others just want a long-distance joyride. In either case, most phreaking is on the fringe of legality, and AT&T does not like to be goosed. Now that the legal system is coming out of the rotary Dark Ages, the telecom honeymoon is over, and phreakers are being nailed to the wall.

Plan (noun)   A file that netters see when they finger an e-mail address. Netters may use their plan files for personal updates ("My heavy metal band's world tour will hit the following cities this fall . . ."), meaningful quotes, political manifestos, PGP public keys, or other useful and/or amusing data.

Post   1. (noun) A Usenet or bulletin board article. 2. (verb) To author and file a post ("Will someone please post Billy Idol's e-mail address? There's this e-mail-bomb program I've been working on . . .").

Poster (noun)   Someone who posts to a bulletin board or Usenet forum.

Re: (interjection)   "Hello" in IRC. An abbreviation of greetings.

Sig (noun)   An electronic signature, usually a set of words and/or ASCII graphics set off by a border and automatically appended to a netter's Usenet posts and correspondence. Nearly all sigs include the sender's name (or handle) and e-mail address, so that readers don't have to skip back to the header to see who authored the post. Sigs may also include a snail mail address, phone number, institutional affiliation, and quotes, according to the netter's personal taste and the momentary popularity of certain bons mots ("Yours is not to question why, yours is but to brew or die"). The sig is also a canvas for ASCII artists, whose elaborate letter-pictures sometimes dwarf the posts that precede them. While such flourishes are an admitted waste of bandwidth, a great piece of sig art is a thing of beauty and a joy forever, especially when combined with *Star Trek* humor:

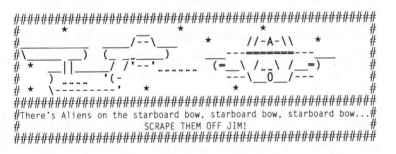

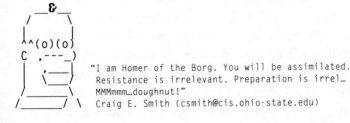

"I am Homer of the Borg. You will be assimilated.
Resistance is irrelevant. Preparation is irrel…
MMMmmm…doughnut!"
Craig E. Smith (csmith@cis.ohio-state.edu)

Snail Mail (noun)   Mail that travels through the postal system. Paper, as opposed to e-mail ("You mean I have to wait three days for you to send it snail *mail!!!*")

Snarf   1. (verb) To grab, absorb, or inhale wholesale, as in "I snarfed the *entire* roadmap GIF of lower Manhattan off the NYU archive." 2. (verb) To post to a forum with a highly prized benchmark article number—post number 1000, or post number 1234, for instance. The higher the round number, the more valuable the snarf. Palindromes also count. 3. (noun) An example of such a post. 4. (noun) The act of snarfing.

Spam (verb)   To flood someone else's home file or screen with useless garbage. On IRC, this usually translates into annoying beeping sounds or nonsense character sets. E-mail pranksters often make their targets the recipients of endlessly generated automatic reply messages of mammoth text files that overload the target's account quota. Spamming is often doled out as punishment for behavior that runs against the grain of Net culture—corporate advertising, say, or posting a chain letter, or producing an ersatz cyberpunk album ten years after the last ember of your musical creativity has faded.

Telnet   1. (noun, verb) A Net function that allows one to log onto a remote computer from a local account. From his home system, a user types the telnet command, clicks his heels together three times, presses the enter key, disappears in a puff of electrons, and appears at the designated Net address, *I Dream of Jeannie* style. Telnet makes it possible to stand with one foot in New Mexico and the other foot in New Zealand or to circumnavigate the globe in a matter of minutes ("I telnetted from New York to Norway to Australia to Seattle, all the way back to New York. *Major* lag").

Thread (noun)   A chain of comments linked by the follow protocol. Threads are ostensibly linked by a common topic, but the subject matter of a given thread tends to drift as it gets longer. It's like the telephone game—sooner or later you'll read a post about trace toxins in White House drinking water under the heading "V.Fast 28.8 Glitch, Please Advise."

(tm) The trademark symbol, invoked for ironic effect after product name-dropping or whenever a general sneer is called for ("Golly, another Data Superhighway (tm) article! Clip it for me, won't you?").

Usenet (noun) The Net's bulletin board system, consisting of more than three thousand discussion groups and distributed internationally. Usenet is vast—the information it pumps through global information arteries in a single day would take a human being months to digest. The system is divided into boroughs: the unmoderated free-for-all "alt" playground; the "biz" district; the technical "comp" corner; the hobby-oriented recreational groups; the "sci" science fair; the multicultural "soc" smorgasbord of languages, religions, and nationalities; the "talk" section (the AM band of Usenet); and regional 'hoods like "aus" (Australia) and "ucb" (U. Cal. Berkeley).

Warez (noun, plural) Software (usually pirated) available for download off a bulletin board or Net site. This term is often used to lambaste cyber-wannabe poseurs. ("Ooh, Lord Vogar says he has some kEWl wAReZ on his BBS").

Wizard (noun) In the context of MUDs and other virtual environments, a programmer or high-level player who has special privileges and/or administrative power. Wizards are the Net's landlord/superintendents, responsible for building, maintenance, support, and mediation of tenant disputes.